ANDREW ADONIS

IT'S THE LEADER, STUPID

CHANGEMAKERS IN MODERN POLITICS

I'm always glad to hear from readers. Do please email me on adonisa@parliament.uk if you have any comments or questions or would like to support any of my causes, including European Movement UK, which I chair. I write a weekly political newsletter for Prospect magazine which you can get (free) by signing up at https://www.prospectmagazine.co.uk/politics/sign-up-to-the-insider.

AA

I've searched all the parks in all the cities and
found no statues of committees

G.K. Chesterton

CONTENTS

1

IT'S THE LEADER, STUPID

Leadership is what matters above all in politics: everything else is secondary. That is the argument set out in this chapter and then in profiles of leaders of modern Britain, the United States, France, Germany and India, drawn from my writing over the last thirty years.

I have a theory of national elections. The best leader wins and nothing else matters. It's that simple.

This applies to all "two-horse" national elections in stable democracies where elections lead to the formation of a government with a single person in charge.

Of course, there is hardly a political historian or election analyst who doesn't attribute some importance, often a lot, to leadership. Leadership ratings are part of the mix of things regularly polled and leaders dominate coverage of election campaigns. But my theory is different. It is that leaders are basically all that matter.

What about ideas, policies and political parties? After all, they are a large part of what politicians do: debate ideas, frame and implement policies, and engage in party organisation. All this is true. But all this is subordinate to leadership and none of it succeeds without successful political leaders. "People do not believe in ideas: they believe in people who believe in ideas," writes the political columnist Jonathan Freedland, and I entirely agree. He expresses the fundamental truth that the battle of ideas in politics—indeed in life—cannot be comprehended separately from the people who advocate those ideas. As an insight into the nature of government it is as profound as Hobbes on power ("covenants, without the sword, are mere words") and Machiavelli's dictum that "it is better be feared than to be loved, if you cannot be both." Political parties and movements stand or fall by their leaders.

It is remarkable, and supportive of this insight, that most of the world's ideologies and religions are named after a person, usually their founder, sometimes a champion or interpreter. Christianity, Buddhism, Marxism, Leninism, Keynesianism, all hail from individual leaders or writers. Great intellectual or religious doctrines do not generally stand alone in a platonic realm of ideas; they are pinned to a particular person.

Equally, where political traditions are taken forward by a prominent leader, this often earns a personalised hybrid label—"Disraelian conservatism" and "Gladstonian liberalism"—or a descriptor comprised entirely of the leader's name—"Reaganomics", "Thatcherism", "Blairism" —or a slogan drawn from the leader's catchphrase – the "New Deal" (FDR), "Great Society" (LBJ) and "Third Way" (Blair again).

Human beings have not evolved to think easily in abstractions, and it is human nature to view political ideas through the prism of their prime advocates. Besides, successful leaders not only adopt ideas: they fashion them and combine them anew to suit their needs and times. Margaret Thatcher in the 1980s and Lord Salisbury in the

1880s and did not believe the same things, although both called themselves Conservatives and led the Conservative party. Tony Benn and Tony Blair didn't remotely believe in the same "socialism" even in the same decade. A rose by any other leader does not smell just as sweet.

It is the same with political parties. The leadership-driven essence of political parties is much underappreciated because these institutions often keep the same names over time, even generations, while in reality they are franchise operations in the hands of their leaders pro tem, not vehicles for stable bodies of policies and ideas. The Labour party of Tony Blair and Jeremy Corbyn may have had the same name, largely the same constitution, and even a substantial continuity of members and activists, but its creed and positioning changed so radically between the two leaders, in the space of less than a decade, that it would be more meaningful to call it the "Blair Party" and the "Corbyn Party", much as Charles de Gaulle, the dominant leader of modern France, dubbed his party "Gaullist".

Political parties are most obviously franchise operations in the United States, where each of the two major parties is transparently auctioned to the highest electoral bidder every four or eight years in a "primary" election. This results in an overnight change of leadership, personnel and policies. So little does ideology or affiliation matter that the successful leader—like Donald Trump in 2016 and Dwight Eisenhower in 1952—may not even be a member of the party that they go on to lead until they enter the primary election.

So critical is the leader to a political party's fortunes that a new leader can transform a party's electoral prospects, for good or ill, within days of taking over. Narendra Modi is the supreme modern instance, a Hindu nationalist outsider who in 2014 broke through seventy years of Nehru/Gandhi dynastic politics to win a landslide election in India, the world's largest democracy, and then repeated the exercise five years later – an incredible story, whatever you think of Modi, told in Chapter 5. In the United States, of the available leaders of the Democratic party in 2020, quite possibly only Biden could have beaten Trump, the story of Chapter 4.

In Australia, famous for its brutally snap changes of party leaders, Bob Hawke seized the Labour party leadership on the very day the 1983 election was called and proceeded to win it with a huge swing. An everyman Australian of vast charm, guile and ruthlessness – an ex-trade union leader who had also been an Oxford Rhodes scholar and held the world beer-drinking record, downing two and a half pints of beer in 12 seconds – Hawke had enormous charismatic reach and went on to win three more elections on the trot, "basking in what he believed was a never-ending love affair with the people," as one journalist put it.

Olaf Scholz pulled off a similar coup in Germany in September 2021, winning the succession to Angela Merkel as chancellor although only recently chosen as candidate of a party (the SPD) which was third-placed when the election campaign started barely weeks before. How he did it, and the political significance of Scholz, is described in Chapter 17.

Ditto Justin Trudeau, who seized the Canadian Liberal leadership in 2013 and stormed a general election two years later, quadrupling his party's parliamentary tally and more than doubling the party's vote from 19 to 40 per cent. This was just four years after the party's worst ever defeat under the hapless Michael Ignatieff, who demonstrated that successful political leadership is not synonymous with either charism or celebrity. Dubbed "a blend of Marlon Brando and Napoleon" by Barbra Streisand, Trudeau's rise was a unique blend of nepotism, charisma and daring, including a boxing match (literally) with a pugnacious political opponent. According to an analyst of his rise, after the boxing match in 2011, which he won ("Brazeau suffered a knock-out with half a minute to go in the third round") Trudeau's media image changed overnight from "reed-thin, pedigreed Dauphin" to "a public figure of toughness, strength, honour and courage." He went on to win the next two Canadian elections in 2019 and 2021 by more modest but still decisive margins.

Equally, new leaders without the skill can also lose elections within days. Francois Fillon looked set to be crowned president of France in 2017, having secured the nomination of the Gaullist successor party riding high against Francois Holland's unpopular socialists. So toxic was Holland that he didn't even run for a second term. But engulfed in scandal over his wife's employment as an aide at public expense, Fillon was edged out by the smart, charismatic, daring Emmanuel Macron, a 39 year-old former Hollande minister who projected himself as a tough centrist through a new personal party—*En Marche* —whose initials were deliberately his own.

What, more specifically, are the leadership qualities which count in electoral politics? They can be assessed, I suggest, on two dimensions. There are the quintessential attributes of human leadership: charisma, confidence, acumen, empathy, presence, glamour. Few would dispute that in their prime Churchill, Roosevelt, de Gaulle, Thatcher and Blair had some of these in abundance, albeit in different combinations. There is also the ability to personify the "spirit of the age", which can sometimes propel less rousing and glamorous leaders to victory. Among modern leaders, Attlee and Adenauer top this second league. The very word personify says it all.

The table opposite summarises every US presidential and UK general election since 1944. There are no party labels or vote tallies here. Instead, leadership points are given to the two principal leaders contending for power, on a 15-point scale. Up to 10 points are awarded for raw leadership talent, and up to another 5 for fitting with the times. The "winner" is the candidate with most points.

I can already hear the objections from the school of social scientists who are given to physics envy and crunching raw data. Obviously, these leadership points are wholly subjective. But I have endeavoured to be fair, and not to let my political preferences colour my judgements. Kennedy is a hero of mine, whereas Nixon sends a shiver down my spine, but on the basis of Nixon's greater experience and authority I rank the pair as tied in 1960, while Trump, who I detest, was in my view appreciably stronger than Hillary Clinton as a leader in 2016 on this 15-point scale. In the British context, I feel more affinity with Gaitskell than Thatcher in their respective primes, but that has not stopped me scoring the Iron Lady more highly.

UK

Election:	Leaders:	Intrinsic:	Spirit of the Time:	Total:
45	Attlee	7	5	12
	Churchill	9	2	11
50	Attlee	8	4	12
	Churchill	9	3	12
51	Churchill	9	3	12
	Attlee	8	3	11
55	Eden	9	4	13
	Attlee	6	3	9
59	Macmillan	9	5	14
	Gaitskell	6	3	9
64	Wilson	8	4	12
	Douglas-Home	6	4	10
66	Wilson	8	5	13
	Heath	6	3	9
70	Heath	6	3	9
	Wilson	6	3	9
74	Wilson	6	2	8
	Heath	5	2	7
74	Wilson	6	3	9
	Heath	4	2	6
79	Thatcher	6	3	9
	Callaghan	5	2	7
83	Thatcher	8	3	11
	Foot	3	1	4
87	Thatcher	7	3	10
	Kinnock	5	2	7
92	Major	6	4	10
	Kinnock	5	3	8
97	Blair	9	5	14
	Major	4	2	6
01	Blair	9	4	13
	Hague	5	2	7
05	Blair	7	3	10
	Howard	5	2	7
10	Cameron	6	3	9
	Brown	5	2	7
15	Cameron	7	3	10
	Miliband	4	2	6
17	May	5	2	7
	Corbyn	4	2	6
19	Johnson	6	4	10
	Corbyn	2	2	4

US

Election:	Leaders:	Intrinsic:	Spirit of the Time:	Total:
44	Roosevelt	10	5	15
	Dewey	6	3	9
48	Truman	7	5	12
	Dewey	6	4	10
52	Eisenhower	9	3	12
	Stevenson	6	3	9
56	Eisenhower	8	4	12
	Stevenson	6	3	9
60	JFK	7	4	11
	Nixon	7	4	11
64	Johnson	8	5	13
	Goldwater	4	1	5
68	Nixon	7	3	10
	Humphrey	6	3	9
72	Nixon	8	4	12
	McGovern	4	3	7
76	Carter	6	3	9
	Ford	5	2	7
80	Reagan	7	3	10
	Carter	5	3	8
84	Reagan	8	4	12
	Mondale	5	3	8
88	Bush Sr	7	3	10
	Dukakis	5	3	8
92	Clinton	7	4	11
	Bush Sr	6	2	8
96	Clinton	8	4	12
	Dole	6	2	8
00	Bush Jr	6	3	9
	Gore	7	3	10
04	Bush Jr	7	3	10
	Kerry	7	3	10
08	Obama	9	5	14
	McCain	6	3	9
12	Obama	9	4	13
	Romney	7	3	10
16	Trump	5	3	8
	Clinton	5	2	7
20	Biden	7	4	11
	Trump	4	2	6

Although leadership ability is about more than popularity, there is a correspondence between my scores and polling on "the best leader" in these electoral contests, and others I consulted awarded points similarly on the 15-point leadership scale. Try it and see how many, if any, of the 41 elections you would award differently using the 15-point scale.

We shouldn't be surprised at this level of agreement. After all, it is nowadays accepted that all sorts of personal abilities can be meaningfully assessed; businesses spend serious money on psychometric tests for recruitment and the more senior the post the more store they place on them. If you can reasonably confidently rate the leadership capacity of potential chief executives then why shouldn't you be able to rate charisma, competence and other leadership attributes in aspiring presidents and prime ministers?

The one charge I cannot counter is the bias of hindsight. The 15-point scale is also of limited use in estimating the prospects of third party or wild card candidates, whose prospects depend upon being able to get seriously into the race at all. The most popular leader in the 2021 Canadian election was Jagmeet Singh, the Sikh leader of the third-placed NDP. But the NDP, like Britain's Liberal Democrats, isn't regarded as a credible governing party under the first-past-the-post electoral system which both countries use, and he couldn't get into the race between Trudeau and his less popular sergeant-major opponent Erin O'Toole.

However, I am confident enough in the 15-point leadership scale to suggest it as a reliable guide to the outcome of future elections, where one leader is clearly superior leader among the top two parties. In the original 2017 *Prospect* version of this essay, I predicted that Jacinda Ardern, the charismatic new leader of New Zealand's Labour party, would become prime minister in the imminent election there, and that Jeremy Corbyn, who had just lost the 2017 UK election to Theresa May, although improving Labour's position, would lose the next election "decisively" if the Tories ditched May and chose a better leader. So it proved in both cases. Corbyn lost the 2019 election to Boris Johnson by one of the biggest margins in electoral history. In New Zealand, Ardern didn't win the popular vote but came to power by momentum gained through a barnstorming campaign and a decisive electoral advance against a staid Tory opponent, which led the third party, holding the balance of power, to put her in office. Arden went on to win the next election, in 2020, by a landslide.

On my scores in the table on p.7, there is a clear leadership "winner" in 38 of the 41 post-war elections in the US and UK. In only one case—the US presidential election of 2000, which I award 10-9 to Al Gore over George W. Bush on leadership points—did that winner fail to become president. Maybe this is the exception to prove the rule, for Gore won the national popular vote, and may have gone on to win the states-based Electoral College too had the Supreme Court not sided with Bush in a partisan 5:4 ruling which awarded a knife-edge result in Florida to Bush without a full recount.

Generally, too, the balance of leadership points not only indicates the winner but also the scale of the victory. On my leadership points Blair defeated Major 14-6 in 1997 and Hague 13-7 in 2001; Boris Johnson beat Corbyn 10-4 in

2019, Roosevelt scored 15-9 over Dewey in 1944, LBJ 13-5 over Goldwater in 1964, Nixon 12-7 over McGovern in 1972 and Obama 14-9 ahead of McCain in 2008. All these elections were landslides.

Leadership points are not constant: the talent of leaders changes over time as they age, change and face different opponents and situations. For some, experience improves the capacity to inspire and lead; for others, it breeds hubris or simply exhausts. The fresh, dynamic Harold Wilson who in 1964 personified the "white heat of the technological revolution" (12 points) had become a jaded and compromised 8-point leader in the industrial strife of the 1970s. Trump's exiguous 8 points of 2016 (just enough to beat Hillary Clinton) slid to just 6 in Covid-infested 2020 (insufficient to beat Biden). Nonetheless, an initially successful leader like Wilson or Trudeau will generally retain enough charisma and ability to fight repeat elections, and very often win. In the two near dead-heat British general elections of 1974, his fourth and fifth as Labour leader, Wilson skilfully edged it over Edward Heath both times, although leading a bedraggled party. Trudeau similarly edged it for a third time in Canada in 2021.

First-term US presidents usually stand for re-election, and since they were the previous winner – or, in the case of Truman in 1948 and Johnson in 1964, previously selected as vice president partly on the basis of leadership qualities – it is no surprise that they generally get re-elected. Even Donald Trump, maybe the most preposterous candidate ever to win the US presidency, lost re-election in 2020 by only 51 to 47 per cent despite America's soaring Covid death rate and his own manifest incompetence. With his sky-high national profile from 14 series of *The Apprentice*, his Marmite-style appeal strongly attracting a white, blue-collar electorate, and his "spirit-of-the-time" appeal to the angrily dispossessed, he commanded a big following.

However, 9 of the 13 presidential bids for re-election since 1944 have succeeded, and it is a fair bet that many successfully re-elected presidents would have won a third, maybe even a fourth term, had they been eligible to stand. Eisenhower, Reagan, Clinton and Obama would have been safe bets for a third term, health permitting; Roosevelt might even have won a fifth had he survived in reasonable health. It was to prevent re-elected presidents becoming semi-permanent that, after FDR, the 22nd amendment to the US constitution prohibited any future president serving for more than two terms. In the UK, with no term limits, Wilson fought five elections and won four, Margaret Thatcher and Tony Blair fought three elections and never lost. Blair might have won a fourth in a row had he not stood down in the middle of his third term in 2007 after ten years in power. I would have rated him higher than David Cameron in leadership points for an election in 2009 or 2010, unlike his successor Gordon Brown. Angela Merkel is the supreme modern example of the constant winner, triumphing in four German elections in a row from 2005 to 2017, over a different opponent each time. She would almost certainly have won had she competed for a fifth term in 2021.

This brings me to my next leadership maxim: failed leaders resign or are sacked—or they go on to lose again.

For just as winning once is a good predictor of winning again, so losing once is a good predictor of future defeat. Two of the three UK party leaders in recent decades to lose a first election yet survive for a second—Labour's Neil Kinnock and Jeremy Corbyn—lost their second one too. Similarly, two of the three two losing US presidential candidates of recent decades to fight subsequent elections went on to lose them —Thomas Dewey who lost to FDR and Truman in succession (1944 and 1948) and Adlai Stevenson, who lost to Eisenhower twice (1952 and 1956). Stevenson was dubbed "egghead" for his baldness and detached intellectual air. "Eggheads of the world unite; you have nothing to lose but your yolks," he joked, but it summed up why he was massacred twice by Eisenhower.

Only one of the 15 first-time US losers since 1944 has subsequently won the presidency: the irrepressible Nixon, who tied with Kennedy in 1960 on my leadership points, then defeated Hubert Humphrey eight years later having wisely sat out the intervening election which LBJ won by a landslide after Kennedy's assassination. Similarly, only one first-time loser in the last 70 years has gone on to win in Britain: Edward Heath, who defeated Wilson at the latter's third election in 1970, after six turbulent years in government. However, Heath went on to lose to Wilson in the two following elections, making the overall score 3-1 in Wilson's favour.

Hillary Clinton belongs in the serial loser camp if you put her long and failed primary campaign against Obama in 2008 alongside her general election defeat by Trump in 2016. Hillary Clinton's defeat by Obama in the Democratic Party's 2007-8 primary was decisive on my leadership points (13-10). Eight years later, I gave her a tiny leadership points lead over Bernie Sanders (9-8) in the primaries, but she ended up with an 8-7 leadership points defeat by Donald Trump in the national election. On the "losing leaders must go immediately" rule, it was foolhardy for the Democrats to select Clinton in 2016, just as it was absurd for Labour in the UK to have gone into a second election with Corbyn as leader in 2019. Two years previously he had lost to Theresa May, despite her fighting one of the most disastrous election campaigns of recent times (as one wit said, "it was the first time in history there had been a personality cult around a non-personality"), so there was never much prospect of him defying gravity thereafter.

What of that leadership giant Winston Churchill, who lost his first two elections (1945 and 1950) and only scraped victory in his third in 1951?

Churchill is exceptional as a party leader in that he didn't fight his first election until the sixth year of his premiership, in July 1945 after the end of the war. Had the election due in December 1940 not been cancelled because of the supreme national emergency which made him prime minister, he would surely have won an overwhelming popular mandate at the start of his premiership. On my estimate, he beats Attlee 14-7 in leadership points in 1940.

I accept, however, that of all 21 British general election outcomes since the second world war, Churchill's landslide defeat by Attlee in 1945 is the one where leadership points correlate least well. There are explanations aplenty. The war was practically over by July 1945. Attlee personified a yearning for post-war reconstruction without the mass unemployment of the 1930s, associated with the Tories. I accordingly give Attlee a one-point leadership edge over Churchill in 1945. It is only when Churchill reconnects with the times five years later, accepting the Attlee settlement of the National Health Service and welfare state while promising to build on it, including a shrewdly judged "bonfire of controls" still hanging over from the war five years later, that he again becomes a credible contender.

Nonetheless, I confess the blatant intervention of Captain Hindsight in all these judgements on Churchill. In truth, his political resurrection after 1945 is a remarkable testament to still formidable leadership skill and aura. The Conservatives gained 90 seats in the 1950 election and another 23 in the election a year later, when Churchill returned to power. So within just six years of abject humiliation, he had increased the Tory vote from 36 to 48 per cent and increased the party's seat tally by nearly 50 per cent, which few would have thought possible in 1945. Churchill's stamina and resilience, in the face of most of his senior Tory colleagues wanting him to retire immediately, are utterly exceptional.

Churchill is in a class of his own, an exotic exception to almost every rule except, ultimately, the one that is central to this book: that in politics, leadership matters above all.

2

GLADSTONE v. MARX

In a 62-year parliamentary career, William Ewart Gladstone (1809-98) was chancellor of the exchequer and prime minister four times each, personifying the Victorian era as powerfully as the Queen herself. Gladstone largely created today's representative parliamentary system based on a mass, ultimately universal, adult electorate. This enabled Britain – although not Ireland, which it ruled until 1922 – to transition peacefully towards democracy, without the revolutions which gripped continental Europe.

No one did more to foster revolutions than Gladstone's contemporary Karl Marx (1818-83), who fled from Prussia to London after publishing his Communist Manifesto *and campaigning for violent regime change. On reading Marx's collected writings, I was astonished to find that the communist polemicist was obsessed with Gladstone. He saw Britain's Liberal leader as the epitome of the intelligent reformer who by skill and guile kept revolution at bay. Gladstone was the refutation of practically everything Marx stood for. The story of Marx's hatred of Gladstone has never been told before, maybe because it is so uncomfortable for Marxists. So here is Gladstone v. Marx, and why the Liberal leader triumphed, first in Britain and ultimately across the West.*

Karl Marx's funeral at Highgate in March 1883 was attended by Engels and some ten others. Fourteen years later William Ewart Gladstone, Queen Victoria's longest serving Liberal prime minister, lay in state for four days in

Westminster Hall so that vast crowds could pay their respects. Yet, claimed E.H. Carr in his 1934 biography of Marx, the future lay in Highgate. "Marx could see, as hardly anyone else of his time could see, that not only Metternich and Bismarck, but Bright and Gladstone, belonged to an outworn epoch. Marx proclaimed the coming of the new age. He knew that its leaders and heroes would be men of another mould, of other traditions and of other methods."

Now that Marx has joined the outworn epoch, liberals and social democrats in search of traditions and methods for guidance might do well to exhume Gladstone, one of Britain's pre-eminent liberal leaders. Marx himself would not have been surprised, for he never regarded Gladstone as yesterday's man. On the contrary, from his arrival in England in 1849 until his death 34 years later, during Gladstone's second government, the German revolutionary was obsessed by the character and methods of Britain's political colossus. Gladstone features on 307 pages of the Lawrence & Wishart edition of the Marx-Engels collected works, mostly in Marx's letters and journalism. Even in illness, the Liberal leader was an obsession. "He is still very, very unwell," Jenny Marx told Engels when Karl was laid up in May 1854. "There can be no question of writing. He labours over Gladstone's long speeches and is very annoyed at not being able to write just now when he's got enough material on Mr Gladstone and his SCHEMES."

There is a curious parallelism about the two men. Of their fathers, the Liverpool merchant was richer than the Trier lawyer, yet their sons were both in the vanguard of the early 19th century's rising bourgeoisie. Both were classical scholars with a journalistic bent and a political mission; both were intellectuals in politics, concerned to establish first principles; both radicalised with age, roused to passion by injustice, alienation, and imperialism, with plenty of "honest idiocy of flight" in both cases. But for the suppression of his *Rheinische Zeitung* in 1843, Marx might never have ended up a Marxist. Although ignorant of Hegel's dialectic, Gladstone held an essentially dialectical conception of political progress leading to greater freedom, and was remarkably dialectical in method, trying one thing, then another, then another. Marx once compared his method with Gladstone's: "I am a machine, condemned to devour books and, then, throw them, in changed form, on the dunghill of history. A rather dreary task, too, but still better than that of Gladstone's, who is obliged, at a day's notice, to work himself into 'states of mind', yclept 'earnestness.'"

All in all, Marx was far more akin to Gladstone than he cared to admit. Gladstone's great political departures invariably followed the relentless amassing of facts, books, opinions, and a subtle perception of the balancing action needed to right the status quo towards an attainable liberal mean. Marx noted in *Kapital* that the investigation of social and economic statistics, critical to his work, was a prime British trait not followed on the Continent. It was a Gladstonian trait *par excellence*.

Gladstone's view of Marx can be stated simply. He had none – at least, none is recorded. The index to the 21,000 books and pamphlets noted in Gladstone's diary, which covers a remarkable range of political and historical literature, contains no entry for Marx. Gladstone read German, but mostly books on theology and the classics. *Das Kapital* appeared in English only a few years before his death. Although based largely on British sources, *Kapital* attracted minimal notice in Britain and there is no evidence that Gladstone was aware of it. An 1881 article in the *Contemporary Review* noted the "curious and not unmeaning circumstance" that for all their impact on the Continent "the writings of Marx are hardly better known in this country than those of Confucius."

The *Contemporary Review* believed the explanation for this ignorance to be "obvious." Marxism was rooted in the "long Continental struggle for political emancipation." In Britain, by contrast, "the course of politics has long run very smooth; none of the questions of the day have forced the fundamental principles of the existing system into popular debate ... and the working classes are preoccupied with the development of trade unions." Marxism could only flourish "either by the injudicious obstinacy of those in power, or by the direct teaching of influential thinkers." Gladstone was insufficiently obstinate for the purpose: he even refused to ban the socialists. When in 1871 the German ambassador asked Downing Street to follow Continental governments and denounce the First International, foreign secretary Earl Granville, in a letter seen by Gladstone, firmly declined. "It is thought that here, at least, the best mode of meeting any danger which may be feared from the proceedings of the association is to encourage their publicity," he responded with magisterial liberalism.

Gladstone's ignorance of Marx flowed, ironically, from his acute sensitivity to the causes of social strife and his relentless struggle to address them by liberal methods. To Gladstone, the only means to achieve social peace and communal growth was government commanding wide consent, deeply rooted in its local and national society. His entire career, from darling of the "stern unbending" Tories in the 1830s to *bête noire* of the aristocratic Establishment in the 1880s and '90s, was a struggle to reconcile first himself, and then the political class, to the reforms necessary to promote class harmony, broadly based economic growth, and self-government in its widest conception. Like Alexis de Tocqueville, whom he *had* read, Gladstone founded liberal principles of toleration, inclusion, compassion and duty on the Gospels: unlike the French liberal, he wore his faith on his sleeve, infuriating Marx ("pietistic casuistry" is a recurring phrase) and his Tory opponent Benjamin Disraeli in equal measure.

Yet for the mature Gladstone, faith dictated principles not policies. When it came to public policy, he retained into old age an extraordinary suppleness of mind and action, a flexibility exhibited both in his pragmatism and his conception of ripeness: the notion that in applying principles, reform should be adaptive to the status quo and attempted only when circumstances and public opinion were sufficiently ripe for it to secure general acceptance. Ripeness is readily enough the cry of the weak-willed and nakedly populist. But not for Gladstone, who never doubted that the politician's duty was to aid the ripening process; and who never supposed that the implementation of reform would be uncontroversial, however ripe the time.

Marx's own observation of Gladstone bears this out. It takes the form practically of a dialogue between the two men, in which the liberal politician responds to the revolutionary polemicist in terms of action.

Four themes run through Marx's diatribes on Gladstone in his letters and journalism: the working class, foreign policy, Ireland, and the futility of parliamentary politics. It was central to Marx's economics that England's working classes were exploited and getting poorer, and to Marx's politics that Gladstonian liberals were their chief persecutors. As he wrote in 1878, the collapse of the Chartist campaign for full democracy in the 1840s inaugurated a long "period of corruption" during which the workers "finally reached the stage of being no more than an appendage of the great Liberal Party – ie. of its oppressors, the capitalists."

In his inaugural address to the First International (1864), Marx seized on Gladstone's 1863 budget speech for the purpose. Gladstone had lauded the 20 per cent rise in Britain's taxable income between 1853 and 1861 as an "intoxicating augmentation of wealth and power." But, Marx alleged, he went on to note that this augmentation was "entirely confined to the classes of property." When repeated in *Kapital*, these last words were furiously denied by Gladstonians, who cited their non-appearance in the *Hansard* parliamentary record.

The riddle of the missing words says much about the Gladstonian method. The report of the budget speech in *The Times* unambiguously supports Marx, although the key sentence needs to be read with the ensuing remarks on the labouring masses:

> The augmentation I have described, and which is founded, I think, upon accurate returns, is an augmentation entirely confined to the classes possessed of property. Now, the augmentation of capital is of indirect benefit to the labourer,

because it cheapens the commodity which in the business of production comes into direct conflict with labour.

In the *Hansard* report of the speech, the first sentence is radically recast to omit the crude reference to the "classes possessed of property" and to extend property to the labourers, while the second sentence is reworded to magnify the "indirect benefit" to the poor of the rich getting richer:

> The figures I have quoted take little or no cognizance of the condition of those who do not pay income tax; or in other words, significantly accurate for general truth, they do not take cognizance of the property of the labouring population, or the increase of its income. Indirectly, indeed, the mere augmentation of capital is of the utmost advantage to the labouring class, because that augmentation cheapens the commodity which in the whole business of production comes into direct competition with labour.

The *Times* report is verbatim, whereas speeches were revised by MPs before their appearance in *Hansard*. Gladstone evidently rewrote the passage to remove the implication that the working class, unpropertied, had gained only crumbs from a boom for the rich. Gladstone didn't need to read Marx to realise, on reflection, that this was the stuff of revolutions.

However, Gladstone did not delude himself as to the scale of poverty in 1850s Britain and the need for an effective response. His response was two-pronged. The first involved tax reductions for the poor and reforms such as extending the use of the new Post Office Savings Banks to trade unions, to make Victorian free trade and laissez-faire more palatable to the working class. His confidence was to be supported by the return of growth in the late 1860s.

The second Gladstonian strategy was a redefinition of the whole notion of the political community so as to include most of the male working class. Painting an elevated picture of the fortitude of industrial workers during the cotton famine of the American civil war of the 1860s, he sought to justify their admission "within the pale of the constitution," as he put it. The result was the 1866 Reform Bill to extend the franchise in urban districts, including the typically Gladstonian flourish of a vote to holders of savings accounts of £50 for two years. Limited to the towns, the 1866-67 reform settlement, ultimately enacted by Disraeli in a stroke of celebrated opportunism, was inherently unfinished, and the great work of Gladstone's second government in 1884, a year after Marx's death, was to extend the vote to rural workers.

In all this, Gladstone was the quintessential liberal reformer, making decisive moves towards political emancipation and economic justice. As chancellor in the 1850s, he largely created the modern "budget" as an annual political act of economic reform. His consistent policy was to improve governmental efficiency and achieve a fairer balance between direct taxation and the indirect taxes bearing hard on the middling and lower-income classes, precisely to meet Marx's critique of the oppression of the poor by the rich.

Marx was scathing of Gladstone the "financial alchemist." "There exists, perhaps, in general, no greater humbug than the so-called finance," he snapped after Gladstone's sweeping 1853 budget. "The public understanding is quite bamboozled by these detestable stock-jobbing scholastics and the frightful complexity in details." Yet the alchemy and scholastics delivered political and economic "material" on an enviable scale. Gladstone's governments were generally perceived by "Middle England" of the day as holding the ring fairly honestly between competing interests. Confidence in governmental competence and fairness remained high, while for the public at large, politics was sport between competing parliamentary idols.

For Victorian aficionados, Gladstonian bric-a-brac still haunts the antique shops, not revolutionary memorabilia. Instead of stoking anti-regime riots and passing anti-socialist laws, late-Victorian ministers and union leaders in general behaved with mutual respect, seeking to reach accommodations and to maximise their autonomy vis-à-vis their less disciplined followers on left and right. There were plenty of industrial disputes, but as Marx put it of Britain in 1879: "strikes take place which, victorious or otherwise, do not advance the movement by one single step." To Marxist irritation, Gladstone legalised Britain's trade unions, making them forces for reform not revolution. Up-and-coming late-Victorian working-class leaders spent their leisure in such activities as imitating the speechifying Gladstone in "mini-parliaments" across the land. Parliament and the party system possessed an ideological strength which steadily increased throughout the 19th century. As the Labour historian Ross McKibbin puts it in a celebrated essay on the question "Why was there no Marxism in Great Britain?'":

The demand for the vote, the emphasis on the instrumentality of enfranchisement, made it difficult to conceive of any other form of political action as legitimate, or indeed, of any other form of political action.

Marx told the First International in 1864 that "the great duty of the working classes" was "to conquer political power." In Britain Gladstone was their chief ally in the conquest. His 1884 Reform Act, while not making Britain a full democracy, created a majority male working-class electorate. But in Britain, numerical dominance never became class dictatorship, or any attempt at it. Although Keir Hardie, with his cloth cap, served in Gladstone's last parliament (1892), it was another 14 years before the nascent Labour party won more than a handful of parliamentary seats and even then it only did so at the behest of an electoral pact with the Liberals. It took the social and economic upheaval of two world wars, and a bitter split in the Liberal party between rival leaders Asquith and Lloyd George – recounted in Chapter 10 – before the first majority Labour government took office in 1945. A leading light in that government was Ernest Bevin, whose intense struggle with Stalin over the post-war fate of western Europe is the subject of the next chapter. Bevin was a youthful disciple of Gladstone's, who became Britain's greatest trade union leader and foreign secretary – and was passionately anti-Marxist.

In international affairs Gladstone, like Marx, recognised that harmony required justice and consensus on norms, not just a "balance of power" or superpower policemen. In the succession of crises he confronted over the disintegration of the Turkish Ottoman Empire – the last Sultan of Turkey's interior minister was Boris Johnson's great-grandfather, murdered by revolutionaries in 1922 – Gladstone evolved notions of collective security and European cooperation which, as Henry Kissinger recognises in his book *Diplomacy*, laid the foundations in statecraft for Woodrow Wilson's efforts after the first world war to reconcile national self-determination with peaceful co-existence. They also presaged today's European Union.

Gladstone's espousal of a modern notion of European values evolved through heated experience. In his 1851 campaign against the brutalities of the Neapolitan government, while he was still a Tory, he appealed to the conscience of the Bourbon regime and spoke as a Conservative "compelled to remember that that party stands in virtual and real, though perhaps unconscious, alliance" with established governments. By 1876, as a Liberal, he was appealing to the conscience of the British masses to uphold the rights of Bulgarians to revolt against oppression, urging the eviction of their Turkish rulers "bag and baggage." As one historian remarks, by the mid-1860s Gladstone's "mature European sense" had "fused with his new democratic sympathies. They formed a highly combustible compound." "Modern" is perhaps a better word than "combustible."

It is in relation to Ireland that the Marx-Gladstone dialogue is most striking. For Marx, exploitation of the nationalist and economic grievances of the Irish was the key to, indeed the only likely cause of, an early social revolution in Britain. "After studying the Irish question for years," he wrote in 1870, "I have come to the conclusion that the decisive blow against the ruling classes in England ... cannot be struck in England but only in Ireland." Gladstone concurred. Hence his preoccupation with Irish reform, which grew with each passing year after the mid-1860s until by 1887 he was writing in his diary: "Now one prayer absorbs all others: Ireland, Ireland, Ireland."

In 1868 Marx saw controversy over the future of the established Anglican Church of Ireland as the likely ignition for social upheaval, because of its status as "the outpost of the Established Church in England as a landowner." So did Gladstone. After his election victory that year, his first legislation was to disestablish the Church of Ireland, a measure carried against bitter church and landowner resistance. Next came the agricultural land crisis. Gladstone's 1870 Land Bill, with its tentative safeguards for Irish tenants of (mostly English) aristocratic landlords, did little to contain the Land War taking place across the country, but it was a first step. But Marx lighted on the real problem, writing to Engels when the bill was before the Commons:

> The best bit of Gladstone's speech is the long introduction, where he states that even the 'BENEFICENT' laws of the English always have the opposite effect in practice. What better proof does the fellow want that England is not fit to be lawgiver and administrator of Ireland!

On this premise, Marx urged that England's working class "not only make common cause with the Irish, but even take the initiative in dissolving the Union, substituting a free federal relationship for it." Gladstone proposed just such a "free federal relationship" three years after Marx's death, stating categorically that "England is not fit to be lawgiver and administrator of Ireland." Immersed in the literature of federalism and Irish nationalism, he saw the rise of a conservative nationalist elite under Charles Stewart Parnell's "Home Rule" party, which for the first time won the great majority of Irish seats in the 1885 election, after decades in which coercion and church and land reform had failed to quell Irish discontent, as evidence that self-government was both prudent and ultimately irresistible. In the event, bitter Tory opposition and Gladstone's maladroit handling of his Liberal heir apparent Joseph Chamberlain, defeated his first Home Rule bill in 1886. His second, in 1893, was weakened by Chamberlain's defection to the Tories as a "Liberal Unionist," and by Parnell's fall in a quintessentially Victorian sex scandal. After narrowly passing the Commons, it was rejected by the House of Lords at the behest of Tory leader Lord Salisbury by a vote of 419 to 41, foreshadowing the battle between the next great Liberal reformer, David Lloyd George, and the aristocratic bastion of the House of Lords over the People's Budget of 1909, described on pages 197 to 199 below. As for Ireland, 13 years later the Catholic-dominated south became fully independent while most of Protestant Ulster was partitioned and remained uneasily within the UK, with much bloodshed on all sides then and since, largely because Gladstonian home rule was rejected a generation previously.

So Gladstone failed to conciliate Irish nationalism by liberal means. But it wasn't for want of trying.

What fundamentally separated Gladstone and Marx was the notion of inevitable class struggle and experience of liberal political institutions. An "out and out inequalitarian," Gladstone nonetheless worked himself into his most "yclept earnestness" in denouncing national and international oppressors, including (as the aristocracy deserted him) the "upper ten thousand" at home. Ironically, he shared with Marx a conception of class which was altogether too static and coloured by recent history: witness his romantic attachment to the aristocratic Whigs even as they undermined him. Yet the notion of endemic conflict, between classes or nations, aroused his profound repugnance. In part this reflected a Christian view of the "bonds of mutual sympathy" transcending classes and nations. Equally important was his faith in the power of sound institutions and expert politicians to yield a government sufficiently class neutral to promote the interests of all classes. Contemptuous of parliamentary politics, Marx was supremely unconcerned about institutional design. By contrast, Gladstone summed up his political life as "greatly absorbed in working the institutions of his country."

Marx was an acute, as well as caustic, critic of the Gladstonian style. Here he is on "Gladstone's eloquence":

> Polished blandness, empty profundity, unction not without poisonous ingredients, the velvet paw not without the claws, scholastic distinctions both grandiose and petty, quaestiones and quaestiuniculae [minor questions], the entire arsenal of probabilism with its casuistic scruples and unscrupulous reservations, its hesitating motives and motivated hesitation, its humble pretensions of superiority, virtuous intrigue, intricate simplicity, Byzantium and Liverpool.

Yet Marx's invective, for all its telling thrusts, failed to make the connection between Gladstone's method and his phenomenal success in uniting and inspiring social coalitions broader than virtually any other in modern British politics. For Gladstone, the art of politics was as much process as policy. He set high store by the processes of professional politics – rhetoric, debate, persuasion, electoral and parliamentary procedure – and was a master of them all.

Procedure, it has been said, "is the only constitution the poor English have." Gladstone was a procedural bore, yet he never confused the respect due to established forms with the imperative to ensure that the substance met contemporary exigencies. Indeed, his profound empathy with old forms and new imperatives exigencies was one of his hallmarks. "Byzantium and Liverpool" went the jibe. His ruling conviction, he told his early Tory mentor Sir Robert Peel in 1841, was "that it is possible to adjust the noble and ancient institutions of this country to the wants and necessities of this unquiet time." This made him at once one a great liberal patriot and a stickler for time-honoured institutions – not least the monarchy, which he defended despite Queen Victoria's deep loathing of him.

What of Gladstone's legacy to modern progressives? Foremost is the method: being "greatly absorbed in working the institutions of the country." It means resisting the belief – the bane of modern left and right alike – that the destruction of broadly well-functioning institutions (most recently a European Union including Britain) is fair populist game. It means talking up, not down, to the electorate. It means the cultivation of expert politicians, in the sense of politicians who are professional at the job of working institutions, formulating good policy, and interacting with elites, interest groups and voters. It means government by discussion and consideration, not by soundbite and prejudice.

Above all, it means leadership by liberals unafraid to make their case and act boldly in defence of progressive values.

Gladstone sought to leave his society more democratic, open, prosperous and cohesive than he found it. And so should we. Motivated by no Utopian vision of social or political perfection, he nonetheless defined ambitious beneficial reform projects for his own age, and he largely achieved them. As he put it to the Commons, introducing his 1884 Reform Bill to extend the vote to the working class:

> Ideal perfection is not the true basis of English legislation. We look at the attainable; we look at the practicable; and we have too much of English sense to be drawn away by those sanguine delineations of what might possibly be attained in Utopia, from a path which promises to enable us to effect great good for the people of England.

Which takes us back, full circle, to E.H. Carr's 1934 biography of Marx, published in the year of Stalin's Great Purge and Hitler's Night of the Long Knives. "In the epoch of humanism," Carr wrote, "there had been individual liberty, except for the despised and unimportant masses who lay outside the pale." In the Marxist epoch of mass rule, individual liberty would of necessity either be meaningless (as automatic acceptance of the mass will) or noxious (as a revolt against it). But, Carr concluded wistfully, the time would come for a new revolution in human thought. "The inveterate tendency of man to individualise himself will ultimately reappear; and unless all historical analogies are false, a new differentiation of the mass will lead to a new renaissance of humanism."

Thanks to Gladstone, and leaders like him, the renaissance of humanism is the civilisation of modern Europe.

3

BEVIN v. STALIN

Ernest Bevin (1881-1951) is a neglected giant: Britain's greatest trade union leader who went on to become Churchill's right-hand man as minister of labour in his wartime coalition and then transformational foreign secretary in Attlee's post-war Labour government.

Bevin described himself as "a turn-up in a million": son of a farm labourer, orphan at the age of eight, who left school at eleven yet achieved more in politics than most prime ministers. As foreign secretary he largely created NATO and the Federal Republic of Germany, following his victory over Stalin in the siege of West Berlin in 1948/9. For 323 days the world held its breath before the Soviet dictator lifted his blockade: a trial of strength as potentially cataclysmic, before it was triumphant, as the Cuba missile crisis 14 years later.

Bevin v. Stalin, like Gladstone v. Marx, is one of the seminal but previously untold leadership contests of modern Europe. Here is the story, from my Ernest Bevin: Labour's Churchill (2020).

Bevin stood up to Stalin sooner and more effectively than any other post-war Western leader. Better even than Churchill and far better than Roosevelt and Truman. He was decisive, maybe indispensable, in keeping Stalin out of Western Europe, and in the process he led the creation of the Federal Republic of Germany, NATO and the transatlantic Western alliance that continues to this day.

The policy of "containment" – seeking to contain Soviet Russia, rather than appease it – was Bevin's unwavering policy from his first day as foreign secretary, 27 July 1945, immediately after the 1945 election, until his last day, 9 March 1951, shortly before the end of Attlee's Labour government. These were the six years which largely shaped today's Europe. He was successful because of his adroit exertion of Britain's continuing world power and the decision of the United States to adopt the same policy from 1947 rather than continuing to seek an accommodation with Stalin a US policy change nurtured and then exploited to the full by Bevin.

Containment is usually credited to George Kennan, American deputy ambassador to Moscow, in his "long telegram" of 22 February 1946. But containment was Bevin's strategy from July 1945, and it was another crucial year after the February 1946 long telegram before containment was fully embraced by the Truman administration. Until then, particularly on the future of Germany, the United States triangulated between Britain and Soviet Russia. But for Bevin, Stalin might have been long past containment by the time Truman was converted to it. And but for him, the consequence might have been a Soviet-dominated Germany, that is West Germany as well as East, destroying political freedom and the whole balance of power across Western Europe.

Bevin had the measure of communism and Stalinism long before he became foreign secretary. From his earliest days leading his Transport and General Workers' Union after 1922, he grasped communism as an existential threat. He sought to root communism out of the British labour movement at every turn. After 1933, he saw communism and fascism as equal threats to democracy, peace and international order. He never made the mistake of thinking that Hitlerite fascism was worse than Stalinist communism. As totalitarian ideologies with criminal, murderous thugs as leaders, they were the same.

Bevin set out his uncompromising views on international communism as far back as the 1927 TUC conference in Edinburgh, when he opposed the creation of joint international trade union institutions with the Soviet Union. This process was already underway until he and Walter Citrine, the new general secretary of the Trades Union Congress, put a stop to it. "Bevin looked pale and grim, as he always did in major debates, when he got up to speak," recalled an observer. "You have to appreciate that running through these things there are two distinct moral standards," Bevin told the conference, getting straight to the heart of the matter:

> One is the moral standard accepted by the British movement: to differ but to hammer out their differences, and when a decision is arrived at, to loyally and honourably abide by it. That is the British standard. The Russian standard, as I see it, is that the end justifies the means. That has been our experience on the General Council. Now these two moral standards cannot be reconciled in the promotion of a unified movement.

The next passage of his 1927 speech is prophetic and compelling on how Stalin and his henchmen Molotov, Beria and Vyshinsky behaved before and after 1945, as well as why Bevin got the measure of them from his first day at the Potsdam conference in 1945:

If you turn down this resolution [rejecting collaboration with Soviet trade unions] it means that the General Council would be expected to meet the Russians on the joint committee. How would we meet them? If you had been called a traitor, a twister, a liar, and everything else that can be thought of, and you had to meet the man that called you that, would you meet him as a friend or as an antagonist? That does not promote international unity; that is the wrong way to assemble for a conference.

Bevin's resolution was carried by four to one. Britain's trade unions kept clear of their Soviet counterparts thereafter and the central plank of Bevin's foreign policy after 1945 was in place.

So far as I am aware, Bevin never once expressed admiration for Stalin while foreign secretary, as opposed to bromides about seeking a working relationship. He issued the bromides in the cause of unity in a Labour Party with strong pro-communist elements and, like much of the international community, an overwhelming belief in the early post-war years that unity was possible and necessary between East and West. But he didn't actually believe this himself and he didn't let it affect policy, in sharp contrast to Roosevelt, Truman and Jimmy Byrnes, Truman's disastrous secretary of state for Bevin's first two years at the Foreign Office.

Roosevelt regarded Stalin in 1945 not just as an ally but as a comrade. "Of one thing I am certain", he told the exiled Polish Prime Minister of the Yalta agreement, "Stalin is not an imperialist". And to the ex-US ambassador to France:

I have a hunch that Stalin doesn't want anything other than security for his country, and I think that if I give him everything I possibly can and ask for nothing in return, noblesse oblige, he won't try to annex anything and will work for a world of democracy and peace.

Churchill was not immune to the Soviet monster's charms and Bevin was privately critical of him on this score, even while the war was ongoing. "Stalin I'm sure means well to the world and Poland," Churchill told the War Cabinet after the Yalta conference in February 1945. The Cabinet note-takers record him continuing: "Premier Stalin had been sincere. He [Churchill] had a very great feeling that the Russians were anxious to work harmoniously with the two English speaking democracies," particularly after Stalin "had given the Polish people a free and more broadly based government to bring about an election." This alarmed Bevin, who knew all about communist "elections." He told the Tory cabinet minister Leo Amery that he was "fed up with Winston over a good many things," including his softness towards Stalin. Five months later, foreign secretary Eden thought Churchill's opening performance at the Potsdam conference was appalling: "He is again under Stalin's spell. He kept repeating 'I like that man' and I am full of admiration of Stalin's handling of him."

However, both Bevin and Churchill grasped Stalin's essential barbarism. The same was not true of Potsdam's novice in international communism, Harry Truman. The new American President, on arriving in Potsdam on 16 July, was polite to Churchill but wary of him. "He gave me a lot of hooey about how great my country is and how he loved Roosevelt and how he intended to love me etc., etc." Truman wrote in his diary of their first meeting. "I am sure we can get along if he doesn't try to give me too much soft soap." Whereas the following day, meeting Stalin for the first time, he was starstruck and took all the beguiling Soviet dictator's soft soap. "I can deal with Stalin. He is honest – but smart as hell." Truman proceeded over the next fortnight to triangulate between Churchill and Stalin on the fate of Poland and much else, as had Roosevelt at the Yalta meeting of the Big Three five months previously. He also stuck to Roosevelt's policy that the United States would withdraw entirely from Europe within two years.

"After ten days in Potsdam, Truman was much taken by the Russian dictator," writes the editor of his presidential papers. "A dozen years later, the President in retirement recalled in a letter to Dean Acheson [secretary of state after 1949] how he had been an innocent at Potsdam, believing that the Soviets desired peace; as for Stalin, he had 'liked the little son-of-a-bitch'."

The one thing Bevin wasn't, at Potsdam or later, was an innocent, and he never liked "the little son-of-a-bitch." Almost every other democratic leader who met Stalin was worsted by him, as by the equally magnetic Hitler. Bevin had no personal dealings with Stalin in the last years of the war, which was probably a blessing as Russia was then, of course, Britain's ally, which was obviously a factor with Churchill and Roosevelt. But Bevin was always unimpressed by the charisma of others, and he was not remotely attracted to Stalin, or impressed by him, in his personal dealings after 1945. From Potsdam onwards, he was blunt and direct with the Soviet dictator, and still more so in his constant dealings with his coffin-faced foreign minister Molotov.

By the time Bevin and Attlee arrived at Potsdam in the afternoon of 28 July, as the new Labour ministers in place of Churchill and Eden, it was too late to affect the big decisions. The conference had already been going for ten days. There had been nine plenary sessions, and Stalin and Truman were anxious to get away. Soon after the start of the conference, Truman had learned of the successful test of the US atomic bomb and its potential to bring a rapid end to the Japanese War. The atomic bomb was dropped on Hiroshima on 6 August, four days after the Potsdam conference ended.

But this didn't stop Bevin putting down markers. "I'm not going to have Britain barged about," he said to General Pug Ismay on landing in Berlin. In particular he wasn't going to be barged about by Stalin. "He said he was quite familiar with the tactics of the Communists because he had had to deal with them in his own labor unions in England," he told James Forrestal, Truman's secretary of the navy, soon after arriving, and he made this immediately plain in the first plenary session with Stalin and Truman.

As soon as the plenary started at 10.30 p.m., Bevin "repeatedly questioned Stalin's remarks in an aggressive manner." When the dictator made a vaguely worded proposal to recognise Soviet-controlled governments in Eastern Europe, Bevin replied that in order to be "perfectly straight with the House of Commons" he would not "quote things in words of doubtful meaning." Attlee nodded throughout but left the talking to his foreign secretary, demonstrating his adage: "If you had a good dog like Ernest Bevin, there was no point barking yourself."

The following morning, 29 July, Stalin developed a "cold" that resulted in a two-day suspension of plenary sessions. It was an anti-Bevin chill: "His cold may have been a device to avoid having to deal with the truculent Bevin while working out compromises with the more accommodating Americans," writes a historian of the Cold War.

When Stalin's chill abated sufficiently for him to return to the conference table, Bevin did not let up. To get a sense of the drama, here are the heated Stalin–Bevin exchanges on the Soviet dictator's claim for massive reparations from Germany, at the heart of his post-war strategy to plunder and control the Ruhr in British-occupied north-west Germany. There had already been a provisional agreement on reparations earlier in the summit between Stalin, Churchill and Truman, but Bevin was setting out his stall. Even in the dry official transcript it comes alive:

> **Mr Stalin** said he hoped the British and Americans would meet the Soviet wishes.
>
> **Mr Bevin** should have in mind that the Russians have lost much equipment. They should receive a small part of it back then. Mr Bevin said that the British had had in mind equipment after determination of the amount needed for the maintenance of the [German] economy.
>
> **Mr Stalin** said this was in his proposal. If he thought it over, Mr Bevin would accept it.
>
> **Mr Bevin** replied that he could not. He had used the words 'equipment not needed for peacetime economy'. This was not in the Soviet document.
>
> **Mr Stalin** reread the Soviet proposal on this point.

Mr Bevin said he did not give the basis on which the determination would be made.

Mr Stalin insisted it was the same thing.

Mr Bevin asked if he would then accept the British wording and said he did not want a misunderstanding.

Mr Stalin said the Russians had in view 15 per cent of the equipment to be removed which was not necessary for the peacetime economy but was not clear about it.

Mr Bevin again cited the British language which he said reflected the views agreed upon by the British and American delegations...

Mr Stalin observed that the U.S. was willing to meet the Soviet wishes – why was Britain unwilling?

Mr Bevin said that because they were responsible for the zone from which the Soviet claims were to be satisfied [i.e. the Ruhr]. They were also responsible for satisfying the claims of France and other countries.

Mr Stalin pointed out that France had signed an armistice with Hitler and had suffered no real occupation. France should be satisfied with a small amount. He said that 150 divisions had been sent to Russia from France or had been supplied from France.

Mr Bevin repeated that they had to satisfy France, Belgium, Czechoslovakia and Holland. The British wanted nothing except raw materials ... He said that the percentage the Soviets asked plus reparations from their own zone gave more than 50 per cent.

Mr Stalin insisted that it would be less than 50 per cent and pointed out in addition that they were supplying goods to the equivalent of 15 per cent. The Soviet proposal was a minimum. The Soviets received only 10 per cent – the others got 90 per cent. He agreed to 15 per cent and 10 per cent and thought it fair. The Americans agreed. He hoped Bevin would support them.

Mr Bevin said 'All right then.'

Mr Stalin expressed his thanks.

The final exchange is especially significant. Bevin's problem in resisting Stalin in the crucial first year after the war was that Truman and Byrnes had already conceded the points at issue, making it hard for Britain to revisit them. US appeasement of Stalin was one of Bevin's biggest problems at Potsdam and after.

Byrnes reciprocated the distrust. Bevin's manner at Potsdam was "so aggressive," he wrote, "that both the President and I wondered how we would get along with this new Foreign Secretary." The answer is that they didn't try too hard. Truman and Byrnes saw Britain as "a bankrupt imperialistic power," in Giles Radice's brutal description, and they acted to hasten insolvency. Within a month of Labour taking office, on 21 August, they ended Lend–Lease financial support to Britain, which had provided an open-ended credit card for vital British imports from the US. This caused the "financial Dunkirk" which forced Britain to seek a large emergency US loan, secured by Keynes over the next year with immense difficulty and on onerous terms. Truman also declined to share atomic research with Britain when Attlee flew to Washington in November 1945, which was a decisive factor in his and Bevin's decision to initiate a British nuclear weapons programme.

Bevin's elemental skill, knowledge and grasp of the international scene is captured in James Forrestal's full account of their conversation at Potsdam:

Found Bevin in very good form. He said in answer to my question that the only industries they proposed to nationalise were power, railroads, mines, and textiles up to the spinning mills. He indicated he had no use for Laski. He spoke highly and appreciatively of Anthony Eden. He said he was quite familiar with tactics of the Communists because he had had to deal with them in his own labor unions in England.

I asked him a question about the Emperor in Japan, whether he thought we ought to insist on destruction of the Emperor concept along with the surrender. He hesitated and said this question would require a bit of thinking, but he was inclined to feel there was no sense in destroying the instrument through which one might have to deal in order to effectively control Japan. He then made a rather surprising statement—for a liberal and a labor leader: 'It might have been far better for all of us not to have destroyed the institution of the Kaiser after the last war—we might not have had this one if we hadn't done so. It might have been far better to have guided the Germans to a constitutional monarchy rather than leaving them without a symbol and therefore opening the psychological doors to a man like Hitler.'

He said he was determined to get going what he called the three historic axes of European trade—the Baltic axis, that is to say, the old Hanseatic League; the Antwerp axis, and the Genoa axis. He said these three were the classic foci of European trade for hundreds of years back, that if they could be restored to activity, it would do much to bring about revival of commerce in Europe.

Bevin knew how to cultivate the tough Forrestal, who was soon to become US secretary of defence and a crucial ally. At home Labour would be bold, but not extreme. Abroad, he wasn't any taking nonsense from Stalin, and he knew the Soviet game. The priority was to get Europe working again, reviving its principal trade routes. The comments about the Kaiser and the Emperor of Japan are arresting: a bit left field, like much of Bevin's conversation, but making striking points on what had gone wrong after the first world war and the lessons. He was possibly right about constitutional monarchy in Germany. As on reparations, he sought to avoid repeating the mistakes made after the first world war and he had thought through what they were. He pointed the way towards the decision to keep the Emperor of Japan: seventy-five years later, that looks a good decision.

Germany was the main battleground on which Bevin fought Stalin for the whole six years of his foreign secretaryship. Hitler had committed suicide in his Berlin bunker only eleven weeks before Potsdam and the Reich was now divided and governed by Britain, Russia and America. North-west Germany was to be Britain's last major colony and maybe the only one where British rule was an unmitigated success, ending in 1949 with the creation of a strong, democratic West German state. The Federal Republic of Germany was essentially Bevin's creation. From this distance it all seems inevitable, yet it was anything but. It resulted from an intense six-year struggle for power which Bevin won and Stalin lost, and at every stage it was incredibly close-run.

It is impossible to overstate the physical and moral wreckage of Germany in May 1945. The cities were piles of rubble, the devastation and desperation akin to Hieronymus Bosch's vision of hell. Column after column of civilians, soldiers and concentration camp inmates marched and shuffled with little but their clothes towards home, or towards somewhere, anywhere, because they had to go somewhere, anywhere. Starvation, desperation and death were everywhere. Never before in Germany had so many people been killed in so short a time, not even in the Thirty Years' War. "Everywhere there is great demand for poison, for a pistol and other means of ending one's life," reported the SS at the end of March. "Suicides due to depression about the real catastrophe which is expected with certainty are an everyday occurrence."

For Germans conquered by Stalin, it was like the fall of Constantinople to the Ottomans in 1453: panic, rape, murder, pillage, frenzy, violence, destruction, arbitrary horror at any place and at any moment. Millions in eastern Germany fled from the Russians in fear for their lives. Millions of Germans in territories further east marched and shuffled westwards, brutally expelled from their *Heimat.*

In 1944, Churchill, Stalin and Roosevelt decreed that after unconditional surrender Germany would be dismembered, with each of them governing a third of the country. The plan, drawn up by FDR's adviser Henry Morgenthau Jr, was for swathes of Germany to be given to France in the west and Poland in the east. The industrial Ruhr, its plants and factories, would be dismantled and then turned into an international zone, with its inhabitants encouraged to migrate. What was left was to be divided into two rump, rural states of northern and southern Germany.

The Morgenthau Plan was adopted by Churchill and Roosevelt at the British–American Quebec conference of September 1944. Churchill did one of his masterly rewrites of history in the light of future events, but the record is clear that he and FDR agreed to a dismembered, de-industrialised Germany. They committed to "eliminating the war making industries in the Ruhr and the Saar, looking forward to converting Germany into a country primarily agricultural and pastoral in its character."

Roosevelt, for all his wide and generous sympathies, was a Germanophobe at the end of the war, drawing on his unhappy schooldays as a nine-year-old in Germany. In one of his last conversations, in April 1945, he told General Lucius Clay, about to depart for France as Eisenhower's deputy, of his "early distaste for German arrogance and provincialism." FDR wrote to Queen Wilhelmina of the Netherlands in August 1944:

> There are two schools of thought, those who would be altruistic in regard to the Germans, hoping by loving kindness to make them Christians again – and those who would adopt a much 'tougher' attitude. Most decidedly I belong to the latter school, for though I am not bloodthirsty, I want the Germans to know that this time at least they have definitely lost the war.

He and Stalin had little difficulty agreeing on this point.

If Roosevelt and Truman had been the lead players in Germany in 1945, events might thus have panned out very differently than with Bevin in the lead. But a key decision at Yalta in February 1945 was the allocation of the economic heart of Germany – the Ruhr, the Rhine, Hamburg and Bremen – to Britain as its zone of occupation. The British zone was also in population terms by far the largest of the four, and by far the most strategic in its proximity to France and the Netherlands. It became still more so after the flight of Germans westwards. The Yalta zone allocation decision reversed the previous plan for Britain to take the more rural south of Bavaria, Baden and Württemberg, while the US occupied the industrial north-west. Churchill negotiated hard for this exchange, which gave Britain the dominant role in post-war Germany and Europe. By mid-1945, 29,000 British officials were in Germany, taking control of the huge British zone under the leadership of Field Marshal Montgomery, who was appointed by Churchill as its governor on 8 May.

By Potsdam, Britain's military and Foreign Office analysts had few illusions about Stalin's intentions. Alan Brooke, Churchill's chief of the Imperial General Staff, wrote in his diary as early as 27 July 1944:

> Should Germany be dismembered or gradually converted to an ally to meet the Russian threat of twenty years hence? I suggest the latter … Russia is the main threat. Therefore, gradually build her up and bring her into a Federation of Western Europe under the cloak of a holy alliance of Russia, England and America. Not an easy policy.

The Potsdam Declaration, agreed by Stalin, Truman and Attlee on 2 August, was Morgenthau-lite, based on "four Ds": de-militarisation, de-Nazification, de-industrialisation and democratisation. It was the first three that mattered most; democratisation was last and least. The immediate step was the abolition of all existing German rule and dismemberment of the Reich. The Polish/German border was shifted 120 miles west and Alsace-Lorraine returned to France, reducing German territory by a quarter compared to 1937. Germans east of the Oder-Neisse line were summarily expelled, as were all Germans in Poland, Czechoslovakia and Hungary. Berlin, like the rest of Germany, was divided into four zones under direct rule by the Big Three and France.

Bevin's approach to containing Stalin after Potsdam was his classic formula of hard, egotistical but pragmatic trade union bargaining with all comers, be they Soviets, Americans, French and Germans, or the Treasury, fellow ministers and parliamentarians at home, on the basis of not giving an inch to Moscow except where *force majeure* left no choice.

This required a robust attitude not only to the US but also to France, which in the immediate post-war years sought to stop the creation of a viable West Germany. De Gaulle had been Churchill's *bête noire* almost from his first day in London in 1940. Now, together with Georges Bidault and Robert Schuman, his successors as leader of France after he retreated to Colombey-les-Deux-Églises in January 1946, de Gaulle sought to enlarge France, beyond the Yalta and Potsdam agreements, at the expense of western Germany. This caused constant tension with Bevin.

For Bevin, the problem with the United States in 1945 was fundamental. Truman inherited FDR's commitment to leave Europe within two years, and the general view of his policy makers, especially Byrnes, was that this required a peace treaty with Stalin. This would include concessions on Central and Eastern Europe, agreement on emasculating the British Empire and a joint administration for the whole of Germany.

Bevin was never anti-American when it came to resisting Stalin. '49th STATE? NO THANK YOU, MR CHURCHILL' was *Tribune*'s headline after Churchill's Iron Curtain speech of March 1946, which applied equally to its view of Bevin. Bevin's view of the United States oscillated. Britain was the "last bastion of social democracy in Europe," he argued in a Cabinet paper of 1946, and the British Empire was all that stood between "the red tooth and claw of American capitalism and the communist dictatorship of Soviet Russia." But when it came to resisting Stalin he never doubted that it had to be "two against one," and he regarded much criticism of America as profoundly ignorant. With his knowledge of the American trade union movement dating back to his first fraternal visit to the American Federation of Labor convention in 1916, he saw America, for all its libertarian zealots, as a republic teeming with workers fighting the same fight as the workers of Britain, France, Germany and the world over. In an exchange about Marshall Aid in the House of Commons with a communist MP, one of the few elected in 1945, Bevin let rip:

> When you strip all these things down which produce political ideologies and get down to the masses, what do they want? They want to live! They want to be free, to have social justice, to have individual security, to be able to go home, turn the key in the lock and not be troubled by a secret police. Why not let them live? Why set them at each others throats? That is the basis of my approach to the problems of a war-scarred Europe and world.

But in 1945 Marshall Aid was still two long years away. After Potsdam, Bevin had to contain Stalin, entice America and stabilise Germany. These were parallel challenges: stabilising Germany and encouraging the US were critical to curbing Stalin and vice versa. And they had to be done in the teeth of opposition from much of the British left, which wanted to appease Stalin or positively supported him. And the right was not immune. Lord Halifax, having spent the late 1930s appeasing Hitler, wanted to do the same with Stalin after 1945 as ambassador to Washington. He declared himself "intensely irritated" with Churchill's Fulton speech in March 1946, which was "a waste of Churchill's commanding position" and "cut off any progress towards an accommodation with Russia." Bevin was with Churchill.

As the new colonial power in the Ruhr and the industrial northwest of Germany in 1945, Britain's immediate objective was, in the words of General Brian Robertson, Montgomery's deputy governor of the British zone, "not to batter Germany down – she was sprawling in the dirt already – but to rebuild her up and do so wisely. We had to save Germany physically from starvation, squalor and penury, and spiritually from despair and communism."

To replace anarchy with stability, the factories, the mines and the farms of West Germany had to start working again. In the summer of 1945, Germany was importing 70 per cent of its food: famine was the looming catastrophe. Bevin's policy was to empower Montgomery and his administration in Germany to act with ruthless pragmatism to restore normality to the British zone, while resisting Stalin's relentless campaign for punitive reparations. Bevin's economic adviser, Alec Cairncross, told him: "At the end of the last war Lord Keynes familiarised us with the truth, which experience is now reiterating, that Germany was the heart of the entire European economy and that upon her prosperity the prosperity of Europe in large measure depends." Bevin made this the core of his policy. It meant stopping Russia and France from seizing coal and steel from the Ruhr. It also meant lifting production quotas, which had been capped tightly at Potsdam and immediately afterwards, against Bevin's better judgement.

Having confronted Stalin personally, Bevin wasn't fazed by Molotov, his foreign minister. He deliberately mispronounced the apparatchik's name ("Mr Mowlotov"), and told him straightout in one bruising early encounter that his attitude and policies were "reminiscent of Hitler." The two men crossed swords throughout the first four years of his foreign secretaryship in the institution of the Council of Foreign Ministers, the rolling summit of the four victorious allied powers charged at Potsdam with negotiating the post-war peace treaties and managing great-power diplomacy. The council held nine summits between 1945 and 1949, each of between ten days and six weeks. Bevin, the only minister to be a member of the council throughout the four years, was its dominant personality.

London hosted the first meeting of the council in September 1945. From the outset Bevin's strategy was to keep Stalin completely out of West Germany and West Berlin, despite the Potsdam Declaration which stated the opposite. He also sought to contain Stalin across the rest of Europe and the Middle East. Obviously this put him in conflict with Molotov. More problematically, it also put him on a collision course with Jimmy Byrnes.

Now historically overshadowed, Byrnes was a key figure in the Roosevelt and Truman administrations. Variously congressman, senator and governor of South Carolina in the old confederacy, he had expected to be FDR's vice-presidential nominee for the 1944 election before losing out at the last minute to Senator Harry Truman of Missouri, who was unencumbered by southern political baggage. Dubbed "my assistant president" by FDR, Byrnes was an assertive director of war mobilisation at the end of the war, becoming Truman's secretary of state just before Potsdam.

Byrnes had been at Yalta with Roosevelt and inherited FDR's belief that compromise deals could be done by personal diplomacy with Stalin, although he was lacking the maestro's subtlety and intuition. He was "prima-donnish" – the reason FDR gave for not appointing him to succeed Cordell Hull as secretary of state at the end of 1944 and why he and Truman ultimately fell out (he called the president "Harry" even in front of subordinates). However, for the crucial nineteen months between July 1945 and January 1947, Byrnes was the principal diplomat of the United States and the main shaper of its foreign policy. This wasn't just because "Byrnes had decided that he was going to run foreign policy and he would casually tell the president about it," as Truman's press secretary recalled. It was also Truman's express will. On appointing Byrnes, the president said in his diary that he would go with Byrnes, the "hard hitting trader on the home front," and not with "the smart boys in the State Department" including Edward Stettinius Jr, the secretary of state sacked to make way for "Jimmy", and ambassadors and diplomats like George Kennan and Averell Harriman.

"I know how to deal with the Russians, it's just like the US Senate," Byrnes breezily told his delegation on board the

Queen Elizabeth travelling to the London Council of Foreign Ministers in September 1945. "You build a post office in their state, and they'll build a post office in our state." Bevin was as much a prima donna as Byrnes, but had no illusions about happily building post offices with Stalin across Europe.

At the London conference, Bevin could not get Byrnes to support a joint Anglo-US statement refusing to recognise Stalinist regimes in Romania and Bulgaria. Even on Austria and Yugoslavia, where they did briefly co-ordinate, Byrnes attributed Russian obstructionism to Molotov rather than to Stalin, telling an aide that there was "no hope of stopping Molotov except by appealing to Stalin," naivety akin to his description of the Soviet monster as "a very likeable person." As one Cold War historian notes drily, "Byrnes came to London with one illusion and left with another."

Illusion soon became dangerous delusion, for in November 1945 Byrnes instigated an unscheduled pre-Christmas meeting of the Council of Foreign Ministers in Moscow, after liaising with Molotov but without even consulting Bevin. He thought he would be able to rapidly broker comprehensive peace treaties, and that he could do this through personal chemistry with Stalin. He told an associate he would achieve "further progress with Stalin in Moscow by means of the compromising American diplomacy of mutual accommodation already practiced by the Hopkins mission [sent by Truman to Stalin in June 1945] and at the Potsdam conference." According to his biographer, "Byrnes presumed that he could 'get through' to almost any individual if only they could meet personally. Hence, on his own initiative shortly after

Thanksgiving Day he called on Molotov to agree to a second meeting of the Allied foreign ministers before the end of December 1945." And he suggested that they meet in Moscow, "where the US Secretary could, if necessary, meet personally with Stalin."

This explicit triangulation, in Moscow itself, astonished and alarmed Bevin, particularly when Byrnes told Stalin, in a conversation relayed to British diplomats, that he had intentionally blindsided Britain. France was excluded even from attending the Moscow conference, at Molotov's instigation. Bevin told Byrnes bluntly that Stalin's aim was to dominate Europe from the Baltic to the Adriatic. He said the same to Stalin himself. When the dictator remarked that Britain and the US had "spheres of influence but the USSR had nothing," Bevin countered that "the Soviet sphere extended from Lübeck [on the German Baltic coast] to Port Arthur [on China's east coast]."

The Moscow conference signified the high-water mark of Byrnes's accommodation of Stalin. By Christmas Eve, after eleven days of sessions and two tete-a-tetes with the Russian dictator, Byrnes had only two tangible achievements: agreement on a United Nations Atomic Development Authority, which rapidly fell apart at the UN on issues of scope and control; and, in return for US recognition of Stalinist regimes in Romania and Bulgaria, the token concession – which Byrnes saw as far more significant – that there should be two opposition ministers included in their communist-dominated governments. Bevin deliberately blocked any accommodation on Germany. For him, the most contentious issue in Moscow was Soviet destabilisation and threats to Iran. Bevin pressed Stalin to withdraw from northern Iran and proposed a mutual early withdrawal of troops. Stalin refused, saying he needed to protect the oil wells at Baku, "whereupon Bevin asked sardonically whether he feared an Iranian attack."

In 1952, by which point Truman had moved decisively against Stalin and sought to deny that he had ever sought accommodation with Moscow, a bitter dispute erupted between Byrnes and Truman about precisely what had happened in 1945 and 1946. Truman claimed he hadn't known what Byrnes was up to in Moscow and, when he learned, "read him the riot act" about turning Romania and Bulgaria into "police states." He claims to have read aloud a letter to his secretary of state, which included the following: "I am not going to agree to the recognition of those governments unless they are radically changed." Byrnes responded that Truman was rewriting history.

There is indeed no contemporary written or third-party record of Truman saying any of this to Byrnes at the time. On the contrary, the circumstantial evidence suggests that Truman supported his chief diplomat at the time. Byrnes did an NBC radio broadcast on 30 December 1945 defending the Moscow conference. "It must be recognised that the Soviet government has a very real interest in the character of the government of these states," he said of Romania and Bulgaria. This broadcast came after he had seen Truman, who praised it in front of guests the following evening when Byrnes was present again. Byrnes said that, had Truman criticised him, "I would have resigned immediately with my deep conviction that there must be complete accord between the President and his Secretary of State," just as he had in fact walked out of previous posts under FDR, Beaverbrook-style, and just as he was to resign thirteen months later. Byrnes's account is the more convincing.

Tellingly also, Truman praised the Moscow conference in his State of the Union address to Congress on 21 January 1946 and made no criticism of Russia. "The agreement reached at Moscow preserves this [human rights] in the making of peace with Italy, Romania, Bulgaria, Hungary and Finland. The United States intends to preserve it when the treaties with Germany and Japan are drawn." All of which was of little comfort to exposed western Germany. The US proceeded to recognise the Stalinist government of Romania on 5 February, nine months before an "election" inaugurated 43 years of dictatorship.

Churchill's seminal "Iron Curtain" speech of 5 March 1946, hosted by Truman in his hometown of Fulton, Missouri, made some impression on the president but it set out only a partial strategy for dealing with the Stalinist menace. Its stirring call for a "fraternal association of the English speaking peoples" was not a policy to resolve the immediate future of Germany, where Stalin already had a firm and growing foothold thanks to Russian domination of the east and the provisions of Yalta and Potsdam.

All this is vital to appreciating the significance of Bevin's stalling tactics in negotiation after negotiation with Byrnes and Molotov throughout 1945 and 1946. In the case of Romania and Bulgaria, occupied by Russian troops, Bevin did not ultimately seek to block the US/Russia deal, but he sought to avoid any US/Russia deal on Germany which might have increased Stalin's leverage and led to the United States withdrawing troops and economic support, as it did after Versailles in 1919.

Bevin was negotiating on a second front too: with Attlee at home. Although Attlee stuck strongly behind Bevin in public and in Cabinet, he was nervous about an overt split with Russia and periodically in 1946 pushed back on Bevin's determination to block any agreement with Stalin. But he shared Bevin's basic assessment of the Soviet dictator and stepped back when Bevin responded robustly. A decisive moment was Bevin's cabinet paper of 3 May 1946 on the government's negotiating position for the forthcoming reconvened Paris meeting of the Council of Foreign Ministers.

Bevin spelt out the extent of the Soviet threat and made an explicit case for the containment of Stalin and building up western Germany as a counter to Soviet Russia. "Until recent months," he told the cabinet in the 3 May 1946 paper,

> we have thought of the German problem solely in terms of Germany itself, our purpose having been to devise the best means of preventing the revival of a strong aggressive Germany. But it can no longer be regarded as our sole purpose, or indeed perhaps as our primary one. For the danger of Russia has become certainly as great as, or possibly even greater than, that of a revived Germany.

In west Berlin, British support for the social democrats was crucial in saving them from "fusion" with the communists, as happened in east Berlin and the whole of Soviet occupied eastern Germany with the creation of the Socialist Unity Party in February 1946. When John Hynd, Minister for Germany, warned Bevin that Germany's social democrats and christian democrats were "rapidly losing their grip on Western Germany and the Communists are going ahead," Bevin agreed. "I never understood why we could not proceed with our own policy in our own zone in the same way as the Russians were proceeding with their policy in their zone," he responded. When Hynd went on to say "the question must be faced whether we should now proceed to establish a [West] German government," Bevin was cautious about timing: "This means a policy of a Western bloc and that means war." But the groundwork for turning the British zone into a self-governing entity had begun by April 1946 and soon became Bevin's next step in containing Stalin in Germany. The alternative was "Communism on the Rhine", said Orme Sargent, a tough anti-Stalinist recently appointed by Bevin as the Foreign Office's top official.

Communist subversion was now relentless across Central and Eastern Europe. Poland, Hungary, Czechoslovakia, Romania and Bulgaria were under intense Stalinist assault and fell one by one to communist police states operating by murder, expropriation and mass persecution. At the United Nations in London in January 1946, a bitter dispute took place between Bevin and Vyshinsky over Iran and Greece. Byrnes stayed silent. John Foster Dulles and Senator Arthur Vandenberg, the leading Republicans present, noted this and were "impressed with Ernest Bevin's impassioned stand against Vyshinsky." In a Senate speech on the question "What is Russia up to now?" back in Washington on 27 February, Vandenburg pointedly praised Bevin as "sturdy" while not mentioning Byrnes. Days later, a Stalinist coup, with Russian tanks and troops, was narrowly averted in Tehran, with Bevin and Byrnes working closely in tandem for the first time because of the imminent threat to the Persian Gulf and Iranian oil supplies.

In public, Bevin continued to pay lip service to the quest for a new global order in partnership with Russia. But in private and semi-private he gave no ground whatever to left-wing appeasers of communism. By now, mainstream Labour MPs could see the pattern of events across Europe and responded positively when rallied by Bevin. But a hostile minority was increasingly vocal and there were many fence-sitters. At a meeting of Labour MPs on foreign policy on 22 March 1946, "after lashing the British Communists as fellow travellers and rounding abusing his critics," he carried the room. Stalin helped with a rare speech in Moscow, on 9 February, asserting that a peaceful co-existence of capitalism and communism was impossible.

The Council of Foreign Ministers reconvened in Paris on 25 April, the first of three meetings in 1946, two in Paris and one in New York, which occupied fourteen weeks between them. Byrnes was still hoping that Paris would yield his peace treaty with the Soviet Union. Since the Iranian crisis, Byrnes had been more alive to the real Stalin behind the façade, but the Soviet–Iranian agreement of 4 April, which ended the immediate threat in Tehran, gave him renewed confidence in his deal-making powers. He still sought a treaty on Germany with the Soviet dictator, which most American administrators in Germany also thought necessary as they couldn't commit to keeping US troops and administrators there long term. Byrnes's 6 September speech in Stuttgart, announcing that troops would stay for the time being, was notably equivocal: "As long as there is an occupation army in Germany, American forces will be part of that occupation army." This begged the question: how long was "as long"? When, in Paris in July 1946, Byrnes asked Bidault what he thought Stalin was trying to achieve in Europe, the Frenchman replied bluntly: "Cossacks on the Place de la Concorde." Byrnes did not respond.

The first Paris conference of 1946 saw Byrnes side with Bevin against the punitive reparations demanded by Molotov from western Germany's steel and coal production. But to Bevin's consternation, the US sided with Molotov in support of setting up pan-German institutions, including possible four-power control of the Ruhr. Bevin rejected this outright. Worse still, Byrnes published proposals to reduce US, British and Russian military forces in Germany, which he proposed would pave the way for a demilitarised Germany to be policed by inspectors. Bevin didn't need Stalin to ask the question, "How many divisions have the inspectors got?"

Bevin kept stalling, making a blunt move to break up any US/Russian bromance on Germany by threatening Molotov with re-opening the question of the Polish–German border. "It has only been agreed that Poland should occupy certain areas pending final settlement," he warned Molotov, "and the United Kingdom would have something to say in view of their experience when the time came to fix them." By these and other feints he managed to get the council adjourned on 16 May without progress on Germany.

Time was Bevin's ally as the situation in Germany went from bad to worse during 1946. The food crisis, with more severe rationing, was leading to a breakdown in relations with German leaders and people in both the British and the American zones, while the subsidies needed to maintain the zones were unsustainable. British and American administrators on the ground were ever more convinced of the need to empower the West Germans themselves. When

Montgomery left Germany in May, handing the governorship of the British zone to General Brian Robertson, he reported to Bevin and Attlee:

> The whole country is in such a mess that the only way to put it right is to get the Germans 'in on it' themselves. We must tell the German people what is going to happen to them and their country. If we do not do these things, we shall drift towards possible failure, and that 'drift' will take the form of an increasingly hostile population which will eventually begin to look east.

Byrnes's attempts at triangulation continued when the Council of Foreign Ministers reconvened in Paris on 15 June. Bevin accordingly kept up the belligerence. In five long and acrimonious sessions on Germany, he used every argument and ploy he could to forestall US/Russian agreement, which again led to a deadlock, as he had hoped. Bevin also had France against him: Bidault wanted to annexe the Saar and put the Rhineland under four-power control separate from the rest of Germany. So tense and exhausting were these weeks that Byrnes had a near breakdown and Bevin had a heart attack on returning to London. All this was on top of his other preoccupations, including the bombing of the King David Hotel in Jerusalem on 22 July. "All the world is in trouble and I have to deal with all the troubles at once," was his characteristically egocentric worldview.

What started out in Paris as a precarious holding operation ended up with a tentative advance. On the penultimate day of the summit, 11 July, in reply to Bevin's robust statement the previous day that Britain would "organise" its zone of Germany in the absence of a four-power agreement, to which he had no intention of agreeing, Byrnes made an offer to join the American zone with any other zone "for the treatment of our respective zones as an economic unit." In practice, this could only mean unity with the British zone. It was a crab-like move towards Bevin's policy of a "bizone" – that is, a united British/American zone with joint political and economic institutions, possibly paving the way for a *de facto* western German democratic state.

However, Byrnes was still riding two horses, for he followed up this bizone suggestion with another proposal for four-power central administrative institutions in Berlin, which Bevin continued to block. More than a year after the war there was still no agreement between Byrnes and Bevin on how to handle Germany, and the United States was still not committed to staying in Europe to contain Stalin.

This intense Anglo-American mistrust is vital to the momentous October 1946 decision, taken in secret by Attlee, Bevin and a small number of cabinet colleagues, to equip Britain with nuclear weapons. Bevin's famous remark that "we've got to have this thing over here whatever it costs, we've got to have the bloody Union Jack flying on top of it," is routinely quoted. However, equally important was Bevin's previous sentence: "We've got to have this. I don't mind for myself, but I don't want any other foreign secretary of this country to be talked at or by a secretary of state in the United States as I have just had in my discussions with Mr Byrnes." It wasn't only opposition to Stalin and the Soviets which precipitated the decision to adopt the British nuclear deterrent, but also acute concern about the United States.

The 26 October 1946 decision to adopt nuclear weapons has become a *cause célèbre* to students of British government, because it wasn't taken by or even notified to the Cabinet, let alone Parliament. But this misses the main point. Decisions of this kind in British government have always been taken by small groups of ministers in secret, whether or not notified to Parliament soon afterwards. In this case, it was not long before the decision was known. The point of substance is what the decision actually *was.* And the point of significance is that, but for Bevin, the decision might have been different. We know this because, by the account of an official present, Bevin arrived late for the meeting, saying he had fallen asleep after a good lunch. Dalton and Cripps argued against a nuclear programme on grounds of cost, and were carrying the point when Bevin reversed the decision in his most brutal method, described by Roy Jenkins: "He simply stopped the engine in its tracks, lifted it up, and put it back facing in the other direction." He barged in, saying, "That won't do at all, we've got to have this,'" as he proceeded to make the remarks quoted above, ending in the decision to go ahead.

So had Bevin not been foreign secretary in 1946, Britain might not have proceeded with the nuclear deterrent. Perhaps Attlee would have driven the decision anyway, over-ruling Dalton and Cripps, and maybe if Dalton had been foreign secretary he would have acted differently. All we know is that, at the time, Bevin was crucial to this decision, and his reasons were directly related to the containment of Stalin.

If the nuclear decision was taken in secret from the British Parliament and media, it was not secret from the White House or the higher echelons of the Truman administration, where it was seen as a statement of British resolve, personified by Bevin, to stand up to Stalin. This can only have encouraged the US to do the same. In the autumn of 1946 Byrnes engaged more positively on the bizone concept, although money remained one of several sticking points. The Americans wanted the bizone financed 57 per cent by Britain, as per the larger population in its zone, while Dalton, as Chancellor, proposed that the US pay four-fifths.

Bevin leapfrogged these disputes with another bold move. On 22 October 1946, in the same week as the nuclear decision and just before leaving on the *Aquitania* for the next Council of Foreign Ministers in New York, he told the House of Commons of his resolve to turn the British zone into a self-governing state, while also lifting the cap on industrial production in the Ruhr. Damning Stalin with faint praise ("we are extremely glad of Marshal Stalin's categorical denial of the idea that Russia might be intending to use Germany against the west"), he went well beyond his previous language of "organising" the British zone to set out a detailed plan to turn it into a de facto state in defiance of East Germany and the Soviet Union. This Bevin Plan set out virtually the entire constitutional structure of what became the Federal Republic of Germany three years later.

"We are striving to stimulate habits of orderly self-government among the Germans," he told MPs, continuing:

> There have recently been elections in the British zone for local councils. There have also been elections in Berlin. Next spring there will be elections for the provincial councils we are decentralising German administration. We have set up a

new province of North Rhineland-Westphalia and intend reorganising the remainder of our zone into two other provinces, Schleswig-Holstein and Lower Saxony. The Hanseatic towns of Hamburg and Bremen will remain separate. Looking ahead, we contemplate a constitution which would avoid the two extremes of a loose confederation of autonomous States and a unitary centralised state. The central Government might consist of two chambers, one popularly elected and the other consisting of representatives of the regional units. There might be a Supreme Court like the United States Supreme Court, with jurisdiction to give rulings on the powers of all central and provincial legislatures.

Bevin was building, as he always built. Here, only seventeen months after the end of the war, are all the key constitutional principles of the Federal Republic of Germany as it functions successfully today: the regional states (*Länder*); power-sharing between the *Länder* and a federal government; a two-chamber German Parliament comprising an elected lower chamber (the *Bundestag*), which appoints the Chancellor; and an upper chamber (the *Bundesrat*) representing the *Länder* to cement the federation. Together with a "mixed member" form of proportional representation, which kept individual constituencies while providing a proportional top-up, it was a constitution that learned from the best of Germany's past and from the best of the Westminster model. It launched West Germany with a constitution now long regarded as a model in its democratic credentials and its spread of political and economic power over a large and diverse country.

Rab Butler, the post-war Tory moderniser, immediately welcomed the Bevin Plan. "Today we have achieved in the foreign secretary's speech the moral purposes which will always be the basis of British foreign policy at its best," he said, recognising also the great significance "that the Rhineland and the Ruhr are to be included in the general bounds of what will amount to a federalised Germany."

This was only a fraction of the work now underway in the British zone to turn it into a successful society and economy – "Trying to beat the Swastika into the parish pump," as one British official put it. Under Bevin's *imprimatur*, German trade unions, media, banks, arts, schools, universities and industry were all revived and modernised to guard against the experience of the Nazis while also applying some British practice. From the creation of *Der Spiegel* and Germany's free media, to industrial partnership between unions and employers (*mitbestimmen*), British engagement was deep and constructive, in many respects more so than in the modernisation of post-war Britain itself.

Armed with parliamentary support for turning the British zone into a *de facto* state, Bevin renewed discussions on the bizone a fortnight later, with Byrnes in the margins of the next protracted Council of Foreign Ministers in New York from 4 November to 12 December 1946. Crucially, they resolved the money issue. Bevin initially tried a weak bluff at Dalton's behest, that Britain might withdraw from its zone if the US did not finance most of the bizone. Byrnes called his bluff by offering to swap zones, adding waspishly – and revealingly of his stand-offish attitude to Britain even at this late stage – that "with American organisation and the potentiality of the British zone they would make it a success in a very short time." The deal was done on 1 December for 50:50 cost sharing. Attlee worried that this was still unsustainable, so weak was Britain's financial position as the American loan ran out. But since the deal paved the way to America's continuing engagement in Germany, Bevin seized it. The 50:50 burden sharing also helped justify an equal partnership between the UK and US in the crucial decisions ahead. In the event, it was supplemented by Marshall Aid, and by the setting up of NATO with a massive, indefinite US military commitment to Germany, so the US ended up picking up the lion's share of the costs.

On the key issue of Germany, Bevin succeeded in keeping the Council of Foreign Ministers stalled for the whole six weeks of the New York meeting. He was still not in agreement with Byrnes, and the absence of France from New York made him all the more anxious to play for time. The reason for the French absence went to the heart of the issues at stake. In the second post-war French election, held on 10 November, a week into the conference, the pro-Stalin French communists became the largest party in the French National Assembly with 28 per cent of the vote. Bidault never made it to New York because of the horse-trading required to put together a precarious anti-communist government. But while the French election made the dynamics of New York more difficult for Bevin, it also demonstrated to the US the gravity and imminence of the Soviet threat deep across Western Europe, not just in Central and Eastern Europe. The threat of communist, even Stalinist, governments across the entire continent, including in France and Italy, was very real.

Another game changer was the mid-term US Congressional elections, held the day after the council opened (5 November). Truman lost control of both Houses of Congress. The rising tide of anti-communism among the

victorious Republicans, and their determination to
weaponise it against the Democrats, decisively shifted US
policy. Joseph McCarthy became senator for Wisconsin in
this election and Richard Nixon won his first congressional
seat after a ruthless red-baiting campaign in California, in
which the future president alleged that his Democrat
opponent – the incumbent – was backed by Radio Moscow.
Days after the end of the New York summit, on 19
December, Byrnes told Truman he was resigning, although
it was a month before he was replaced by George Marshall.

"Any man who would want to be secretary of state would
go to hell for pleasure," was Byrnes's parting shot. It was
more a commentary on Byrnes's lack of staying power than
on the job itself. Unlike Bevin, who never resigned from
any major post and never willingly gave up on any major
endeavour, Byrnes had no stomach for the struggle ahead:
"He realised that the German negotiations would involve
even longer and more arduous meetings, not to mention
political hazards," writes his biographer.

Political hazards were pretty strong in London too. The
left of the Labour Party was now in open revolt at Bevin's
anti-Stalinism, tabling a hostile motion in the House of
Commons while he was in New York, to his fury. Attlee
replied to this debate personally, loyal as ever to Bevin, but
120 Labour MPs abstained in the vote and the mood was
sour. This made no difference to Bevin's policy, nor did the
Keep Left attack, a pamphlet published in early 1947 by
Michael Foot and Richard Crossman. Unlike Byrnes, and
Beaverbrook before him, Bevin had both power and staying
power in resisting his adversaries. In this, as Attlee's
spokesman Francis Williams noted, he had more than a

passing resemblance to the strong man he was confronting in the Kremlin.

Bevin's negotiating brief for Moscow, set out to the Cabinet in a paper of 27 February 1947, was deliberately couched in terms he knew Stalin would not accept. It reiterated the Bevin Plan for the British zone in Germany, raising for the first time the necessity for a new currency for the Western zones as part of the bizone plan, which, he said explicitly, "would be tantamount to splitting Germany into two." He ruled out any early resumption of reparations to Russia until the West German economy was on its feet and gained Cabinet agreement for substantial and immediate increases in West German industrial production. The brief was explicit that the Bevin Plan was compatible with a single state covering the whole of Germany if Stalin accepted all his conditions. But, "If, as is very possible [certain, in Bevin's view] we fail to agree, we could proceed without difficulty to implement the conclusions recommended in this memorandum in respect of the British, American and the French zones only." In other words, the Cabinet was giving the green light to create a fully-fledged West German state.

Bevin's strategy for dealing with Stalin in East Germany was also spelt out in the same Cabinet paper. His priority now was "to keep the Iron Curtain down unless we get satisfaction on all our conditions and build up West Germany behind it." Then, he argued, "there is more chance of drawing Eastern Germany towards the West than vice versa" – a prophecy of what actually happened before and after the collapse of the Berlin Wall in 1989.

Characteristically, Bevin told Attlee and Cabinet colleagues that "the principles at stake are too important for compromise." What he was setting out was in reality a plan of action, not a negotiating brief. He wished, he said, "to bring matters to a head."

Attlee, as ever, supported Bevin in the face of continued sniping from Dalton, Bevan and Morrison. "We shall have to let them [the Russians] do most of what they like in Eastern Europe and Germany," was Dalton's comment on Bevin's paper, which shows how different the fate of Germany and Europe might have been with him as Foreign Secretary. At the same time, Bevin took complete charge of running the British zone, merging the Control Office, which since 1945 had overseen the administration of the British zone, into the Foreign Office. Hynd was sacked as Minister for Germany and Robertson, as governor, became directly responsible to Bevin, a change of form rather than reality.

Bevin's weakness from 1947 onwards was not in his policy, nor in commanding the requisite Cabinet and parliamentary support. He dealt with the Foot/Crossman *Keep Left* attack with a robust rebuttal pamphlet, *Cards on the Table*, written by Denis Healey, by then head of Labour's international secretariat and on his way to becoming a pugilist of Bevinist proportions. The title was a deliberate echo of Bevin's successful speech on foreign affairs to the May 1945 Labour Party conference, when he had said bluntly to Russia and the US: "Do not present us with *faits accomplish* when we arrive [at the peace conference] … If I may use a Cockney phrase, there should be 'cards on the table, face upwards'."

Bevin's problem, rather, was that he was in terrible physical shape in the run-up to the Moscow conference. His now perennial heart condition was exacerbated by the worst winter in living memory in 1946–47 and a fractious Cabinet beset by fears of imminent British bankruptcy. He was so ill, finding it difficult even to get up and down stairs, that he wasn't allowed to fly to Moscow. It took him five days to get to the Russian capital by train, with his personal doctor Alec McCall in attendance. Dalton thought he might not return. Six weeks in Stalin's lair did not look auspicious.

However, once in Moscow, Bevin's spirits and health revived. The British ambassador Sir Maurice Peterson and his wife took great care of Bevin, and isolation from the hurly burly of London, without the social whirl of Paris or New York, had a positive effect. The advent of spring raised Bevin's spirits further. "It cheers one up to see the great thaw and the trees breaking into bud," he wrote to his T&G secretary Ivy Saunders, almost poetically, on 30 March. "Looking out of the windows we look across to the Kremlin with its great golden domes, hideous yet beautiful. Round it is the great wall which is symbolic of its secrecy. Few people enter and who does no one knows what happens within it." There was a run-in with Dr McCall over Bevin partaking of too much champagne at a reception at the Greek embassy: Bevin had to stop the doctor packing his bags. But when they left Moscow he was in better shape than when he arrived, to the relief of Attlee, who badly wanted him to continue at the Foreign Office.

As in Paris and New York, the formal sessions of the Moscow conference were protracted, tense and deadlocked. Molotov gave little ground. Nor did Bevin, who bigged up his verbal confrontations with "Mr Mowlotov" for media consumption. It was a six-week trial of strength (10 March–24 April) which, again, Bevin won. He prevented, for the last time as a realistic possibility with American support, a punitive Soviet reparations regime on West Germany and the creation of a single demilitarised and neutral German state. Molotov helped, with his continued insistence on huge reparations, his opposition to lifting the cap on industrial production in the Ruhr and his insistence on a strong central government based in Berlin – in the middle of the Soviet zone – as part of a new German state, repudiating the power-sharing federalism of the Bevin Plan.

Bevin's big success in Moscow, of all places, was in striking up a good relationship with the new American Secretary of State. George Marshall initially found Bevin's aggression off-putting, but over the next six weeks, as he came to understand Bevin better and what he was up against in Stalin and Molotov, he became increasingly sympathetic and friendly.

Dubbed by Churchill "the organiser of victory" as FDR and Truman's military chief of staff, Marshall was a military genius in the way that Bevin was a trade union genius. They forged a strong two-year partnership from 1947 to 1949, which became transformational with the launch of the Marshall Plan only a few weeks after the Moscow conference. It was all the more remarkable given that each had a precarious domestic base: Marshall was the fourth secretary of state in just twenty-six months, serving an inexperienced US president apparently heading fast towards the electoral rocks. Meanwhile the situation in Attlee's government was barely stronger in 1947–48 as bankruptcy vied with exhaustion. Rarely have two foreign ministers risen further above the fray to do great constructive work.

Tellingly, after their first meeting, Bevin told Ivy Saunders that Marshall was "quiet and firm and very direct with a voice and manner like Ashfield was ten years ago." This was highpraise. Lord Ashfield was the British–American founder of what became today's Transport for London, with whom Bevin did deal after deal as union leader in the 1930s. Bevin and Marshall similarly did deal after deal in the late 1940s.

The three Western foreign ministers each had audiences with Stalin in Moscow outside the plenary sessions. Bevin spoke fairly bluntly to Stalin when he saw him in the Kremlin on the night of 24 March. "I had a good talk, and understandings on many points," he wrote the day after to Ivy Saunders. He appreciated the sensation of dealing directly with Stalin. But never one to mistake words for deeds, he saw no thawing of Stalin's totalitarian ambitions in Europe and Bevin's policy changed not one iota after his last personal encounter with the Soviet dictator.

Crucially, Stalin made a wholly negative impression on Marshall, who delayed his night time audience in the Kremlin until towards the end of the conference, 15 April, when he could see the cards on the table. The dictator was smoothly emollient ("These are only the first skirmishes and brushes of reconnaissance fire," he told the American) but, after five weeks of Molotov, Marshall was unimpressed, particularly as the sessions of the conference the following week were the worst of all. Molotov proposed a big cut in American forces in Germany while leaving

Russia's intact. Since the main issue Marshall had discussed with Stalin was the impasse on German de-militarisation, this convinced him that Stalin did not want compromise but thought he could force the Americans out of Europe and take over Germany. He told Stalin bluntly that he "had reached the conclusion that the Soviet Union did not want such a treaty [based on full demilitarisation in Germany] and would report accordingly to the President."

The breakthrough moment was a Bevin–Marshall meeting on 18 April 1947, after five weeks together and a week before the end of the summit. They had already met privately several times outside in the interminable plenary sessions, but crucially Marshall had by now met Stalin. He had also by now sized up the warring factions in his own delegation. Travelling with a bipartisan delegation in the wake of the Republican takeover of Congress, there were sharp divisions between John Foster Dulles, later Eisenhower's secretary of state, who saw a fundamental battle with Stalinist communism that had to be won in Europe, and General Lucius Clay. Clay was the imperious governor of the American zone in Germany, who had been close to Byrnes and thought Germany, including West Germany, was ungovernable without agreement on joint institutions with the Russians. This co-existed with a jaundiced view of the British, particularly the Labour government's plans for public ownership in the Ruhr, which, Clay told Marshall, "would not be acceptable to the American businessmen and bankers." He didn't spell out how having Stalin in control of the Ruhr would be an improvement on a few nationalised industries, a point Marshall quickly grasped, and Clay left Moscow early.

"The Soviet government were just fooling," Marshall told Bevin in their 18 April meeting. "The US was not going to humiliate herself by remaining in that position [of continuing to seek a German treaty with Stalin]. He was going to tell the President that he did not believe the Russians wanted Four Power Agreement." This was music to Bevin, and what he had been waiting to hear from the US government for two years. He and Marshall resolved to press ahead with the bizone on the basis of practically the entire Bevin Plan, including two crucial advances: firstly, there would be only one political and administrative centre for the bizone, and secondly, the chairman of the bizone's executive committee would hold executive authority. This pointed the way to the creation of a fully-fledged West German government.

In parallel with these discussions in Moscow, Bevin's diplomats in Washington paved the way for the Truman Doctrine, announced by the President to Congress on 12 March 1947. This was a breakthrough for what it said about "the policy of the United States to support free peoples who are resisting attempted subjugation by armed minorities or by outside pressures." But it was also significant because the US implemented this doctrine immediately on taking over from Britain in Greece and Turkey, in order to sustain their precarious governments under constant threat of communist coups.

In Greece, British action to prevent a communist coup had been a key play by Churchill, supported by Bevin, in the last months of the wartime coalition in 1944/5. The significance of the US taking over from Britain in Greece and Turkey is brought out in the account by Francis Williams, Attlee's adviser:

Bevin, shrewdly assessing in his mind the current of American opinion and the cumulative effect upon it of Russian policy, decided the time had come to force the American Administration to a major policy decision. On 24 February he instructed the British Ambassador in Washington to deliver to Mr. Marshall a memorandum informing him that Britain's economic position would no longer allow her to continue as the reservoir of financial and military support for Greece and Turkey. The memorandum created a profound shock in the State Department. It faced the United States with a decision that it had so far been unwilling to meet.

This overdoes the "Bevin masterstroke" narrative but testifies to growing American-British partnership.

From the end of April, back in Washington and London respectively, Marshall and Bevin set off a chain reaction that was to transform Western Europe and seal the containment of Stalin. The initiating move was Marshall's address at Harvard University on 5 June, proposing American economic assistance to stabilise Europe. "I need not tell you, gentlemen, that the world situation is very serious," he told the Harvard students. He then set out pretty much the entire argument that Bevin had been making about Germany and Europe for the previous two years:

> Recovery in Europe has been seriously retarded by the fact that two years after the close of hostilities a peace settlement with Germany and Austria has not been agreed upon … The truth is that Europe's requirements for the next three or four years of foreign food and other essential products – principally from America – are so much greater than her present ability to pay that she must have substantial additional help or face economic, social, and political

deterioration of a very grave character. The remedy lies in breaking the vicious circle … the initiative, I think, must come from Europe.

It is what happened next that precipitated the chain reaction. Marshall had not informed Bevin of what he was going to say, and the Foreign Secretary only heard about the speech from the BBC news on his bedside wireless set. But he immediately grasped its potential to rally and rebuild Western Europe and immediately threw all his energy into conjuring up a European response of sufficient weight and urgency to give substance to Marshall's invited offer of American support.

The "Marshall Plan" was, as a State Department official put it as late as 28 July, "a flying saucer – nobody knows what it looks like, how big it is, in what direction it is moving, or whether it really exists." Bevin determined to convert the flying saucer into a concrete long-term US commitment to Britain and Western Europe. He proposed a joint response to the French, the Italians, the Belgians and the Dutch and flew to Paris to lead it while sending strong personal messages of encouragement and support to Washington. "Britain for eighteen years after Waterloo practically gave away her exports but this resulted in stability and a hundred years of peace," he told the US deputy ambassador in London. It was dubious history but excellent politics.

"The speech which Mr Marshall delivered at Harvard may well rank as one of the greatest in the world's history," Bevin told London's Foreign Press Association on 13 June. "When the United States throws down a bridge to link east and west it is disastrous for ideological and for other reasons to frustrate the United States in that great endeavour." He addressed directly the concern that Britain would not work in partnership with the rest of Western Europe. "We are in fact, whether we like it or not, a European nation and must act as such, as a link and bridge between Europe and the rest of the world," he told the assembled international journalists. It was classic Bevin: realism and idealism jostling, never more so than in this garbled yet crystal clear piece of Bevinese:

> We have been the first in the ring and the last out [in the first and second world wars]. Therefore it has been impossible to maintain our economic and financial position. But if anybody in the world has got it into his head that Britain is down and out, please get it out. We have our genius and science; we have our productivity, and although we have paid the price, I venture to prophesy that in a few years' time we shall have recovered our former prosperity.

"The guiding principles that I shall follow in any talks on this will be speed," Bevin told the House of Commons on 19 June. "I spent six weeks in Moscow trying to get a settlement. I shall not be a party to holding up the economic recovery of Europe by the finesse of procedure. There is too much involved."

Soviet involvement in any American aid plan was an immediate issue. Publicly, Bevin encouraged a positive response from Moscow, but privately he was relieved when Stalin refused, following an exceptionally truculent performance by Molotov, ending in a walkout, at the foreign ministers' meeting in Paris in late June to discuss the response to Marshall. After Molotov's boycott, Bevin countered French moves to maintain dialogue with Moscow on the evolving plan. As he argued, Stalin's decision to impoverish Eastern Europe rather than accept

American aid demonstrated why it was so essential in the first place. After the Paris meeting, Bevin moved swiftly to set up a bespoke West European organisation to plan and administer Marshall Aid with no Soviet involvement: what became the Organisation for European Economic Co-operation (today's OECD). He was anxious to avoid a role for the existing United Nations Economic Commission for Europe because of Soviet membership. Having closed the front door to Stalin, he wasn't going to let him in by the back door.

By leading Europe, forcing the pace and painting the big picture, Bevin rose to the level of Marshall's vision. As with his own plan of 22 October 1946 for a *de facto* West German state, Bevin leapfrogged the all too many issues dividing Europe, and Britain, from the US, to make the bold transformational response that produced Marshall Aid.

Until Marshall Aid, Bevin's fear was that France and Italy, in particular, were on the precipice of communism and that only what he called the "outer crust" of Europe might be saved. Given the trend of elections and politics in Europe from the mid-to-late 1940s, this was no fantasy. As late as April 1948, a strong "popular front" of communists and socialists was fighting the Italian elections, led by the socialist Pietro Nenni, with fellow traveller support from the Labour left in England in the "Nenni telegram", which was signed by thirty-seven Labour MPs. Bevin, fiercely opposed to popular fronts with the communists since the 1930s, supported the expulsion of the organiser – John Platts-Mills, a long-time campaigner for friendship with Stalin – from the Labour Party. It was only two months since the Stalinist coup in Czechoslovakia, which Bevin had earlier thought might be saved from Stalin. The Czech foreign minister colleague of Bevin's, Jan Masaryk, a liberal who survived the Stalinist coup of 25 February 1948 but not the subsequent purge, was found dead in the courtyard of the foreign ministry in Prague dressed only in pyjamas, having "jumped out of a window." It was said that "Jan Masaryk was a very tidy man, such a tidy man that when he jumped he shut the window after himself." Bevin had no hesitation spelling out what had happened and who was to blame. His first Foreign Office private secretary, Bob Dixon, had gone to Prague as ambassador in January 1948 and reported to him after the coup: "The whole character of the state had been changed in less than a hundred hours."

The communists were kept out of government in Italy in 1948, helped by a socialist split over the formation of the Nenni Front with the communists, and by covert British and American support for de Gasperi's Christian Democrats. But the Nenni Front got 31 per cent and as late as 1951 the communists polled 26 per cent in French parliamentary elections. After Marshall Aid, though, the communists generally looked less attractive to working-class electorates in Western Europe; and after the creation of NATO, West Germany and the European Coal and Steel Community over the next three years, the prospect of Stalinist coups receded. And Stalin ended Stalinism by dying suddenly on 5 March 1953. But no one could have securely predicted any of this in the late 1940s.

Bevin shored up his domestic position after the 'failure' of the Moscow conference with his melodramatic "stab in the back" speech to the Labour Party conference at Margate in May 1947, which Dalton said "swept away all opposition."

Left-wing MPs and intellectuals had "stabbed me in the back," he declared, by undermining his foreign policy while he was negotiating in New York and Moscow. "If you are to expect loyalty from Ministers, then Ministers however much they make mistakes have a right to expect loyalty in return. I grew up in the trade union movement, you see, and I have never been used to this sort of thing." The latter point was quite untrue, of course, but the trade unionists in the hall loved it.

The US embassy in London reported to Washington on 11 June 1947, as Marshall and his deputy Dean Acheson weighed up how far to back Bevin's response to Marshall's speech: "We believe that as matters now stand [with Bevin in post], Britain will be on our side in any serious issue." This assessment was crucial to Truman and Marshall's decision to press ahead, despite the Byzantine difficulties of winning the support of the Republican Congress in the autumn of 1947. Bevin made an initial play for Britain to be regarded as a Marshall Aid recipient in its own right, not just as part of Europe, in order to secure a larger share without necessarily creating new European co-operation machinery. His argument was that Britain was Europe's only strong and reliably anti-Stalin democracy. This was true, but it was a pretty humiliating admission of Britain's economic plight, particularly as Truman demurred. Instead, Britain essentially became the lead European co-ordinator when the five-year $12 billion aid programme started in April 1948.

The details of Marshall Aid, and the sums involved, were always secondary in Bevin's mind to the fact that it turned into hard political and economic currency the concept of a "Western Europe" of liberal democracy and rising prosperity, equipped to resist communism. The Marshall Plan for European aid and the Bevin Plan for a West German state were two sides of the same coin, and both depended on seamless British and American action. As Bevin whispered to an aide during the opening of the Paris foreign ministers meeting to discuss Marshall Aid in late June, "We are witnessing the birth of the western bloc."

A string of British–American agreements followed in the summer and autumn of 1947. The "convertibility crisis" of July/August was resolved on 20 August, when Washington agreed to the suspension of the convertibility of pounds into dollars, which for a month had been draining Britain's foreign reserves at an alarming rate. A week later, Bevin agreed with Marshall to substantially increase the level of coal and steel production in the Ruhr, overriding strong objections from Bidault of France, who wanted less German steel and more German coal but only if the coal was for French consumption. There was also agreement that the Western zones of Germany would receive Marshall Aid because, as the Committee of European Economic Co-operation reported with strong British encouragement after the Paris summit, "Other Western European countries cannot be prosperous as long as the economy of the Western Zone [of Germany] is paralysed, and a substantial increase of output there will be required if Europe is to become independent of outside support."

A critical issue, where Bevin and Bidault both compromised with the US in the summer of 1947, was on plans for coal and steel nationalisation in the Ruhr. This was a personal cause of Bevin's and symbolically important to Labour. But on 12 September he agreed with the US that in place of indefinite public ownership there would be a five year "trusteeship" of the coal mines in the Ruhr, with ownership vested in the *Land* of North Rhine-Westphalia. After this, the elected *Land* government could, but not necessarily would, be allowed to decide how the mining industry was to be managed in the future. Bevin agreed this convoluted formula with reluctance. The French did not like it either, fearing it would give too much power to the Germans. It ignited Jean Monnet's seminal thinking on a West European political union, which became official French policy and led to the European Coal and Steel Community as the first step on the road towards today's European Union. But the short-term imperative to secure American goodwill persuaded Bevin to drop mandatory nationalisation. The biggest American concern about the West German bizone was now resolved.

Bevin was now making little pretence of a shared project with Stalin, or of any desire for substantive four-power negotiations for the united Germany presaged at Potsdam. But he did not want a complete diplomatic breakdown with Molotov, which would only heighten tensions further and antagonise the left in Britain and across Western Europe. He handled the second Council of Foreign Ministers meeting of 1947, held in London in November and December, accordingly. As he explained to Bidault beforehand: "At Moscow [in March/April] he had not been entirely certain of public opinion at home. Since then the [Labour] party meeting at Margate and the TUC conference had shown that the country were squarely behind him. People in this country realised what the Russian game was." Marshall told Bevin on 4 December that American public opinion "was now baying for blood" and he could "break off and tell the Russians to go to the devil." This for the first time put him on the hawkish side of Bevin, who lapped it up while agreeing with Marshall not to bring the London conference to an actual breakdown.

Before the conference opened, Bevin and Molotov had a no holds-barred confrontation in the Foreign Secretary's residence in Carlton Gardens. It was vintage Bevin, at least in his retelling of it to the diplomat and diarist Harold Nicolson at a Buckingham Palace reception soon afterwards:

'Mr Molotov, what is it that you want? What are you after? Do you want to get Austria behind your iron curtain? You can't do that. Do you want Turkey and the Straits? You can't have them. Do you want Korea? You can't have that. You are putting your neck out too far and one day you will have it chopped off. You are playing a very dangerous game. If war comes between you and America in the west, then we shall be on America's side. Make no mistake about that. That would be the end of Russia and of your revolution. What do you want?'

'I want a united Germany,' said Molotov.

'Why do you want that? Do you really believe that a unified Germany would go communist? They would say all the right things and repeat all the correct formulas. But in their hearts they would be longing for the day when they would revenge their defeat at Stalingrad. You know that as well as I do.'

'Yes,' said Molotov. 'I know that but I want a united Germany.'

But a united Germany under Soviet tutelage is precisely what Molotov did not get. He and Stalin were never going to get it from Bevin without a war. And not, by now, from the Americans either.

The bizone was now functioning and work was underway on a new West German currency, which was to be another crucial underpinning of the new West German state. The launch of the Deutschmark on 20 June 1948 has gone down in history as the work of Ludwig Erhard, West Germany's founding economic minister, but it was largely the work of British technical experts over the previous two years. Equally vital was the promotion of capable, untainted political leaders for the new West German parliament and government. By late 1947, two leaders were establishing themselves as authentic West German leaders, both of them from the British zone. Konrad Adenauer, the pre-1933 Mayor of Cologne, became leader of a Catholic centre-right alliance, the Christian Democratic Union, while Kurt Schumacher, a pre-1933 Social Democratic Party (SPD) leader based in Hanover after 1945, became leader of an SPD that embraced all the Western zones and West Berlin, refusing to "fuse" with the communists as in East Germany and East Berlin.

Neither Adenauer nor Schumacher had easy relations with the British authorities. They were tough, seasoned politicians who had survived Hitler without compromising themselves, which maybe explains why they were to be so successful in guiding the new West German state after 1949. Adenauer was even briefly banned as Mayor of Cologne in December 1945 after falling out with a British general, which he wore as a badge of honour. Governor Robertson and his team made the relationship work thereafter, and in 1948 Adenauer was elected chairman of the new bizonal executive committee, making him *de facto* leader of the emerging West German state. He went on to be elected founding Chancellor of the Federal Republic at its inauguration on 15 September 1949. Bevin did not seek to influence the election to make a social democrat the first Chancellor. The Attlee and Truman administration supported the new West German government thereafter, not exercising most of the reserve powers they continued to hold. It was a supreme act of democratic statecraft.

To bring it about Bevin had to work hard to secure French consent, first to put the French zone into the new amalgamated Western zones, and then to agree the Federal Republic, which was ultimately approved by the French National Assembly by a majority of only six votes. "Our task was to save western civilisation," Bevin told Bidault in early 1948. "He [Bevin] himself felt that we should have to come to some sort of federation in Western Europe whether of a formal or informal character. As an Englishman, he hoped it would not be necessary to have formal constitutions. Everything should be flexible, but we should act quickly." This appeal to "saving western civilisation" while "acting quickly" is the essence of Bevin at his most masterly. He understood that unless the West became a cause it was nothing, and its rallying cries were freedom, democracy and prosperity. Hence his support for the Council of Europe, established in 1949 with Churchill in the vanguard, despite his opposition to federal arrangements for Europe.

All this took place as relations with Stalin plunged from acute tension to deep crisis. In September 1947, Cominform, the "Information Bureau of the Communist and Workers Parties", was formed from Moscow to unite Stalin's Eastern bloc, amid vitriolic attacks on Western socialist leaders, including Bevin and Attlee who were "attempting to cover up the rapacious essence of imperialist policy under a mask of democracy." Bevin replied in kind. "The free nations of western Europe must now draw together," he told the House of Commons in January 1948. "We shall not be diverted by tyrants, propaganda or fifth column methods from our aim of uniting by trade, social, cultural and all other contacts of these nations of Europe and the world who are ready to cooperate."

On 20 March 1948 Berlin's three-power control council collapsed. Stalin withdrew on the pretext that the introduction of the Deutschmark was undermining the unity of Berlin. On 24 June he blockaded the Western zones of Berlin, which were deep inside the Soviet zone of East Germany and entirely surrounded by it. He also cut off the supply of electricity from East Berlin. This was a bold play by Stalin to expel both Britain and America from Berlin, to take over the entire city and maybe stop the creation of a West German state. His gamble was that Britain and the US would sooner abandon Berlin than undertake the almighty struggle and expense required to maintain their zones, risking another European war. He sensed rightly that unless he evicted the Americans from Western Europe quickly, before they took up permanent residence, he and his communist puppets would be permanently shut out. A thriving democratic West Berlin in the heart of East Germany and Soviet-controlled Eastern Europe was an existential threat to his whole project, so he judged the blockade a risk worth taking.

But Bevin and Marshall never flinched from the moment Russia closed West Berlin's surrounding land borders. They were adamant that Berlin had to be kept – and kept open to the West. In a renewed D-Day spirit, British and American forces worked as one, sustaining a dramatic eleven-month airlift of food, fuel and people. It was heroism, risk and mission to match the greatest moments in history. Up to 7,000 tons of goods were flown into West Berlin every day for 323 days to supply the 2 million inhabitants. Bevin and Attlee's key decision, to allow the US to station in Britain B-29 bombers that were capable of carrying atomic weapons, convinced Stalin of the British–American determination to stay in Berlin. After weeks when the world held its breath, Stalin did not interfere with the airlift and did not escalate to war.

The siege of Berlin was lifted on 12 May 1949, the highpoint and vindication of Bevin's resistance to Stalin.

The Berlin blockade accelerated progress towards a permanent transatlantic military alliance. The North Atlantic Treaty setting up NATO, signed by Bevin in Washington on 4 April 1949, was a phenomenal negotiating achievement. It began as a serious project when Bevin appealed to Marshall on 11 March 1948, a fortnight after the Stalinist coup in Prague, for the British and US governments "to consult without delay" on establishing a transatlantic security pact. Marshall immediately replied, after consulting Truman: "Please inform Mr Bevin that in accordance with your aide memoire of 11 March we are prepared to proceed at once in the joint discussions on the establishment of an Atlantic security system."

American willingness to commit to the defence of Europe in time of peace "marked a revolutionary step in US policy," said Oliver Franks, sent to Washington as British ambassador after successfully executing the negotiations for the Marshall Plan. Franks also negotiated the 1951 agreement by which US military bases became permanent in the UK. Bevin's objective throughout was to create not just reciprocal transatlantic defence and security commitments, but also an institution that would promote lasting solidarity and a real community of interest between leaders and peoples on both sides of the Atlantic. Hence NATO, with the emphasis on the last word: Organisation. This included a parliamentary assembly drawn from all the member states. "If only I'd had time to make the Atlantic Pact into something large, into a wider organism, with a budget and other things for the whole area," he told his ex-assistant Nico Henderson in his last conversation as Foreign Secretary, six weeks before his death. But he did pretty well. Seventy years on, the organism is alive and well.

It now has thirty members: North Macedonia is the latest country to join, in 2020, in one of the most disputed and unstable regions of Europe in 1945, which had caused Churchill and Bevin so much grief after 1944.

The road to NATO included both the Berlin blockade and the Brussels Pact between Britain, France and the Benelux states, signed just a month before the NATO treaty, in March 1948. The Brussels Pact was itself an enlargement of Bevin's Anglo-French Dunkirk Treaty of March 1947, a binding mutual defence commitment, so it was the piecing together of a jigsaw. Vital too was Attlee and Bevin's decision to commit to the Korean War in June 1950, which for all the trauma it caused in sending British troops, demonstrated to the US, in the fraught end-game of Stalinism, that Britain would stand by the United States as well as *vice versa*. In this intense period of British American collaboration, as the only two global democratic powers, it was a genuine "special relationship", however misused the term later became. The new partnership extended to agreement on the devaluation of sterling and further economic support for Britain in September 1949, negotiated by Bevin and Cripps together in Washington in an atmosphere far warmer than for Keynes's loan negotiations of 1945.

This Anglo-American co-operation was enhanced by Bevin's exceptionally close rapport with Dean Acheson, who took over from George Marshall as Secretary of State on 21 January 1949. Acheson had been Marshall's deputy and served in previous foreign policy roles for Roosevelt and Truman dating back to 1941. In 1949, a large part of which they spent in each other's company at long summits in Washington, New York, London and Paris, he and Bevin were almost telepathic, building on four years of shared endeavour and discussion of the Soviet menace dating back to the days of Jimmy Byrnes, whom Acheson had distrusted from the start. It was an uncle–nephew relationship, but with the nephew holding the cheque book. Bevin took to calling Acheson "me boy." After one particularly obscure Bevin intervention in the crucial North Atlantic summit of September 1949, where Bevin couldn't quite bring himself to endorse German rearmament, Acheson suavely remarked: "If Mr Bevin means what I think he means but not what he said, we are in agreement."

Of all Bevin's achievements in his life, the greatest was the one about which he was most reticent: the creation of the Federal Republic of Germany. His goal throughout was to stop Stalin dominating Europe and undermining Western democracy; for Germany itself he had no love. "I tries 'ard, Brian," he told General Brian Robertson, Governor of the British zone, "but I 'ates them."

Throughout these six turbulent years, which focused so much on the future of Germany at the heart of post-war Europe, Bevin only went there once, apart from the Potsdam conference, and that was to Berlin to show solidarity with British troops in the struggle against Stalin during the 1949 blockade. He only met Adenauer once. The new German Chancellor took great offence when, in 1950, Bevin blurted out in the House of Commons that "the Hitler revolution did not change the German character very much. It expressed it." When Churchill protested, it led to some telling Bevinese: "I had to deal with them as well as the right honourable gentleman, as employers, and in shipping, and in many other things where I got into close contact with these gentlemen." Everything came back to the Transport and General Workers' Union.

But Adenauer respected Bevin. When, again in 1950, Bevin intimated that he wanted to speak to the Ruhr miners, the Chancellor responded with an invitation to address the *Bundestag*; the first foreign visitor to be accorded this honour. Bevin was by now too ill to accept.

As for Stalin, he outlived Bevin by just two years. And he kept out of Western Europe.

Bevin won; Stalin lost.

4

BIDEN

Elected at the age of 78, Joe Biden (b. 1942) is the oldest and most experienced politician ever to assume the US presidency. He harks back to FDR, JFK and LBJ as a progressive leader, but will he be a changemaker to match?

Joe Biden saw Camelot before him on his election as one of the youngest ever senators in 1972, hoping to be the next JFK only nine years after the man himself had been shot. Joe had dashing good looks, a glamorous young wife, and three beautiful children. Then days later a truck smashed into Neilia Biden's Chevrolet as she was on her way to buy a Christmas tree. Neilia and baby Naomi were killed instantly; the two under-five boys, Beau and Hunter, seriously injured. Overnight, Joe became "a man of sorrows, acquainted with grief." In the decades ahead, his own near-death from a brain aneurysm and then—later on—Beau's losing battle with brain cancer deepened the acquaintance.

The presidential dream, however, never expired during 36 years in the Senate, including two unsuccessful tilts at the highest office. But destiny seemed to lie in a court ruled by others, apparently culminating in a stint as vice president to Barack Obama.

Then came Donald Trump and Covid-19. The people chose Biden, the oldest, most battle-hardened knight of the

Democratic court, to fell the grotesque, gargantuan monster laying waste to all about. The veteran struggled a little in mounting his steed, but rode out and did it. The creature writhed and lashed out violently to the last, but then was no more. Milton's "happy realms of light" after "darkness visible."

Yet amid the relief and euphoria, the reality in 2021 is a land still beset by plague and locusts. The pandemic has become the worst peacetime crisis for America since the Great Depression. The people's desperate yearning is for a leader who, like FDR, can bring the country out of deep recession and embattled pessimism. And unlikely as it would have once seemed, friends, and even foes too, are projecting this role on their new president. Indeed, he is thrusting it upon himself: Biden constantly invokes FDR as muse and guide.

Fittingly, perhaps, Joe Biden Junior was born in 1942, in the years after the New Deal and Roosevelt's struggles to dig the United States out of depression and lead the world from out of the dark shadow of authoritarianism. Joe Biden Senior moved from Scranton, Pennsylvania to the small port city of Wilmington in neighbouring Delaware in the 1950s, as early prosperity was followed by excruciating downward mobility when his uncle's wartime armaments business evaporated along with later ventures. There was enough money—just—to get young Joe to a Catholic private school and then to college, but the struggle was genuine.

Biden's role model FDR was impulsive, gregarious, constantly dynamic, and managed to dominate the centre-ground while governing radically. The New Deal was a

Keynesian revolt against unemployment and stagnation. FDR was experimental, often incoherent, sometimes outright contradictory, yet he always found a way to win in the face of crisis. A contemporary quipped that he had a second-class intellect but a first-class temperament—by far the more important gift in transformative democratic politics. Biden may not have FDR's charm and command, but he shares something of his temperament and instinct—and in a similar context. Crucially, to my mind, he is also one of the "club of 30": democratic leaders first elected to public office or seriously engaged in politics by the age of 30, "professional" politicians in the sense of being true experts, deeply versed in the institutions of state from their early careers. FDR first got elected at 29, the same age as JFK; LBJ at 28; Clinton at 30. In Britain Churchill was elected to parliament at 25, Blair at 30.

Biden got elected to one of Delaware's three county councils at the age of just 27, then to the US Senate just two years later, in an extraordinary coup against a popular Republican incumbent. He could only take his seat because he attained the 30 years stipulated as a minimum in the US Constitution on a birthday (20th November) that fell between the election and the summoning of the new Congress in January 1973.

Only a handful of politicians who start young and endure for decades are skilled and lucky enough to reach the top. But those few who do become quintessentially public figures, with public lives and public *families* akin in some ways to royalty in their celebrity. They acquire a vital quality of latency—an ability to cut through to voters by being so long imprinted on the public mind—which makes them a constant point of reference, occasionally, as with

Biden, able to stage a dramatic return after their careers appear finished.

For "club of 30" politicians, entering the limelight when barely adults and maturing in the public eye, their frailties as well as their strengths become familiar, even endearing, and integral to their charisma—either that, or their flaws barely register because they don't fit with their already established public persona. (FDR's polio, wheelchair and walking braces would have kept him out of any office, let alone the Oval Office, had he not started out long before they struck, enabling him to master infirmity and its media treatment within an established career). In Biden's case, a penchant for plagiarising Neil Kinnock, Robert Kennedy and assorted poets sank his first presidential bid at the age of 45, a third of a century ago. By the time of his next tilt, 20 years later in 2007, piracy and verbosity were merely harmless foibles, while his Rust Belt popularity and Washington deal-making record eventually made him Obama's running mate in 2008.

Today, that lightly reworked rendition of Kinnock—"Why is it that Joe Biden is the first in his family ever to go to a university?... the first Biden in a thousand generations..."—is a classic; and his quoting Lincoln's "we shall nobly save or meanly lose the last best hope of earth" for the hundredth time was uplifting rather than hackneyed when he denounced Trump and his rabble's assault on Congress. As for RFK, the striking connection now is less borrowed words than a shared quest to unite black and white working-class voters.

While they pale besides the complaints against Trump and even Bill Clinton, there have been claims of questionable conduct towards women in the distant past, and in one case a (strongly contested) allegation of sexual assault. But whatever their truth, most Americans again assign them to a career stretching back to the mores of a different era. Biden's latest biographer, the journalist Evan Osnos, goes for a title, *American Dreamer*, which is pure brand Biden. The most striking flaw that he highlights in his subject—he records Biden speaking for 55 of 64 minutes in a typical vice-presidential meeting—is one that the new President can live with: "If my Achilles heel has to be that I talked too much, not that I'm a womaniser or I'm dishonest or what-not, it's fine." FDR, after all, was an inveterate yarner.

At the heart of the Biden phenomenon, right from the age of 30, is a public mourning and grief that would be mawkish if they did not flow plausibly, apparently naturally, from being stricken in public life. Its centrepiece is the illness and death in 2015 of eldest son and political heir Beau, an Iraq veteran and attorney general of Delaware, while his father was vice president.

Beau was only 46, and with two young children, when his coffin lay in state in the Delaware State Capitol. President Obama gave the eulogy at the Wilmington obsequies. "Joe, you are my brother," he said, embracing his deputy besides the flag-draped casket. There was even a message from the deathbed. "You've got to promise me, Dad, that no matter what happens you're going to be all right," the son told his father, as recorded in the patriarch's bestselling book, *Promise Me, Dad,* published soon after. "Beau was making me promise to stay engaged in the public life of the nation and the world," he writes, in case the message were unclear.

Family tragedy is the story most Americans know of their new President, because it's the story that he tells about himself. In an electric campaign moment in early 2020, an Iraq veteran turned anti-war campaigner asked him: "We are just wondering why we should vote for someone who voted for a war and enabled a war that killed thousands of our brothers and sisters and countless Iraqi civilians?" Biden gently interrupted: "So was my son, was in Iraq, for a year. Not that it matters, right? It matters a lot to me." He stopped to talk to the man while leaving the hall. Everything about Trump was tacky by comparison. Even Fox News couldn't seriously dent brand Biden while attacking his younger son Hunter's questionable Ukrainian business dealings.

Religion is integral to brand Biden. He is the second Catholic president after JFK, with a characteristic twist— Joe wears Beau's rosary around his wrist, calling it his connection with his lost son, and quotes Kierkegaard: "faith sees best in the dark." Morbidity as charisma is a rare and strange thing. It has been Biden's political shield and sword. Whether it continues to cut a swathe through his opponents depends, I suspect, on whether he maintains the vigour of FDR before his final months—rather than as "sleepy Joe" resembling, well, other men approaching 80. Trump identified the Achilles heel, he just couldn't get to it.

Team Biden looks formidable, combining extraordinary longevity, loyalty, friendship and talent. Ron Klain, Biden's 60-year-old White House chief of staff, was Biden's adviser as chairman of the Senate judiciary committee in the 1980s before becoming vice presidential chief of staff to Al Gore and then to Biden himself. Ted Kaufman, the 81-year-old

Biden-Harris transition chief, was one of the original volunteers of Joe's first barnstorming 1972 Senate campaign, and not long afterwards his office chief. He eventually replaced his boss as Delaware senator when Biden became Vice President, and was thought to be keeping the seat warm for Beau. A string of sometimes-younger Biden diehards—Bruce Reed, Cathy Russell, Mark Gitenstein, there is a long list—have reassembled in the West Wing after intertwining with him for decades. Biographer Jules Witcover calls this coterie "his other family."

As to Biden's cabinet, the deeply experienced secretary of state, Anthony Blinken, is a throwback to Cordell Hull, the longest-ever holder of the post under FDR and "father of the United Nations." Paris-educated Blinken, son of one US ambassador and nephew of another, was Biden's perpetual adviser on the Senate foreign relations committee in the eighties, nineties and noughties. They travelled to Iraq together 10 times, and back and forth to central and eastern Europe as Biden agitated, rather brilliantly, for the expansion of Nato to the east, and for military intervention to halt Slobodan Milošević's atrocities in the Balkans. Blinken went on to become Obama's deputy secretary of state under John Kerry—himself a longtime Senate buddy of Biden's, now reincarnated as climate envoy.

Biden's newly acquired talent is as impressive as his old: vice president Kamala Harris; transportation secretary "Mayor Pete" Buttigieg, a gay, energetic young Democrat; attorney general Merrick Garland, Obama's eminent Supreme Court pick, who was denied Senate confirmation by Mitch McConnell at his most partisan; and treasury secretary Janet Yellen, former chair of the Federal Reserve.

The media has focused on "diversity," and the team collectively certainly embodies that. But just as important, each one of these appointments reinforces Team Biden's "tough moderate" and "competent" brand—especially Harris, a former California state prosecutor. So too Lloyd Austin, ear-catchingly announced by Biden as defence secretary as a black four-star general who served with Beau in Iraq. Team Biden is a match for FDR's Harry Hopkins, Henry Morgenthau, Harold Ickes, Frances Perkins, and the "brains trust" which forged the New Deal. It is the sharpest contrast imaginable with Trump's dysfunctional collection of advisers and cabinet members, whom he barely knew and fired on a whim.

However capable this incoming governing machine may be, what are its chances of overcoming Washington's entrenched paralysis? The Democrats have razor-thin control of both houses of Congress since the party's nail-biting two-Senate seat triumph in the Georgia run-off of January 2021. It's not a guarantee of success, but a precondition for it: Obama's only big legislative successes, healthcare and the bold economic stimulus to counter the Great Recession, came in his first two years, when he presided over Democratic majorities in both chambers of Congress.

The arithmetic is tougher this time, turning on Harris's tie-break vote in the Senate, but then thanks to Biden's success in channelling the political, societal and economic emergency created by Trump and Covid-19, the discipline and cohesion of the Democratic Party is unusually strong. And after Trump's rule descended into a doomed proto-fascist attempt to outright cancel the election, Republicans who had followed this morally bankrupt frontman for four long years are newly divided. To exploit this moment, Biden has to generate immediate and continuing momentum in the way FDR did from the moment of his celebrated "the only thing we have to fear is fear itself" inaugural address—"to assume unhesitatingly the leadership of this great army of our people dedicated to a disciplined attack upon our common problems."

Hindsight credits FDR with magical properties in political mobilisation, a world away from the sluggishness of Biden's primary campaign last year. But on inauguration day, 4th March 1933, that's not how Roosevelt seemed even to many Democrats. A scion of the Hudson Valley, he was widely written off as a privileged if affable dilettante. He was also treated as a prize chameleon. "If he became convinced tomorrow that coming out for cannibalism would get him the votes he so sorely needs," wrote the columnist HL Mencken, "he would begin fattening a missionary in the White House backyard."

Biden too is a pretty good chameleon. His party piece is to take Democrat and Republican positions on controversial issues and adopt them both. In the 1960s, he was against the Vietnam War—but against amnesty for draft dodgers. In the 1970s, he was against criminalising abortion—but against federal funding for it. He was against racial segregation—but against "busing" to create racially mixed schools. "I'll be damned if I feel responsible for what happened 300 years ago," was his response to Jesse Jackson's call for positive discrimination in favour of African Americans, even as he lambasted Reagan's secretary of state George Shultz for being soft on apartheid, proclaiming: "I speak for the oppressed, whatever they may be."

In the 1980s Biden was open to the possibility of installing the conservative judge Robert Bork on the Supreme Court—then against him. In the 1990s, he backed Clinton's welfare—or rather, anti-welfare—reforms, and his most notable Senate legislative achievement was the 1994 Crime Bill which massively increased incarceration. Given the heavy racial slant of American criminal justice, liberal critics damned it as "the new Jim Crow." Then in the 2000s he voted for George Bush's war in Iraq—before becoming its fiercest critic. "I do not believe this is a rush to war," he said in the October 2002 debate in the Senate, "I believe it is a march to peace and security," a line right up there with FDR's "I have said this before, but I shall say it again and again and again. Your boys are not going to be sent into any foreign wars"—delivered shortly before Pearl Harbor.

Not being stupid, Biden obviously can't believe his own highfalutin defence of all this triangulation: that the 1994 Crime Act was incidental to America's mass incarceration, or that the Iraq War vote would strengthen the hands of UN weapons inspectors. In both these cases he didn't just go along with the right; he led the right, bragging of his 1994 Crime Act that "the liberal wing of the Democratic Party" was now for "60 new death penalties, 70 enhanced penalties, 100,000 cops and 125,000 new state prison cells."

But here's the thing, just when you think Biden is for power at any price, he surprises. Sure enough, in June 2019, sensing a changing public mood and a Democratic Party sick of Clintonite cross-dressing, he switched against capital punishment, a fortnight after reversing his career-long opposition to federal funding for abortions. There are shades here of FDR's slow, calculating but ultimately decisive shift from his youthful suspicion of organised labour towards signing and making his own the Wagner Act of 1935, which enshrined the legal right to strike.

However you look at it, Joe Biden's record is less compromising than Roosevelt's accommodation with Southern segregationists. "He was the most complicated human being I ever knew," FDR's confidant and long-serving labor secretary Frances Perkins said of him. "Out of this complicated nature there sprang much of the drive which brought achievement, much of the sympathy which made him like, and liked by, such oddly different types of people, and much of the apparent contradiction which so exasperated those associates." The playwright Arthur Miller, another fan, held FDR to epitomise the truth that "in the politics of a democracy, the shortest distance between two points is often a crooked line."

The same is true of Biden. As a student at the university of Delaware in the early sixties he was "a coat-and-tie guy and would do everything correctly" rather than a head-for-the-barricades type, recalls a friend. After a law degree at Syracuse University in upstate New York, he became a trial lawyer, first registering in Delaware as an independent, then voting for a Republican governor in 1968. His first wife Neilia was a Republican. Only in 1969, the year before winning his county council election against an entrenched Republican, did he register as a Democrat.

So Biden's cross-dressing was a habit acquired early—in Delaware. Busing lit the blue touch-paper for the state's white middle class: his first Senate initiative was to seek to ban federal funding for it, in tandem with Delaware's Republican senator, William Roth. He held Roth close until his death in 2003, delivering the eulogy at his funeral.

Without resisting busing, he wouldn't have got elected by a hair's breadth in the Nixon landslide year of 1972, nor in all likelihood been returned in the tricky 1978 Carter mid-term elections. Only then did Biden become a fully-established Delaware fixture. He went on hold a long line of nationally prominent Republicans close, famously speaking at the funeral of John McCain, Obama's opponent in 2008 ("my name's Joe Biden, I'm a Democrat and I loved John McCain").

By such dedicated centrist bonding, Biden made himself—without wealth or Ivy League connections—the 46th President of the United States. Remarkably, he has did so anchored in tiny Delaware, without any power base to rival FDR's New York or Reagan's California. The state has less than half the population of Houston, and is known mainly for gaping tax loopholes and a few beautiful beaches, midway between Washington and New York. And he had never even run Delaware, nor for that matter anything much besides two Congressional committees, before becoming president.

Herein is a stark contrast with Roosevelt, who was assistant secretary of the navy throughout the first world war and later governor of America's then-most-populous state before he got to the White House.

There are nonetheless good reasons for optimism. First, Biden never abstains or goes AWOL. He is always a man in what FDR's cousin Teddy called the "arena," "struggling valiantly"; and he has shown himself capable of leading decisively to the left at key moments. The felling of Trump was not a one-off. As chair of the Senate Judiciary Committee in the 1980s, while he initially indulged ultraconservative Bork, who had been an ally against busing in the Nixon years, Biden moved against him ruthlessly as Reagan's Supreme Court nominee the moment he grasped the political possibility and necessity. "I didn't want," he said, "to be a little asterisk in history." It was the Gipper's biggest reverse.

Second, like FDR Biden is a politician of majorities, not minorities. However honourable, minorities in political institutions always lose, at least in the short term in which presidents deal. The challenge is to assemble majorities behind your own ideas, not just bend to others. In his determination to work from within the biggest political pack, Biden also has much in common with Lyndon Johnson, as well as the great British trade unionist and politician, Ernest Bevin. Neither of these 20th-century titans ever knowingly joined minorities while clambering up their institutions of power. Bevin organised a General Strike he deplored in 1926 in order to keep in the cockpit: two decades later, he was at the pinnacle of the British state building a welfare state. Though biographer Robert Caro calls him "Master of the Senate" in the 1950s, Johnson was in reality more servant than master, cosseting many of the same racists that Biden would later cultivate in the same chamber. LBJ's genuine mastery was as president after JFK's assassination, seizing the moment and two decades of Congressional skill to enact the wave of Great Society civil and welfare rights legislation that took FDR's legacy to a new level. This is Biden's moment to do the same. "Where's the deal space?" a Biden refrain, is pure LBJ.

For like FDR and LBJ, whatever his other tergiversations, Biden is progressive on the core New Deal agenda of jobs and fair shares for America's working and middle classes.

"Amtrak Joe" isn't just an act, although it is that too. He has always been on good terms with the Democratic party's liberal wing and black communities—recall that it was South Carolina's African-Americans who saved his candidacy in 2020, spurning Bernie Sanders and turning out for a man they trusted to stand by them. Tellingly, Sanders preferred Biden to Hillary Clinton, relating how Biden had told him: "I want to be the most progressive president since FDR."

In his 1932 Oglethorpe speech, at the depth of the Depression, FDR declared prophetically: "The country needs, the country demands, bold, persistent experimentation. Take a method and try it. If it fails admit it frankly and try another. But above all, try something." Biden's cast of mind is similar.

FDR coined the concept of a first "hundred days." He called Congress into special session and kept it there for three months. The Federal Emergency Relief Administration, Civil Works Administration, Civilian Conservation Corps, Tennessee Valley Authority, Emergency Banking Act, Farm Credit Act, National Industrial Recovery Act, Home Owners Loan Act, and Emergency Railroad Transportation Act were all launched. Fifteen major bills were enacted by Congress, plus a cascade of executive orders. Prohibition was repealed and America came off the gold standard.

So, writing in late 2021, what of Biden's first year?

So far, the FDR template remains credible. It has been a year of unrelenting presidential energy and focus devoted to state-led jobs growth, infrastructure renewal and social welfare. Biden initially broke the logjam in Congress. A $1.9 trillion Covid-19 stimulus bill was enacted just seven weeks after his inauguration. Enactment of a further $1 trillion infrastructure bill and a $3.5 trillion federal budget boost for health, children and social welfare is in the balance at the time of writing, buffeted by Democrat divisions on whether to go "full FDR" as Biden clearly wishes, but passage of a substantial further package appears likely.

Biden's deal-making skill has been on full display. A bipartisan agreement with Congressional Republicans, including minority leader Mitch McConnell in the Senate, passed the infrastructure bill and facilitated the other spending packages. Crucially, Biden succeeded in splitting the Republicans. Trump helped with his bizarre determination to continue disputing the 2020 election, but equally vital was the new president's deftness in attracting Republican support for a growth plan while playing to the centre, or into touch, on divisive cultural and non-economic issues, including foreign policy.

With echoes of pre-1941 FDR, and in stark contrast to LBJ, foreign policy has been handled with a premium on avoiding entanglement in far-off wars. While keen to nurture allies where practical, Biden's priority is fighting for the condition of America rather than anything else. A defining moment was the controversial withdrawal of American forces from Afghanistan in August 2021, implementing a deal with the militant Taliban negotiated by Trump in his last year. It was Biden saying, like FDR, that jobs and the economy came first and "your boys are not going to be sent into any foreign wars." He used almost exactly this FDR formulation in his broadcast on the day

US troops left and Kabul fell to the Taliban: "I cannot and will not ask our troops to fight on endlessly in another country's civil war."

Like FDR, Joe is a happy warrior, which is part of his appeal. But there is steel and backbone. Obama, proposing him as his running mate in 2008, said "he has stared down dictators." This is literally true. The most impressive story I know of Biden is of his mission to Serbia in 1993 to try and halt Slobodan Milošević's genocide in Bosnia. At one point, Milošević asked: "What do you think of me?" Biden jumped up, jabbed his finger at the tyrant across the table, and yelled: "I think you're a damn war criminal and you should be tried as one."

5

MODI

You don't get to lead a democracy, let alone get re-elected by a landslide, without a mandate to save your country. What distinguishes Indian prime minister Narendra Modi (b. 1950) is that he is a cult salvationist—yet after seven years leading the world's biggest democracy, he has little to show for it beyond the accumulation of votes.

As an outsider distilling the avalanche of controversy, hagiography and verbiage, I am struck most by Narendra Modi's congenital ambivalence. This is a thoroughly 21st-century party leader beamed as a 3D hologram into thousands of election meetings and rallies, fiercely partisan and constantly accusing his opponents of disloyalty to India. Yet he is also a man who decamps to a cave mid-campaign, cameras in tow, to contemplate the meaning of life and impart spiritual wisdom. While earning rapt adoration all the while.

This ethereal hologram—brutal modern politician as prophet and guru—has won two successive election landslides across a vast, extraordinarily diverse country of 1.3bn people. But who is the real Modi? In trying to find out, I kept coming back to three key questions. Which country does he see himself as leading: India or Hindu India? Is he saving Indian democracy or is he subverting it? And is he, as he insists, a true economic moderniser—or a fanatical religious nationalist for whom modernisation is a tool to assert supremacy, with reforms proposed, chopped and changed for sectarian advantage?

I have come to the view that these questions can't be resolved, unless he lurches to extremity thereafter, because chronic ambiguity *is* Narendra Modi. A fervent Hindu militant in his teens, he now operates within a quasi-western political framework which he half accepts and half rejects but has not sought—or at least has not yet been able—to fundamentally change.

Ambiguity is also in India's DNA. Since its refoundation as an independent state in 1947, India's prime ministers have been a mix of strong men—plus one strong woman—and weak caretakers. They have ruled a just-about democracy characterised by multi-party elections and formal constitutional liberalism but equally by extreme instability and endemic political violence—including regular assassinations—all flowing from two bitter centuries of British imperialism. Modi represents this continuing congenital ambiguity of the Indian state itself.

Modi's western admirers call him the Thatcher of India, and claim he is reversing 70 years of state regulation. This is risible given his paltry and contradictory economic record, starting in 2016 with the chaos of a botched demonetisation: removing 86 per cent of cash from the economy overnight, for no good reason. He also claims to be founding a "second republic," replacing the one forged by the Nehru-Gandhi dynasty. Yet while Modi has defeated the latest gilded Gandhi—Rahul—in two successive elections, and may have ended the family's political ambitions, I am struck by his resemblance to Rahul's grandmother Indira. Prime minister for most of the two decades (1966-1984) between Modi's formative 16th and 34th years, Indira was similarly contradictory on both democracy and reform. She lurched in crisis to an "emergency" dictatorship in 1975-1977, then drew back and unexpectedly surrendered power after losing the 1977 election under her father Jawaharlal Nehru's constitution. She returned on winning the following election three years later, serving until her assassination by Sikh bodyguards in 1984.

In his mid-twenties, Modi was an underground runner in the resistance to Indira's emergency. Ironically, his rule since 2014 has itself been called an "undeclared emergency." This is inaccurate: he hasn't resorted to the draconian repression and mass imprisonment of opponents of Indira's 21-month dictatorship. But the constitution has been pushed to the limit and manipulated, as under Indira and her son Rajiv, including the blocking of social media, the arrest of journalists and even a comedian, serious if localised violence with a nod and a wink from Modi's minions, and the suborning of the Supreme Court, the state media and the Electoral Commission.

Then there are Modi's peremptory "modernisations," accompanied by alternating aggression and retreat: the latest is an increasingly botched "big bang" deregulation of agriculture, India's largest industry. Again, this is eerily reminiscent of Indira, whose *pièce de résistance* was a mass forced sterilisation campaign spearheaded by her other son, Sanjay, carried out in the name of modernisation.

Modi's India, like Indira's, is thus in many ways a continuation of the republic founded by Nehru 74 years ago. It has all the tensions and contradictions embodied in

Nehru himself, a Harrow- and Cambridge-educated barrister turned freedom fighter and authoritarian ruler. Nehru's republic is in parts socialist, elitist, democratic, secular and Hindu, nurturing a dynamic and sophisticated middle class, yet perpetuating massive inequality and divisions.

Yet in his love-hate relationship with Nehru's republic, Modi offers two populist twists—abandoning the inclusive language of secularism to rally the religious majority against India's huge minorities, and rallying anyone feeling downtrodden against the old elite, and most especially against the Nehru-Gandhi dynasty itself. Breaking from hereditary rule sounds like progress, but whether even this turns out to be so will depend on how Modi organises his eventual succession, and whether he hands over to one of the more extreme Hindu nationalists in his political "family," like his right-hand rottweiler Amit Shah, his interior minister.

On the spectrum of contemporary populists, Modi is more proletarian, professional and indeed popular than Erdoğan of Turkey and Bolsonaro of Brazil, and leagues more so than Trump. He is a vigorous 71-year-old whose tenure has no end in sight. Rahul Gandhi resigned the leadership of the opposition Congress party in 2019 with many of its members, nationally and in state assemblies, having in effect defected to Modi's party, the Bharatiya Janata Party (BJP).

Modi's brand of populism is described by Arvind Rajagopal of New York University as a "simulacrum", defined as:

> a media artefact regarded as more true than any amount of information and, in fact, capable of correcting that information. Modi is the leader who will drag the country out of its trouble and propel it to greatness: accepting this basic premise amounts to political realism today.

Neelanjan Sircar of Ashoka University puts it more starkly: "The murkier the data, the easier it is for him to control the narrative." However, three artefacts of the Modi phenomenon are truly solid. First, his journey from poverty to power. His rise from the bottom half of Indian society is unique in a country historically ruled by moguls, princes and—for the first half-century of independence—largely through one family.

Within India's labyrinthine caste gradations, Modi is an OBC ("Other Backward Caste"): sort of lower middle class. His dad was a *chaiwala* (tea vendor) with a stall on the station platform in small-town Vadnagar, sustaining a family of eight in a three-room house without windows or running water but able to get his children a decent education. In Indian terms, Modi's background is similar to Joe Biden's, another son of a struggling lower middle-class small-town salesman (of cars). At school both had a love of debating, argumentation and, say contemporaries, a propelling stubbornness.

Modi's mission is power, not money or dynasty. Although he courts and is courted by the Hindu mega-rich who fund his party at home and abroad, especially in Britain and the US, he does not enrich himself or his relatives. "I am single: who will I be corrupt for?" is one of his lines. An arranged marriage was effectively dissolved by him, unconsummated, when the ascetic teenager abruptly departed Vadnagar, aged 17, on the first of several nomadic nationwide quests. He has apparently been celibate ever since. As monk-leader, implacable yet worldly-wise, he reminds me of both Archbishop Makarios, priest-founder of independent Cyprus, and Lee Kuan Yew, authoritarian guru-founder of Singapore. "Dynasty or democracy," one of his 2014 slogans, successfully branded Rahul Gandhi a "prince" (*shahzada*). Another saying of his was "I am proud I sold tea, I never sold the nation," which struck home.

Modi has an electoral Midas touch. No one else in history has won a total of nearly half a billion votes in fairly free multi-party elections—and he isn't done yet. His BJP is the world's largest political party, claiming 100million members: twice the size of the Chinese Communist Party. Two huge national victories since 2014 followed three equally sweeping elections as chief minister of his native Gujarat, a state bigger than England on India's northwest coast. In 2014, he nearly trebled the BJP's tally in the directly elected Lok Sabha (lower house) of the Indian parliament, giving the party, which everyone had assumed was fated to remain a perpetually minority party, its first ever overall majority. It was also the first single-party government of any party in India since the 1980s. The BJP has now become Modi's party in the way that New Labour was Blair's and Germany's CDU became Merkel's—only much more so.

But it is important to understand that Modi is not a De Gaulle or even a Macron who summoned their own political party into being: his rise came through a movement which had deep historic and cultural roots, even if he has transformed its appeal. Like so many of the world's election winners, Modi is in the "club of 30" as a professional politician since his twenties. He started as an apprentice in the Rashtriya Swayamsevak Sangh (RSS), a religious nationalist movement which believes in the essential Hinduness of India—an ideology known as "Hindutva"—and went on to join the BJP, founded as the movement's electoral wing in 1980. He started in the army of RSS volunteers before becoming an organiser, after which he was drafted to become chief minister of Gujarat amid a leadership crisis in the local BJP.

Modi knows India, socially and geographically, better than perhaps any other Indian alive, and from the bottom up. He has mastered modern democratic arts and his ubiquitous social media presence includes a Modi app, flashing up every speech, event and opinion to millions with a professionalism that leaves Trump in the gutter. "India saved itself with a timely lockdown, travel restrictions, shows recent study. Read more here!" runs the latest notification on my phone, the fourth of today.

"Speaking in Hindi, Modi is the finest speaker I have ever heard; his oratory is mesmerising," one opponent who does not wish to be named tells me. To my surprise, given his dictatorial reputation, he is a considerable parliamentarian, capable of graceful tributes to opponents, albeit only when they are retiring or have been defeated. "We stand for those who trusted us and also those whose trust we have to win over," he declared after his 2019 landslide. His bitterest political critics typically pay tribute to his skill and crave his attention even as they attack him.

Each day features another socially distanced mass Modi event, typically in a different state. Whether launching a toy festival in Delhi or a railway scheme in West Bengal, the white-bearded sage declaims an impassioned homily combining political message with spiritual guidance and lifestyle advice. Addressing newly graduating doctors, after thanking them for their efforts in the pandemic, he urges them to "keep a sense of humour, do yoga, meditation, running, cycling and some fitness regime that helps your own wellbeing," and invokes Hindu saint Sri Ramakrishna Paramahamsa's mantra that "serving people is the same as serving God." "In your long careers, grow professionally and at the same time, never forget your own growth. Rise above self-interest. Doing so will make you fearless," he preaches.

"Modernisation not westernisation" is another Modi slogan—he has a slogan for everything—yet his political packaging, including that hologram, is done with the help of slick BJP professionals trained in Britain and the US. He plays the west, using the right language and commandeering the wealthy and influential Hindu diaspora like an army. Britain's populist Home Secretary

Priti Patel, a fellow Gujarati, jokes with her friend "Narendra" in Gujarati. He calls virtually every western leader "my friend," and they reciprocate. Whatever their concerns about sectarianism, western leaders desperately want the Indian leader onside. After his inauguration, Biden called Modi before Xi Jinping: escalating crises in Myanmar, Afghanistan, Hong Kong, Taiwan and the South China Sea give the prime minister leverage, which he shrewdly exploits.

Is Modi within or beyond the democratic pale? In his personal language generally within—although under his rule an anti-Muslim and anti-secular culture war has been stoked, amplified by Amit Shah and BJP activists. Yogi Adityanath, a Hindu priest cloaked in saffron robes and the BJP chief minister of the northern state of Uttar Pradesh, infamously proclaimed: "If Muslims kill one Hindu man, then we will kill a hundred Muslim men." Modi himself doesn't go there: modernisation and Hindu ancestor worship are his public rhetoric, and he rarely attacks opponents for much more than being divisive and unpatriotic, which is pretty much what British Tories have been doing for two centuries. In parliament in February 2021, Modi called the farmers encamped in Delhi protesting the agricultural reforms "people who cannot live without protests" and "parasites," which is about the limit of his public invective.

However, the BJP culture war he leads is increasingly vicious, seeking to erase India's Mughal past and repress Muslims in the present by renaming towns and cities, rewriting and "saffronising" Indian history, and asserting cultural, religious and legal ascendancy, including through beef and alcohol bans. In the Hindutva mind, "their" India has been invaded twice, by the Muslims and then by the British, and both invasions need to be repelled. A defining event was the BJP-inspired 1992 attack on the Mughal-era Babri mosque in Ayodhya, Uttar Pradesh. Demonstrators razed it to the ground and attempted to erect a Hindu temple to Rama, an event which radicalised the whole Hindutva movement. This is the backdrop to Modi's discriminatory social and cultural policies—in 2019, the Supreme Court ordered the site of the demolished mosque be handed over to Hindus to build a new temple—as well as his symbolic gestures, like his scheme to rebuild Lutyens' colonial complex in New Delhi.

The bigger issue is whether Modi is not only sectarian but an outright inciter of violence and underminer of the constitution.

Four charges are laid against him on this score. First, that in early 2002, shortly after becoming chief minister of Gujarat, he stoked a Hindu-on-Muslim pogrom in reaction to the murderous attack by a largely Muslim mob on a train passing through Godhra, in Gujarat, conveying Hindu pilgrims from Ayodhya. Second, there is the 2019 imposition of direct rule from Delhi onto the country's one Muslim-majority state, Jammu and Kashmir, which neighbours Pakistan. Third, a new citizenship law, also introduced in 2019 shortly after his re-election, giving Hindu but not Muslim immigrants a fast track to Indian citizenship. And fourth, the 2020/1 farm reforms, which have anti-Sikh overtones because they particularly affect Punjab, "the breadbasket of India."

Poring over accounts of these four cases, my verdict—surprise, surprise—is that Modi's responsibility for bloodshed and excesses is ambiguous. It is what happens in his penumbra, rather than by his explicit or overt direction, which is so murky. During the 2002 Gujarat riots, more than a thousand people were killed, mostly Muslims, with 200,000 people displaced and 230 historic Islamic sites vandalised or destroyed. No national official inquiry indicted Modi, even though his opponents were running the government in Delhi, and there was no repetition in the next 12 years of his chief ministership. But it was on his watch, and some of his associates were implicated and prosecuted.

In Jammu and Kashmir, the verdict is again ambiguous. Communal strife long predates Modi. Nehru unilaterally asserted sovereignty over most of the briefly independent state in the 1950s, before partitioning it jointly with Pakistan. Modi's 2019 imposition of direct rulefollowed decades of endemic instability and paramilitary outrages on both sides, akin to Northern Ireland during the Troubles. Nor has democracy been entirely suspended there. Multi-party elections in the region continue, including ones announced for a new Jammu and Kashmir legislative assembly.

Of the four charges, the anti-Muslim citizenship reform is the most partisan, and entirely of his own making. It is nakedly targeted at Bangladeshi Muslim immigrants. But on any comparative perspective even this explicit racism is probably within the ambit of contemporary democratic action, It is a less sweeping alteration to existing immigration law than Trump's anti-Mexican measures and far less so than the UK government's abolition of free movement of people to and from the European Union with

Brexit, even if the religious sectarianism is an aggravating factor.

Modi's farm reforms are ambiguous for a different reason. There is no disputing their legitimacy in principle. Independent observers and modernising politicians, including Modi's Congress Party predecessor Manmohan Singh, the Oxbridge-educated Sikh economist who made his name as a deregulating finance minister in the 1990s, have long urged and periodically attempted the liberalisation of India's command-and-control economy, including its agricultural sector. Reforming an ossified regime of "minimum support prices" and state "agricultural produce marketing committees," and introducing private agri-purchasing companies, is not inherently wrong or indefensibly partisan.

There are accusations that BJP-supporting middlemen will reap fortunes and screw over the farmers, and the handling of the farmers' protests in Delhi has been terrible. However, as journalist Shekhar Gupta puts it, the first-order issue isn't the legitimacy of the reforms—"at various points in time, most major political parties and leaders have wanted these changes"—but rather the executive incompetence that means they have been so mishandled, watered down and delayed that they will probably make little impact. "The Modi government has lost the battle for these farm laws," he writes. "These laws are dead in the water."

This chaos is typical of Modi's "modernisations." The disastrous 2016 demonetisation, a populist but unjustified attack on "black markets," was followed by a new goods and services tax (GST), forcing small businesses to digitise their payment systems, despite chronically poor preparation and support. Four years later, medium-sized and small businesses, the backbone of the Indian economy, are still struggling. India's unemployment rate was 3.4 per cent when the GST was introduced in July 2017. It is currently over 8 per cent; even before Covid-19, growth had stalled.

As for Thatcherite-style privatisation, it might be controversial if it had actually happened but, wary of opposition and loss of patronage, Modi's biggest privatisations are announced and re-announced but don't take place. The next ones are supposedly of Air India, hardly a good post-Covid prospect, and of as yet unnamed public-sector banks. It is the same story—namely the lack of any consistent story—with international trade. The seminal moment was in November 2019, when at the last minute Modi pulled out of a trade deal with the 15 Asian members of the Regional Comprehensive Economic Partnership, leaving China supreme in the organisation. Ditto with industrial policy, which oscillates between liberalisation and protection. The latest incoherence is two trillion rupees ($27bn) in "production-linked incentives" to assorted domestic and foreign firms for a period of five years.

Asian economic commentary is no longer about the (always disputed) "Gujarat miracle" that Modi was going to transplant from his home state to the whole country. Gone is the talk of a delayed continuation of Manmohan Singh's modestly deregulatory 1991 budget with its grand paraphrase of Victor Hugo: "No power on earth can stop an idea whose time has come. The emergence of India as a major economic power in the world happens to be one such idea." The discussion now is about post-Covid China again accelerating away from India economically, when the per capita income of this colossal neighbour is already several times higher. And about the consolidation of "crony capitalism" as business backers of Modi's—like India's wealthiest man Mukesh Ambani and fellow billionaire Gautam Adani—get richer while nothing changes for ordinary Indians. Even the campaign to "sanitise India," ending open defecation in rural areas, has stalled.

The god Rama is the ultimate Hindu embodiment of the supreme values of love, compassion and justice. Modi claims to stand for a new "Rama Rajya," invoking Mahatma Gandhi. But the Mahatma, before he was assassinated by an RSS militant, wrote: "By Rama Rajya I do not mean a Hindu state. What I mean is the rule of God," where the weakest would secure justice. He was unambiguous about that: not a hologram.

6

BLAIR

Possibly the most gifted natural politician to have become prime minister of Britain apart from Lloyd George, and with fewer personal flaws, Tony Blair (b. 1953) held the supreme office continuously for ten years, a tenure exceeded only by Margaret Thatcher in the democratic era. His impact on the British state is matched or exceeded since the second world war only by Thatcher and Attlee.

Tony Blair was an electoral genius. He won all three elections he fought as Labour leader, two by landslide majorities (1997 and 2001). His third victory, in 2005, was the first time the Conservatives had lost three elections in a row since the introduction of the democratic franchise in 1918. The common view at the time, that "any" Labour leader would have won the 1997 election, and might have carried off the other two as well, looks less plausible in the light not only of the party's poor previous electoral history but also of the four elections since 2005, all won by the Conservatives over Labour despite unspectacular Tory leaders and unfavourable economic and political conditions in the 2010s.

Blair's greatest governmental achievements were lasting peace and power-sharing in Northern Ireland, devolution to Scotland and Wales, the refinancing and transformation of the National Health Service and England's public education system, and the introduction of a national minimum wage. These fortified the progressive tradition of Liberal and Labour governments since Earl Grey's Great Reform Act of 1832. However, like most Liberal and Labour governments since Palmerston, Blair also became embroiled in bitter disputes with left-wing and liberal supporters over the use of military force abroad as he wrestled with Britain's security and global role. His decision to participate in George W. Bush's invasion of Iraq in 2003 created deep and lasting controversy on a par with Gladstone's conquest of Egypt in 1882, Asquith's entry into the first world war in 1914, and Attlee and Bevin's military resistance to Jewish immigration and the creation of the state of Israel after 1945.

Anthony Charles Lynton Blair was born into a comfortable professional family on 6 May 1953. His father, a youthful communist, became an establishment barrister, law lecturer at Durham University and aspirant Conservative MP. He set his younger son on a similar path, sending him to a prestigious private prep school in Durham followed by Fettes College, an Edinburgh public school. From there Tony progressed fairly effortlessly to St John's College, Oxford to study law, like his father and elder brother, who also became a barrister. His early years were privileged but not untroubled: his father suffered a stroke when Tony was ten, putting an end to his parliamentary ambitions, and his mother died of cancer when he was twenty-one.

The young Blair's preoccupation at Oxford was pop music not politics, in which he evinced little interest until he reached the Bar. A serious side developed at Oxford from engagement with Christian socialism at the behest of a charismatic Australian graduate theologian Peter

Thomson, who introduced Blair to the communitarian philosopher John Macmurray. His later speeches, especially on international affairs, contain frequent biblical phrases and overtones.

Following the family tradition to the Bar, Blair fortuitously got a pupillage in the chambers of Derry Irvine, a dominant and domineering barrister well connected with the Labour leadership as a friend of fellow Scots lawyer and ex-cabinet minister John Smith. A fellow pupil barrister, with whom he was soon going out, was Cherie Booth, a politically driven Liverpudlian who went on to become a human rights specialist.

Derry Irvine's chambers gave the young Blair the triple whammy of a job, a wife and a political career. Cherie Booth was initially the more politically ambitious of the two, but after fighting the 1983 election in a safe Tory seat she concentrated on her legal career and the couple's two boys and a girl (a third son followed much later, in 2000, when they were in Downing Street). Irvine remained a powerful influence and ally, and was later to drive the radical constitutional reform legislation of his ex-pupil's government as Lord Chancellor, including a Human Rights Act and freedom of information. Lord Irvine of Lairg, as he became, also had an eye for the fine things of life, which left its mark on both his pupils.

Blair quickly built an employment and commercial law practice, including trade union work, and he joined the Labour Party as the Callaghan government limped to defeat in 1979. In 1981 he was sufficiently Labour-connected and left wing not to defect to Roy Jenkins' SDP, as so many aspirant politicians with backgrounds like his did. Instead, in 1982 he fought a by-election for Labour in unwinnable Beaconsfield, impressing party leader Michael Foot. His personable and energetic performance helped him gain the last-minute nomination a year later for the then safe Labour seat of Sedgefield, an ex-mining constituency in County Durham. Winning the selection contest by a single vote after the 1983 election had been called, at the young age of thirty he became one of a handful of new Labour MPs in a year when Labour was decimated nationally. Gordon Brown was among the other newcomers.

By such fine margins are political careers forged, even the foremost. Election at the age of 30 also puts Blair in the politically masonic "club of 30" described earlier (on p.93), alongside the equally precocious Joe Biden, Bill Clinton, FDR, JFK, LBJ and Churchill. Olaf Scholz and Boris Johnson are in the club, as described in later chapters.

Blair was content to go along with the left orthodoxies of the day: he stood on a platform of leaving the EEC in 1983, and in these years was also a member of the Campaign for Nuclear Disarmament. Left conformity was partly why he was able to rise so smoothly through Labour ranks in the 1980s and ultimately accede to the party leadership just eleven years after election to Parliament: the same interval between first election and party leadership as for John Major, his sparring partner for his first three years as leader, although Blair, aged 44, became prime minister three years younger than did Major.

Tony Blair was a rare, exotic creature on the Labour benches in Neil Kinnock's party after 1983: youthful, charming, articulate, informal, with matinée-idol looks, a young family, sensible judgement – and English. He was quickly promoted into deputy leader Roy Hattersley's shadow Treasury team, and was widely tipped for the top from the outset because he was so well attuned to "Middle England". At a time when Labour needed to advance massively in suburban England to stand any chance of power, being quintessentially modern English middle class was a huge asset in a shadow cabinet top heavy with Scottish and Welsh MPs, including all four – electorally unsuccessful - party leaders between Harold Wilson and Blair (Callaghan, Foot, Kinnock and Smith).

Elected to the shadow cabinet in 1988, Blair worked closely with Peter Mandelson, Herbert Morrison's grandson, who became Kinnock's media manager and increasingly his "modernisation" strategy director too. A decisive break came a year later when he was appointed shadow employment spokesman. This pitched him into the most sensitive area of Labour policy – relations with the trade unions – in the aftermath of the Thatcher trade union reforms and the industrial militancy of the early and mid-1980s. Over three years up to the 1992 election, he accomplished a delicate political balancing act of vigorously opposing Thatcher's trade union reforms while not committing to reversing them, all the while projecting a strong positive public narrative of industrial partnership and renewal.

He repeated the performance, on a bigger canvas, as shadow home secretary under John Smith, who became leader after Kinnock's defeat by John Major in 1992. His mantra, "tough on crime, tough on the causes of crime" resonated and was thought to be politically brilliant, while his ethical "broken society" response to a moral panic sparked by the murder of a Liverpool toddler, James Bulger, by two ten-year-old boys in 1993, struck a national chord.

John Smith's sudden death on 12 May 1994 was the moment of Blair's rise to leadership. Opinion polling showed him far ahead in public preferences for the succession and it was soon clear that party members, as well as Labour MPs, backed him en masse as the candidate most likely to win power for Labour after fifteen years in the wilderness. At this stage he had few enemies and his nickname was Bambi. Gordon Brown, Shadow Chancellor under John Smith, regarded himself as far more heavyweight, but he saw the writing on the wall and the political siblings did an uneasy deal – the "Granita pact", after an Islington restaurant near Blair's home – whereby Brown said he would not stand for the leadership in return for an assurance of the chancellorship and an indication that Blair would not go "on and on" in the event of a Labour government. What this actually meant was much disputed in future years, but Blair would have won the leadership in any event. However, by choice it made him beholden to Brown, who in the second and third Blair terms claimed he was owed the succession.

Blair's relationship with Gordon Brown was the crux of his leadership, like Attlee's with Ernest Bevin and Asquith's with Lloyd George. It was to be one of his greatest assets, because of Brown's force and command at the Treasury and beyond, but it also caused endemic frustration, especially when the political siblings started arguing over domestic policy and the leadership after 2001. Brown constantly underestimated Blair's resilience and will to power. He mistook an easygoing temperament for lack of drive and purpose, and overly disdained as superficial the political arts – charisma, rhetoric, persuasion – that made Blair so formidable, not least on the rebound.

Brown apart, Blair was separated oceanically from other British politicians and elite leaders for nearly a decade between 1994 and the Iraq war of 2003. Elected Labour leader in 1994 by a landslide, a year later in 1995, by another landslide, he carried a symbolically and strategically significant Labour conference vote to change the highly charged Clause 4 of the party's constitution from a commitment to public ownership to a social-democratic statement of communitarianism. From now on, the party's name changed from "Labour" to "New Labour", and it was treated as if it was indeed a new party of the centre and centre left, unlike anything that had gone before. Major and the Tories hadn't a clue how to counteract the Blair phenomenon, and few ad campaigns have bombed as badly as their "demon eyes" posters against him in the 1997 election. "Weak, weak, weak", and "I lead my party, he follows his", Blair's refrains on Major, pierced Major to the political core, while his two slogans summing up his mission – "education, education, and education" and the still endlessly recycled "tough on crime, tough on the causes of crime" – gave him compelling urgency and freshness behind the cause of "New Labour for a New Britain." Major was reduced to the quip that on education he had the same three priorities but not necessarily in the same order.

Blair proceeded to win the 1997 election with the greatest landslide in seats gained by any party since the second world war (416 Labour, 165 Conservative), then repeated the coup in 2001 (413 Labour, 166 Conservative). In his first term, Blair also won four transformational referendums rewriting key parts of the British constitution: to implement power-sharing and a devolved assembly in Northern Ireland, building decisively on Major's brave rapprochement begun in 1993 and bringing an end to the civil war in the province that had been ongoing since the late 1960s; and to create a devolved parliament for Scotland, a devolved assembly for Wales, and a mayor of London, an office with the largest direct democratic mandate in Europe besides the president of France.

Blair despatched four Conservative leaders. The three after Major (William Hague, Iain Duncan Smith and Michael Howard) never became prime minister, the only Tory leaders of whom that was true since 1922. His reach extended even to the monarchy, the aristocracy and the military. The death in a Paris car crash of the recently divorced and highly popular Diana, Princess of Wales, on 31 August 1997 left the monarchy reeling. Lauding Diana as the "people's princess" in a pitch-perfect tribute on the Sunday morning of the crash, outside his parish church in Sedgefield, Blair orchestrated the dramatic national and royal mourning.

In the first Blair term, the hereditary aristocracy was mostly removed from the House of Lords and its inbuilt Tory majority was ended, a reform no previous Liberal or Labour government had been able to accomplish. The Lords became a largely nominated chamber and did not trouble Blair thereafter. The military top brass were equally deferential and readily subscribed to his escalating wars, notably interventions in Kosovo (1999), Sierra Leone (2000) and Afghanistan (2001), which paved the way for the Iraq war in 2003. All three interventions were in explicit pursuit of a neo-liberal "doctrine of liberal interventionism" annunciated in a Blair speech in Chicago on 22 April 1999, which asserted an expansive and quasi-imperial military role for Britain, beyond keeping Russia out of western Europe, for the first time since Suez.

Blair forged a wary but working relationship with media mogul Rupert Murdoch, whose lowbrow *Sun* and highbrow *Times* newspapers, hitherto fiercely hostile to Labour, were fairly supportive throughout his leadership. Murdoch supported Blair partly because he was a winner. His editors were also cultivated intensively by Blair's ebullient communications director Alastair Campbell, the most prominent No. 10 media spokesman in history, who was widely regarded as deputy prime minister until his departure in the wake of Iraq in 2003.

It was the received wisdom of the time that Blair maintained a cautious approach to tax-and-spend policy and relations with the European Union in order to appease the right-wing media, Murdoch in particular. This is to underplay Blair's charismatic skill at playing both sides of electorally sensitive issues – "you shouldn't be in this game unless you can ride two horses at the same time", he used to say – and his skill in securing a progressive policy when he wanted to while appearing to appease the right. Equally, he sometimes located policy to the right by design, particularly on law and order, while carefully neutralising the left. He had these qualities in common with Bill Clinton, president from 1993 to 2001, who was a "third way" model for Blair and became a friend and collaborator for the first four years of his premiership.

With a strongly growing economy, Blair and Brown were able to increase spending on public services substantially in their combined thirteen years of office, especially on health and education, by the expedient mostly of pegging taxes rather than increasing them, in an environment where a Thatcherite Tory government would have cut them. This enabled a trebling of spending on the NHS and a doubling of state spending on education, substantially renovating these key public services without appreciable direct tax increases. Spending also doubled on overseas aid, a cause of both Blair and Brown.

Alongside extra investment Blair championed radical reform of the public services. The key elements were ambitious performance targets and data, workforce expansion and upskilling, and the promotion of consumer choice and higher standards through radically reformed institutional structures (independently managed "foundation trusts" within the NHS and independently managed state schools, called academies, to replace failing comprehensive schools). Some of these reforms were strongly opposed by trade unions and a discontented left, including some ministers within his own government and increasingly by Gordon Brown, who after 2001 exploited the unpopularity of public service reform on the left to tweak and weaken Blair. In a celebrated speech (7 July 1999), Blair talked of "scars on my back" from public service reform, but partly from this perception of struggle he generated wide public and media support for his "invest and reform," "something for something," "investment not cuts" strategy, and it made a highly effective rallying cry and dividing line with the Conservatives in the 2001 and 2005 elections.

Blair's most controversial state reform in England was the introduction of student tuition fees of £3,000 a year for university education in 2004, justified as the quid pro quofor a substantial increase in student numbers. This provoked a massive Labour back-bench rebellion, encouraged by Brown, and the legislation only passed the House of Commons by a majority of five on 27 January 2004. But the reform endured and was generally seen as progressive. Fee levels were trebled by the incoming Conservative/Lib Dem coalition in 2010, using the Blair legislation.

Blair's policy on Europe was highly consequential and highly ambiguous. Like Major before him, who had agreed the framework for European monetary union with Helmut Kohl in the Maastricht Treaty of 1991, including a British right to opt in, he was anxious to keep British membership of the new Euro currency in play should Germany and the other core members decide to proceed, as happened in 1999. But in the event, Blair did not take Britain into the Euro, and it was only with difficulty that he managed even to maintain UK support for the Brussels institutional reforms necessitated by EU enlargement, culminating in the Lisbon Treaty signed shortly after his resignation by his successor. Brown symbolically and deliberately arrived at midnight in Brussels to do so with no media coverage, and with no other European leaders present

Ironically, there was near universal political and media support in Britain for the enlargement of the EU to include the former community states of central and eastern Europe after 2004, after a treaty negotiation also begun under Major after the collapse of the Berlin Wall in 1989, although this gave rise to the substantial immigration that was to turn British Euroscepticism into a mainstream political movement at the behest of Nigel Farage's United Kingdom Independence Party, culminating in Brexit. Ironically also, Blair had attacked Major before 1997 for being weak and irresolute on Europe, although his policy of rhetorically projecting Britain at "the heart of Europe" without being so was the same as Major's and he took no political risks as great as had his predecessor at Maastricht. On the contrary, his decision to go to war with Bush in Iraq in 2003 vitiated the geopolitical unity with France and Germany, for which Blair was to pay a high personal price, undermining his ambition to become president of the European Council, a key new EU post created by the Lisbon Treaty, after his time at Downing Street.

Blair anguished about whether Britain should join the Euro. There was disagreement between him and Brown about how definitely to express Britain's refusal to sign up, but not about the decision itself. However, at the time Blair was far keener to join than his retrospective account in his 2010 memoirs suggests. Between 1997 and 2007 no issue preoccupied his inner team in Downing Street so much and for so long as the Euro. At a No. 10 policy unit "awayday" at Chequers in July 2001, after one of his frequent riffs on wanting to "do" the Euro, I recall in my diary asking him over lunch what his game plan was to get there, with the following sequel:

He promptly disappeared into sun-drenched rose garden, scribbled notes, and came back to give us pep talk at the start of the afternoon session. 'If we can we should do the Euro in this Parliament. I am absolutely clear how I see this. There are two sides to the British character: the cautious and the adventurous side. The cautious side has dominated us for the last 40 years and done untold damage. John Major and David

Owen epitomise it perfectly. It is the cautious side which wants us to wait another four to six years, to wait and see how it all goes, but I tell you if we do that – and I can already see all the forces of caution uniting, on our side also – we will repeat the mistakes of the past . . . We should do it in this term. There is no point being Prime Minister unless you take risks to do the right thing. If we don't go in, we will be a supplicant in five or six years' time.

But it was not to be. After years of to-ing and fro-ing between Blair and Brown, a formal government statement by Brow n on 9 June 2003, shortly after the Iraq invasion, ruled out British membership of the Euro for the foreseeable future. Even after this 2003 announcement, Blair still thought it might be possible to re-open Brown's negative Treasury assessment of the "economic case" for membership and hold a referendum in 2004. But this option silently disappeared in late 2003 without being explicitly abandoned.

Blair had come to power in 1997 on a manifesto that was ambiguously negative on the Euro. "There are formidable obstacles in the way of Britain being in the first wave of membership if EMU takes place on 1st January 1999", it stated. Anxious not to lose media or provincial English support during the election, which he thought would be far closer than transpired, he reinforced even this negativity during the election campaign, with Campbell placing an article in Murdoch's *Sun* a few days before the poll under the headline: WHY I LOVE THE POUND. But Blair's ardent desire – riding two horses at the same time – was nonetheless to find a way to take Britain into the Euro, and he said this frequently and with great earnestness to Roy Jenkins, Britain's only president of the European Commission, who launched European monetary union in

1977, and who had become his friend and mentor by the mid-1990s. In the event, for all his natural charisma, Blair lacked the agility and maybe the imagination to transfer from one political horse to the other at the moment of greatest urgency, in the manner of the greatest modern master, Franklin Delano Roosevelt. The same was perhaps true of his dealings with George W. Bush on Iraq.

The decision not to join the Euro, and the decision to invade Iraq, were the two determining international acts of the Blair government. From the outset, Iraq set him against France and Germany. This is reflected in Blair's memoirs, where he undiplomatically attacked Chirac of France and Schröder of Germany, with whom he previously had a good relationship, for being

> brilliant at ringing statements of intent, which then evaporated into thin air when the consequences of seeing them through became apparent. In truth, without the US, forget it; nothing would happen. That was the full extent of Europe's impotence.

Chirac replied in kind in his memoirs (2011):

> Having tried, on coming to office, to free himself from the control of Washington, Blair had not been long in bowing down to it. What saddened and angered me, to be frank, was that he did not make greater use of the former experience that his country had of the Middle East and of Iraq in particular. By immediately rallying to the American side, Blair unfortunately deprived himself of any real ability to influence the analysis made by the American government of a regional situation that it knew less well than Britain.

The watershed moment for the Blair premiership was the Islamic terrorist attack on the twin towers in New York on

11 September 2001, shortly after Bush had replaced Clinton in the White House, which was also a target for the 9/11 terrorists. The events of that day led to the invasion of Afghanistan, where the terrorists were based, a relatively uncontroversial international decision taken with United Nations support, although one that became increasingly problematic, as the pacifying not only of terrorist-related activity, but also of hostile and provoked indigenous communities, proved far harder than anticipated, and indeed was never accomplished before Biden's withdrawal two decades later. Nonetheless, before this was clear, Bush decided to move on from Afghanistan to invade Iraq, also in the name of quelling Islamic terrorism orchestrated by the Al Qaeda organisation of Osama bin Laden.

Bush's motive for invading Iraq was always transparently to remove the Iraqi dictator Saddam Hussein, left in place by his presidential father George H.W. Bush after the Kuwait war of 1990/1, to the filial disapproval of his son and, more particularly, the younger Bush's ultra-hawkish vice-president Dick Cheney and defense secretary Donald Rumsfeld, both pugilistic veterans of the Nixon administration. For all his crimes against his own people, Saddam was not an Islamic terrorist, so from the outset his removal proved a difficult and controversial mission for Blair to share. He was, however, determined to do so, partly to stick close to the United States for political and security reasons, partly from a belief that Saddam was an urgent and imminent security threat – on this the case in international law for removing him by invasion crucially depended – and partly in pursuit of his own by now neo-imperial doctrine of liberal interventionism.

The frenetic diplomatic and political activity in the months leading up to the Iraq invasion of 19 March 2003 was fraught, as bitter in its domestic political argumentation as the events surrounding the Munich conference in 1938, with similar language deployed on both sides. Blair was confident that the invasion would be a success, fortifying British prestige as well as security, but it was not to be.

The intervention started auspiciously, with the passage of a parliamentary vote in favour on 18 March 2003 by an overwhelming 412 to 149, as most Labour MPs stayed loyal and the Conservatives swung behind Blair. Public opinion was also majority supportive at this stage. The initial invasion removed Saddam with less Iraqi military opposition, and far fewer British and American casualties, than expected. But the US-British position rapidly disintegrated as troops got bogged down in a desperate guerrilla war with insurgent forces militarily supported by neighbouring Iran and its continuing anti-American revolutionary government. Well-publicised atrocities took place on both sides. The failure to find "weapons of mass destruction" steadily sapped Blair's moral authority, particularly after the suicide of British weapons inspector Dr David Kelly on 17 July 2003, who was hounded after speaking to a journalist about his long-standing doubts as to the existence of WMDs. All this reignited domestic opposition, manifested before the war in a march in central London of more than a million anti-war protesters. The liberal left defined itself against the Iraq invasion with a bitterness and intensity not seen since Eden's Suez invasion of 1956. Successive judicial and public inquiries into governmental decision making in the run-up to the war dominated Blair's last years in office and his long post-premiership.

In Iraq, Blair wanted his Falklands but got his Suez. It was "never glad confident morning again," although he did a political Houdini in surviving with substantial political authority for four more years in office. He not only contained growing internal and international opprobrium but also won the May 2005 election, gaining a new lease of political life until September 2006 when Brown, deploying lieutenants to threaten a leadership challenge, forced him to set his departure for 27 June 2007. This period saw the successful British bid for the 2012 Olympic games, pipping Paris for the honour after a highly personal duel between Blair and Chirac.

One of Blair's greatest regrets is that he was not able to take Britain into the Euro, while his engagement with George W. Bush was deeply fraught. So the big counterfactual of his leadership is: what if he had expended the huge political capital he amassed in 1997 on the Euro instead of Iraq? Having been in No. 10 working for him, it is possible to imagine this; the margins were fine in both cases. Britain and maybe the world would be fundamentally different had he gone for the Euro, not Iraq. Ultimately, Blair poses in especially stark relief the profound remark of Pierre Mendès-France, who got France out of Vietnam: "To govern is to choose."

7

LINCOLN, FDR AND HEIRS

It is not unusual to conceive of US presidents as modern Caesars, but it is a brilliant idea to take Suetonius's The Twelve Caesars, *his collective portrait of the rulers of Rome from Julius Caesar to Titus and Domitian, and to make it the template for a collective portrait of modern America's leaders. This is the achievement of Nigel Hamilton in his* American Caesars *(2010), portraying the twelve US presidents from FDR to George W. Bush.*

However, the first Caesar was Abraham Lincoln, born in the same year as Gladstone and Darwin (1809), who fought a civil war of almost unparalleled scale and bloodshed. Here is my collective portrait inspired by American Caesars *and BY biographies of LBJ and Lincoln.*

Suetonius inspires more than the theme of imperial power: he provides the biographical form. Each of his portraits of the Caesars is divided into three parts: an account of how they rose to power; their public life as emperor; and finally, their private life. Nigel Hamilton does the same for his twelve presidents. The effect is a compelling rhythm and a good sense of proportion between the public and the private. For the Romans, tales of the emperors' scandalous private lives was new and shocking. Today, when the private life of political leaders tends to overwhelm their public policy and deeds, in the media and in biographies alike, it is a refreshing counter-revolution in approach to put the public life first.

Hamilton has previously written biographies of John F Kennedy and Bill Clinton, legends in their own bedrooms, and he acknowledges the discipline this brings. "Every modern biographer is *de rigueur* a disciple of Freud, and must lace a modern understanding of the subject's psychology into the gradual unravelling of the subject's life story, from the start, to satisfy public expectation." However, by following Suetonius and putting the public career first, it is possible to see each president "initially in the context of his historic imperial role, and then, by contrast, as a man with a private life story."

Hamilton highlights public reputation with a pithy tag at the head of each portrait. FDR, Harry Truman, Dwight Eisenhower and JFK are "later deified." Lyndon Johnson, Richard Nixon and George W Bush are "later reviled." Gerald Ford is "respected," Jimmy Carter "mocked but later respected," Ronald Reagan "later deified—by conservatives." This is probably too harsh on LBJ, who retains liberal respect for his "great society," and far too kind to Carter, who in parallel with Reagan can at best be described as "later respected—by liberals." George HW Bush and Clinton are not given tags, presumably because Hamilton thought it too soon to make definitive judgements. I would suggest "mocked yet respected" for the elder Bush, and "middling" for Clinton.

FDR is judged "the greatest Caesar of them all." Mobilising the full resources of the US empire and his office as no president in history apart from Lincoln, he was the saviour of the West in the 1930s and '40s. Hamilton believes "his political, strategic, industrial and diplomatic skill in guiding the US not only on the sidelines of the world war, but with a clearly articulated moral framework for the world that would come thereafter, was—and remains—perhaps the greatest example of presidential leadership in American history." It says it all that Biden's aspiration and highest compliment 2021 was to be "a new FDR" in the depths of the Covid-19 catastrophe.

One of FDR's best decisions was his choice of successor. True to FDR, Truman eschewed the isolationism of post-first world war America. And he proved equally tough. There is an evocative description of Truman flying 14,000 miles to meet Douglas MacArthur after the general's victory at Inchon in the Korean war. "Every fibre of his humble Missouri background cautioned him against hubris. There, like Julius Caesar attempting collegial relations with Pompey, the president tried to be civil and get to know, face to face, the notoriously vain, self-seeking general. The result was disaster." But the ultimate victor was Truman.

The best portraits are of Eisenhower and Carter. Far from the conventional view of him as laid back and nonchalant, Eisenhower is portrayed as a brilliant and (in retrospect) almost faultless geo-strategist, directing his administration with strength and clarity at almost every key juncture. Eisenhower put in place much of what we now consider the "west wing," including the first strong chief of staff in Sherman Adams, regular press conferences and weekly national security council meetings.

It is a startling fact that General Eisenhower, almost alone of the emperors between FDR and Bush Junior, kept America out of foreign wars after his deft settlement in Korea. In forcing a decisive halt to British-French-Israeli Suez adventurism of 1956, he rejected the advice not only of his own secretary of state, but more tellingly of LBJ, then majority leader in the Senate, who urged him to "tell them [the British and the French] they have our moral support and go on in." "Go on in" is precisely what LBJ was to do in Vietnam, on a scale Hamilton is fairly sure that neither Eisenhower nor Kennedy would have done.

As for Carter, his West Wing was chaos, and his good works in retirement take on the hue of a penance for the underappreciated dark side of his foreign policy. It is not generally known that it was Carter who instigated the destabilisation of Afghanistan, arming and funding the Islamic revolutionary Mujahedin with the intention of provoking a Russian invasion which the president then condemned while lying about US involvement. "The CIA operation was a wonderful idea," his national security adviser Zbigniew Brzezinski said, for "it succeeded in luring the Soviets into the Afghan trap." And who, largely in consequence, got trapped in the Afghan hills and mountains for two decades when the country became a terrorist training camp thereafter?

Afghanistan and Iraq were bad, but America's worst imperial venture of the post-war era was by some margin LBJ's war in Vietnam, as unnecessary as it was catastrophic. Johnson's presidency is portrayed in Roman style in Robert Caro's magisterial biography. Its most compelling insight – which holds true of most leaders – is that his legacy, good and bad, was determined by bold moves and decisions made within a matter of days of coming to power on 22 November 1963.

"To watch Lyndon Johnson during the transition is to see political genius in action," says Caro. No sooner had he returned from Dallas to Washington on Air Force One – sworn in on the plane, photographed with Jacqueline Kennedy by his side in pink bloodstained dress – than, amid the solemn obsequies and national mourning, he set to work on an emergency address to Congress. Delivered five days later, this set the course for his whole administration.

By November 1963, every major legislative proposal of the Kennedy administration was stalled in Congress, including his flagship Civil Rights Bill. Racial conflict was boiling over, yet a Senate coalition of southern Democrats and Republicans continued to block virtually all civil rights legislation, as they had for the quarter of a century since FDR, including during LBJ's leadership of the Senate in the 1950. Kennedy's "softly, softly" strategy with southern Democrats was going nowhere and his only hope was that re-election, if it happened in 1964, would give new momentum.

LBJ was urged by his own advisers, as well as Kennedy's, to avoid controversy in his emergency address to Congress on 27 November, in particular not to highlight civil rights. He did the opposite. Seizing on the national crisis, he put civil rights at the core of the speech. "No memorial oration or eulogy could more eloquently honour President Kennedy's memory than the earliest possible passage of the Civil Rights Bill for which he fought so long," he told the solemn assembly, rewriting history in those last six words. "We have talked long enough in this country about equal rights. We have talked for a hundred years or more. It is now time to write the next chapter and to write it in the books of law."

What followed was a masterclass in political management. Using every ounce of his tactical prowess, powers of persuasion and personal knowledge of individual senators and congressmen, Johnson created unstoppable momentum. The prelude was a tactical victory secured in the Senate the day before even his emergency address to Congress, just four days after the assassination and a day after JFK's funeral. Legislation to ban the sale of US wheat to Russia was about to be passed in the Senate. This seemingly second-order measure, which JFK had sought (but failed) to stop, because of its curtailment of presidential powers in foreign affairs, was turned by Johnson into an immediate trial of strength for precisely this reason. Making it an issue of confidence in him personally, and in the forces of constitutional order during a national crisis, he cajoled, bullied and wheedled senators, telling them he wanted the legislation "murdered." And it was, by a hefty margin of 57 votes to 36.

Congress now knew who was in charge. Martin Luther King could see power in action and rallied strongly to the new president and the Civil Rights Bill was enacted in just six months. But Johnson did not stop there. His next move was to broaden his social programme dramatically, which he did in his State of the Union address to Congress on 8 January 1964.

This is the speech, delivered only 47 days after he took office, which launched LBJ's "war on poverty" and set in train all the legislative measures of the "great society". Again, there was deliberately Kennedy-esque rhetoric, drafted by Ted Sorensen, Kennedy's speechwriter. "This administration today, here and now, declares unconditional war on poverty in America." LBJ inserted the four key words of urgency and action – "today, here and now" – into Sorensen's draft. Also, Caro notes, "in sharp contrast to John Kennedy's State of the Union addresses, only about a quarter of Johnson's speech was devoted to foreign policy, and it was the last quarter. None of that portion was newsworthy or even particularly significant." Which, again, was by design, as was LBJ's pledge to cut the budget, alongside his "unconditional war on poverty", appealing adeptly to the right as well as the left.

Behind the words, real substance followed fast. "The atmosphere surrounding the anti-poverty programme bore little resemblance to the atmosphere that had existed before 22 November," writes Caro. Driven forward like a military campaign, measure by measure, it was summed up by the presidential memo sent to cabinet members with a list of detailed proposals on 6 January 1964 – two days before the speech – with this instruction: "Your preliminary written reactions are required before close of business, Thursday 9 January." Washington had seen nothing like it since the early days of FDR.

The 1964 state of the union speech sealed the transition from Kennedy to Johnson. LBJ's administration was now secure and strong, with an urgent, compelling programme. He faced no challenge for the Democratic nomination that year and won re-election by a landslide in November.

Caro's point is that just seven weeks previously, on that plane back from Dallas, this outcome was not remotely assured. Locked in bitter rivalry with Robert Kennedy – "one of the great blood feuds of American history" – and distrusted by the left of the Democratic party as surely as he had come to be regarded as ineffectual by left and right alike, after three years as a marginalised vice-president, Johnson could easily have become a weak, stop-gap president, as Gerald Ford did after Richard Nixon's resignation eleven years later.

Unlike Ford, however, Johnson had superlative leadership powers. Part of this was a reform agenda, honed from a lifetime's experience. He sensed that he could break the decades-long logjam on social and racial change and required no think tanks or focus groups to tell him what that change should be. The Great Society grew out of his roots in the poor Texas hill country and his struggle to get on, and to help others get on, which went back to his days as a young teacher of penniless Mexicans. It went hand-in-hand with a fierce, if concealed, resentment of those he called "the Harvards" who filled Kennedy's "Camelot", liberals who knew poverty only from books and seminars.

Caro remarks that if power corrupts – and it certainly corrupted Johnson—"what is equally true is that power always reveals." As Walter Lippmann put it, Johnson "knows about the hidden and forgotten American poor" and was "showing himself to be a passionate seeker with an uncanny gift of finding, beneath public issues, common ground on which men could stand."

Equally, within days of Kennedy's assassination, the seeds of the Vietnam catastrophe were also sown. This was the opposite of "genius in action."

JFK's greatest achievement had been his handling of the Cuban missile crisis in 1962, when he secured the withdrawal of Russian missiles from Cuba while circumventing the hawks in his administration, who wanted an immediate invasion of the island, which could easily have escalated into a war with Russia. Then, Johnson was among the hawks. He supported invasion and opposed negotiation with Nikita Khrushchev. Trading Russian missiles in Cuba for American missiles in Turkey—even though the latter were obsolete—amounted, he argued, to saying, "I'm going to dismantle the foreign policy of the United States to get those missiles out of Cuba." This is crucial background to Vietnam. In response to a memo in Christmas 1963 from Mike Mansfield, his successor as majority leader in the Senate, which called for a political rather than a military strategy in Vietnam, Johnson countered bluntly: "Do you want [Vietnam] to be another China? I don't want these people around the world worrying about us. They're worried about whether you've got a weak president or a strong president."

What he meant by "a strong president" was made clear a few days later when he backed Robert McNamara's call for "more forceful moves" against North Vietnam, including covert operations to escalate the war. A national security action memorandum would normally have been signed by the president in such cases. None was ever signed.

So, within days, the imperial course of the Johnson administration abroad was set, and its triumphs and its disasters equally foretold.

The theme of cataclysmically fateful, defining decisions of supreme leadership in the initial days of office harks back to the most imperial presidency of all – Abraham Lincoln's in the days after his inauguration on 4 March 1861.

Lincoln has been deified practically since the day of his assassination, but he was every bit the calculating politician in his rise to power. (Lincoln is also a leading member of the "club of 30": he was first elected to the Illinois House of Representatives at the age of just 25). He won the 1860 election with less than 40 per cent of the popular vote, brilliantly manipulating Democrat divisions while outmanoeuvring the Republican front-runner by adopting a less abolitionist tone on the future of slavery.

On his policy as president, his biographer David Donald's interpretation is summed up in the 1864 Lincoln quotation he places at the front of his biography: "I claim not to have controlled events, but confess plainly that events have controlled me." But this is nonsense. The civil war could have been averted when Lincoln took office in March 1861, had he recognised the secession of the southern states and the confederate government they had already established. His Democrat predecessor, the hapless James Buchanan, had practically done this by the start of 1861, and even considered ceding the confederates Fort Sumter, a federal garrison in the deep south at Charleston, South Carolina. Lincoln chose not to continue Buchanan's policy but instead to start a war with the confederation. Whether one agrees or disagrees with Lincoln's actions, he controlled these crucial events, they did not control him.

The *casus belli* for the American civil war was Lincoln's decision to defend Fort Sumter. The only reason for doing so was to start a war to reverse a secession from the United States which was already an accomplished fact. A secession which was plausibly constitutional, and carried through by meetings of elected popular conventions. His decision followed the putting of this specific question to his cabinet.

"Assuming it to be possible to now provision Fort Sumter, is it wise to attempt it?" The response was evenly divided. William Seward, his secretary of state, told Lincoln bluntly that such a step would "provoke combat and probably initiate a civil war," but the new president determined to proceed. When Doris Kearns Goodwin argues, in a book too often taken at face value, that Lincoln formed a "team of rivals," this misses the fundamental point that he in fact formed a team to fight his real rivals, namely Jefferson Davis and his new confederate government.

Lincoln was careful to limit his declared goals in 1861, which did not extend to the abolition of slavery. He knew, in March 1861, that many Americans considered the union to be worth fighting for, but far fewer would support a war against the southern white planters' way of life. From the start, Lincoln invoked the Almighty and declared the union sacred. But his war, like all wars, was an act of leadership, not an act of God.

8

FARAGE

Nigel Farage (b. 1964) is the most significant changemaker in modern Britain never to have been an MP, let alone a minister. He accomplished a reverse takeover of the Conservative Party as audacious as it was triumphant. This is how he did it.

We have not successfully rolled back the frontiers of the state in Britain only to see them reimposed at a European level with a European superstate exercising a new dominance from Brussels," was the key sentence of Margaret Thatcher's Bruges speech of 20 September 1988. Bruges set off a chain reaction which led to Nigel Farage's reverse take-over of the Conservative party, without even becoming a Conservative MP, and ultimately to the Brexit vote of 23 June 2016. Faragism became the animating philosophy of the Conservative right, and because of the weak, inept leadership of David Cameron and Theresa May, and the connivant leadership of Boris Johnson, it progressively took over the party as a whole.

On 24 June 2016, when David Cameron resigned, Farage became de facto leader of the Conservative party until the completion of Brexit in January 2021. It is the most extraordinary reverse takeover of a political party by an outsider in modern Britain.

The story begins with Margaret Thatcher. Until the late 1980s there was a European project in which Thatcher believed. Obliged by Cold War imperatives, she formed a triumvirate with Helmut Kohl and Francois Mitterrand to resist the Soviet Union and then to hasten its disintegration under Mikael Gorbachev. At this stage she went with the economic right not the nationalist right. Hence the Single Market, ironically the one transformational British project in the UK's 45 years of EU membership. The aim was to build on Europe's customs union, eliminating tariff barriers to trade, by removing invisible non-tariff barriers to trade, so creating the world's largest, richest single market. It was a breathtaking ambition, largely realised.

Thatcher was okay with – even briefly enthusiastic about – the EU while it was mainly about "markets". But not when it moved on to "social Europe" and political integration. She snapped when Delors came to Bournemouth in early September 1988 to address the Trades Union Congress on the "social dimension of Europe." Delors wowed the unions and the Labour Party, but Thatcher was appalled. As a direct riposte she promptly rewrote a speech she was due to give to the College of Europe in Bruges twelve days later, inserting the passage above attacking the supposed development of a "superstate", which she also branded a socialist state.

Two years after Bruges, in 1990, Thatcher was forced from power by a revolt of her MPs. She fell partly because of her poll tax, described in Chapter 16, and partly because of her bristling opposition to "Brussels" and Germany. These were two facets of the same domineering "control or abolish" philosophy (her hostility to local government at home and to Brussels abroad). Douglas Hurd, her last Foreign Secretary, noted: "Cabinet now consists of three items: parliamentary affairs, home affairs, and xenophobia." She was barely restrained even in public. "We beat the Germans twice and now they are back," she told fellow heads of government after the fall of the Berlin Wall. It took a war of attrition by Hurd and the grandees to get her to desist from trying to prevent the reunification of Germany in 1990.

Unmuzzled and out of office by the end of that year, Thatcher railed against her hapless moderate successor, John Major, for signing the 1992 Maastricht Treaty even though Major secured an opt-out from its key tenet, the single European currency. Symbolically, her last vote in the House of Commons, in 1992, was at the head of a rebellion against Major calling for a referendum on Maastricht. Only 20 Tory MPs supported her, but she had raised her standard and "Euro-scepticism," as it was then called, spread across the Conservative party like a virus, especially the grass roots.

The conversion to Brexit of the Conservative party was gradual and not fully accomplished until after the 2016 referendum, but it was nonetheless relentless from the early 1990s. The collapse of the Soviet Union in 1991, followed by Maastricht a year later, were key moments. Now that the Soviet threat had evaporated, German predominance and the Euro became the issues. While Mitterrand and Kohl sought to situate Germany within a strong, quasi-federal Europe, Thatcher was implacable: 'no, no, no.' Enoch Powell had by now long retired, his last 13 years in the Commons sitting for an Ulster constituency as a Unionist, so it was viable for her to follow her instincts and head the nationalist neo-liberal right without controversies about racism and out-and-out xenophobia.

The credo of Thatcherites, young and old, was now simple: 'UP YOURS, DELORS, in the words of the Sun headline on 1st November 1990, just days before Thatcher's defenestration. "Sun readers are urged to tell the French fool where to stuff his ECU," began a rant about plans for a single currency. "*The Sun* today calls on its patriotic family to tell the feelthy French to FROG OFF!"

"Brussels" was by now shorthand and scapegoat for everything the Thatcherite right-wing hated. They were generally circumspect in public, making arguments about sovereignty and later immigration, not about the extension of Thatcherism. Nigel Lawson's boast in the *Financial Times* that "Brexit gives us a chance to complete the Thatcherite revolution," came only in the hubristic aftermath of the 2016 referendum. But Thatcher's visceral anti-state, deregulating, low tax creed drove Brexit from the outset supported by the Tory media, led by Rupert Murdoch's *Sun* and Paul Dacre's *Daily Mail*, which went Eurosceptic solidly and early.

By 1997, the electorate had sickened of the Tories, their divisions and the evident fissures in British society Thatcherism had generated. The youthful Tony Blair offered a fresh non-socialist alternative, proclaiming "one nation." The Tories were reduced to a rump. However, among the survivors, Thatcherites and now Thatcherism now reigned supreme. Major's successor, William Hague, was one of them. In a speech drafted by Daniel Hannan in the 2001 election, Hague took official Tory Euroscepticism to a new high. Labour would turn Britain into "foreign land" for the British; this was the last chance for the British people to "remain sovereign in their own country."

After Tony Blair's second landslide in 2001, Hague was succeeded by Iain Duncan Smith, the darling of the Eurosceptics who had led the Maastricht rebellion in the 1990s. IDS's leadership soon imploded from sheer incompetence; he was replaced by Michael Howard, similarly Thatcherite, just more capable. In these successive leadership contests the most qualified and electorally popular figure was the unThatcherite Ken Clarke: jazz-loving-man-about-town, MP for the East Midlands city of Nottingham, and successful Chancellor under Major. But every time he stood for the leadership, Clarke's Europeanism made him unelectable by rank-and-file Tory members, who since 1998 selected the leader.

In 2005, David Cameron became the fifth Tory leader to face Tony Blair. A PR executive, he knew the Tories' obsessive image had to go and told his first party conference to "stop banging on about Europe." But he too told the party he was Thatcherite – by now there was no other credible Toryism on offer. As a pledge of allegiance he withdrew Tory MEPs from the main centre-right European People's Party group in the European Parliament; instead they allied with far-right populists including Latvian fascists and Austrians in favour of banning gay pride marches. Leaving the EPP typified Cameron's policy for his eleven years as Tory leader: periodically throwing red meat to the Eurosceptics, while hoping the consequences could be contained. They couldn't. And the reason they couldn't was because by 2005 Nigel Farage and his populist anti-Europeanism was steadily taking control of Cameron's party beneath him.

Like Enoch Powell, Nigel Farage was a professional, elitist demagogue years in the making.

The origins of his party, UKIP, lie in the fringe organisations which sprouted after Thatcher's Bruges speech. Shortly before the 1992 election Alan Sked, a London School of Economics professor, left the Bruges Group, which he considered too loyal to John Major's Conservatives, to found the Anti-Federalist League. In the 1992 election Sked won just 117 votes in Bath, the seat lost by Chris Patten, who went on to become vice-president of the European Commission. A year later the Anti-Federalist League founded UKIP. The founding meeting largely comprised anti-European academics, with two notable additions: Julian Lewis of Conservative Central Office, later a Tory MP, and one Nigel Farage.

Farage grew up in awe of Margaret Thatcher. He joined the Tories in 1978 after Keith Joseph, Thatcher's radical free market mentor, spoke at his south London public school, Dulwich. A brash public school semi-rebel – "a wind up merchant", "bloody minded" and "difficult", according to his school reports – Farage planned to coin it in the City without bothering with university. Heading to a City metal trading floor in 1982, Thatcherism became his philosophy of life.

By now a nuance free Thatcherite contemptuous of the EU, Farage got active in the Bruges Group in the late Eighties, and through it UKIP. "You've hit on the right word – nation," he declared in his first election campaign in 1994. "We are the only party trying to stop all you fight for being thrown out of the window. We are witnessing a case of national suicide." He took Thatcher's line on John Major: weak and useless. Euroscepticism was the reclamation of Thatcherism.

"The more I read about the history of the Tory party, you realise that Thatcher wasn't a Conservative at all, she was a radical economic liberal," Farage told one interviewer. Asked if that was what he was, he replied, "Absolutely." "If you look at TV footage of Mrs. Thatcher being interviewed in the Eighties it actually takes your breath away," he said. "She had conviction, passion, belief. She was forthright. She spoke in a language that ordinary people could understand. I was never a Tory. I am a Thatcherite."

In 1994, aged thirty, the same age as Tony Blair when first elected to Parliament, Farage stood for UKIP in the Eastleigh by-election in Hampshire. He polled just 952 votes, on the same day as nationwide European Parliament elections in which UKIP won just one per cent. UKIP vied for fringe attention with the billionaire financier Sir James Goldsmith and his Referendum Party, set up in the same year, whose sole objective was an in/out EU referendum. Goldsmith had everything UKIP did not: money, connections, and name recognition for its leader.

But Farage soon developed an instinct for campaigning and the limelight. In the 1997 election, he notched up 3,332 votes in Salisbury. He was rising to the top of the UKIP pack. On its own that didn't mean much, but then he had two strokes of luck. Two months after Tony Blair's landslide, Goldsmith died. His Referendum Party disintegrated and UKIP became the sole Euro protest party. His second, equally vital and lucky break was Blair's decision to change the electoral system for the 1999 Euro elections from first-past-the-post to proportional representation.

Blair's switch to PR for Euro elections was designed to appease the Lib Dems and the pluralists within the Labour party. But as with Mitterrand's tactical decision to switch the French electoral system to PR in the mid-1980s, intended to wrong-foot his right-wing rival Jacques Chirac but which rocket-boosted Jean-Marie Le Pen's National Front, the main beneficiary was the populist right. UKIP now secured seats, status and salaries in Brussels in a way they couldn't at Westminster, partly because of first-past-the-post but also because in Westminster elections their vote was invariably too low and evenly spread to win seats. Euro elections, by contrast, were protest votes, and what better protest vehicle than a populist party whose mantra was opposition to the very European institutions whose irrelevance and perceived extravagance symbolized the elite that people wanted to protest against in the first place?

By now well-funded by ex-Tory donors, UKIP fielded candidates in all eleven constituencies for the 1999 Euro elections. It was first mid-term blues for New Labour. The Tories came first; UKIP was fourth with 6.5 per cent, but under the regional list PR system that was enough to elect three UKIP MEPs, one of them Nigel Farage. And so began his 19 years' membership of "a parliament I want no part of, under a system I despise, blinking into the cameras at one in the morning saying how proud I was," he recalled.

Equipped with a platform, a European Parliament salary, staff and generous allowances, and adoring Brexit sugar daddies like Paul Sykes and later Arron Banks, Farage took increasingly control of UKIP. In 2006 he stopped trading metals and became UKIP leader. There were rocky patches. The charismatic ex-Labour MP turned chat show host Robert Kilroy Silk had a brief flirtation with the party when his TV career abruptly halted in 2004. "Kilroy" became a UKIP MEP but lost to Farage in a battle of clashing egos, as did Douglas Carswell, a UKIP defector from the Tory benches in the Commons, a decade later.

Honing his "guy-about-town-with-a-pint-and-a-fag" image, Farage needed a breakthrough issue. "Brussels" itself wasn't sufficient on this score because, under the leadership of the former Portuguese centre-right prime minister Manuel Barroso, the Commission in the 2000s got on patiently with enlargement of the EU to the east, and deepening the Single Market, including the seminal 2006 Services Directive, a British project hard to attack from the free-market right. There were also important concessions to British concerns to promote inter-governmentalism and retreat from grandiloquent supranationalism. Instead of Commission directives the emphasis was on voluntary mechanisms. "Benchmarking" became the vogue word. None of this offered Farage the red meat he needed.

However, there was a new front opening up: immigration. In his early UKIP years, Farage trod warily on immigration, mindful of Enoch Powell. "Powell clearly lost the centre ground with the violence of his language. I have been very conscious not to make the same mistake," he said candidly. Instead, like Thatcher in her nuanced relationship with Powell 30 years previously, he operated by nods and winks – until Blair failed to impose transitional controls on the movement of central and east Europeans entering the EU in 2004. Then, adopting almost identical language to Thatcher in the run-up to the 1979 election, he attacked the Conservatives, as much as the Labour government, for letting Britain be "swamped." "The Europhiles claim that an enlarged EU will bring economic benefits to the UK," he said. "I rather doubt this, though it will bring a flood of people from Eastern Europe seeking benefits." Britain was "FULL UP," UKIP's 2004 Euro election manifesto declared, two months after the flow of immigrants had started. It needed "freedom from overcrowding" and a target of zero net migration. On the back of a £2 million campaign devised by shameless ex-Bill Clinton strategist Dick Morris, UKIP quadrupled its number of MEPs to 12, taking 16 per cent of the vote and beating the Liberal Democrats into fourth place. In September 2004 UKIP took ten per cent of the vote and pushed the Tories into fourth place in the Hartlepool by election, on Peter Mandelson's appointment to the European Commission.

Farage soon had the Tories in tow. Tacking hard right, Michael Howard, ran the Tory 2005 election campaign on the slogan "Are you thinking what we're thinking?," beneath pictures of immigrants. It was a small step to Farage's BREAKING POINT poster of the 2016 referendum featuring a swarm of dark faced actors playing "Syrian refugees," heading remorselessly out of the poster towards the viewer.

As Tory leader after 2005, David Cameron dropped Howard's racist innuendo. But so too, for the most part, did Farage, by now a highly skilled politician adept at strong language while keeping "clear purple water" between UKIP and the out-and-out racist British National Party, which outperformed UKIP in parts of urban England in local elections in the mid-Noughties. A strong line on "radical Islam" became a new theme. Farage made a thing of Sharia law and proposed to ban the burka. He got embroiled in a deliberate row about inviting the populist anti-Islamic Dutch politician Geert Wilders to Parliament.

In the 2005 general election, Blair's last, UKIP polled 2.2 per cent, not a breakthrough but twice the Green vote, and in the first English by-election of the 2005 Parliament, eight months after Cameron became Tory leader, Farage took third place from Labour in Bromley in affluent south London. It's often said that Farage never won a seat in Westminster, as if this was a handicap. But it had the paradoxical effect of making him constantly available to fight them, which he did – seven times in all – from his platform as an MEP in Brussels, keeping himself in the limelight.

As Tory leader, Cameron lived in constant fear of a UKIP surge. For much of his five years as leader of the opposition (2005-2010) it was far from clear he would survive, still less win a general election. His strategy was Brexit-lite: he left the centre-right EPP group in the European Parliament, promised a referendum on the Lisbon treaty, which did further integration, and promised to reform or repatriate everything from the social chapter to free movement, the Common Agricultural Policy and Common Fisheries Policy. He also speculated that he might somehow – though he knew not how – "restore" the sovereignty of Parliament over the European Court of Justice. Everything short of the final concession: a Brexit referendum. Jibes about UKIP – "a bunch of fruit cakes, loonies and closet racists" – were soon dropped.

The 2009 parliamentary expenses scandal, which exploded shortly before the Euro elections of that year, was a gift to UKIP. Norman Tebbit, ardent Brexiteer and Tory party chairman under Thatcher, encouraged Tories to vote UKIP. Gordon Brown's Labour party was pushed into third place and UKIP won 13 MEPs, increasing its vote to 16.5 per cent.

Hence Cameron's pledge in his 2010 manifesto to cut net immigration to just "tens of thousands." Net immigration from all sources was at 250,000 by 2010; with Farage committed to zero, Cameron positioned himself, statistically, about two-thirds of the way towards UKIP, which summed up Brexit-lite. Labour was under pressure too, graphically exhibited by Gordon Brown's disastrous encounter with Gillian Duffy in Rochdale during the 2010 election. Caught on microphone calling her a "bigoted woman", Mrs Duffy responded: "you can't say anything about the immigrants and these eastern Europeans what are coming in."

It was a winding, but not particularly slow, road from Cameron's entry into Downing Street in May 2010 to the referendum of 23 June 2016. The initial lack of a Tory majority put a Brexit referendum on the back burner, but it never left the stove. Brexit-lite continued, crucially in the form of a bill to require referendums on all future EU treaty changes, agreed with his coalition partner Nick Clegg and the Liberal Democrats who, fearing a UKIP surge in their West Country heartlands, themselves wanted to sound tough on "Brussels." This did not satisfy the right, of course. In October 2011, 81 Tory MPs voted for a Brexit referendum, a rebellion twice as large as any against John Major on Maastricht. "From that day onwards it was inevitable that we were going to have a referendum," declared Peter Bone, a self-appointed leader of the awkward squad.

Tellingly, even Nick Clegg's Liberal Democrats were by now committed in principle to a Brexit referendum at an undefined future date. By 2012 UKIP was polling 7-8 per cent. Michael Fabricant, a vice-chairman of the Conservative party, spoke for most Tory activists in calling for an electoral pact with UKIP around a Brexit referendum. Fabricant noted that in 21 seats in the 2010 election the UKIP vote was greater than the Conservative margin of loss. UKIP, he said, was "a major contributory factor to the Conservatives failing to win an overall majority."

The continuing effects of the financial crisis in 2008/9, which spilled into a crisis of the Eurozone in general and Greek debt in particular, later seamlessly morphing into the Syrian refugee crisis, became a backdrop of alleged EU failure. The EU was endlessly portrayed as sclerotic, an economic corpse and, over Greece, selfishly heartless. Germany became the dark spider at the centre of a web of austerity policies prolonging the European recession and imposing impossible economic terms on helpless Greece. This was proof positive, repeated an alliance of left and right alike, of the degree to which a centralized European Union, preoccupied with over-ambitious pan-European policies like the euro, was an elite project against the peoples of Europe.

Buffeted by his party, Cameron chose to indulge his critics and never made the counter case on Europe – instead seizing on openings in the crisis to try to force concessions from EU leaders. Within months of taking office in 2010, with the Eurozone in crisis, he sought to make British support for treaty changes to shore up the Euro, which did not affect Britain at all outside the Euro, conditional upon the UK being allowed to opt out of majority-voting for financial sector rules within the Single Market. He wanted to present this to his euro-sceptic wing as a win against Europe. This manoeuvre irritated without pressurizing Merkel (Cameron had not worked to line up any allies among other less federal-minded EU premiers), and she refused outright. Together with French president Nicolas Sarkozy, she circumvented Britain by doing a deal among the 17 Eurozone members for an inter-governmental treaty. This was agreed at an EPP leaders meeting in Marseilles, from which Cameron was tellingly absent because he had left the EPP.

In coalition with the Liberal Democrats for the first five years after 2010, and therefore insulated from having to act on their rhetoric, Conservative MPs became increasingly extreme on Europe. Brexit-lite Cameron sought any assuaging bone to throw not only to his Eurosceptic MPs but to the ravenously sceptic Conservative constituency party associations, their elderly heads turned by the endless anti–EU propaganda of the right-wing press. In 2012 a "balance of competences" review was launched with the explicit aim of demonstrating beyond peradventure that the legal powers and responsibilities of the EU were excessive, thus necessitating a renegotiation of the treaties. It remains the most comprehensive audit of the workings of the EU ever produced, based on 32 volumes and 3,000 pages of evidence submitted by over 1,500 independent sources, and was widely praised for the rigour and impartiality with which it was carried out. But it did not deliver as Cameron hoped. Far from the coruscating condemnation of the EU, the review found that the EU served British interests pretty well, with any compromises on sovereignty more than compensated for by policy gains with powerful economic and social benefits. Indeed, British business was very satisfied.

Rather than communicate these findings to the public, the government developed a collective amnesia over the whole review. The House of Lords European Affairs Committee came close to accusing Cameron of trying to cover up the review's findings. It observed, critically, that if the purpose of the review were to "ground the public debate on the EU on a strong evidence base" this "seems an unrealistic aim, as long as the public are unaware of the Review's existence, there is no point spending up to £5m of public money on an excellent review and then burying it. People need to know the facts about the UK-EU relationship." Such was the ignorance that even the Remain campaign barely mentioned the Government's own review of the EU in the referendum campaign.

Given the steady build up of Europhobia under Thatcher and Farage, Cameron's fateful announcement of his support for a Brexit referendum, in his Bloomberg speech of 23rd January 2013, seemed almost inevitable. It wasn't a one-off error but the logical conclusion of the Brexit-lite policy he had followed since 2005. Tellingly, although George Osborne claims in retrospect to have been opposed to a Brexit referendum, none of Cameron's lieutenants tried to stop him, Osborne included. They, too, saw further appeasement of Farage as unavoidable. Even in retrospect they maintain the same line. In his recent memoirs, Sir Oliver Letwin, Cameron's policy chief and a Tory front-bencher and adviser going right back to Thatcher's policy unit, where he devised the poll tax, says the Brexit referendum was "right in principle and inevitable in practice." "If we failed to guarantee a referendum, we were more than likely to lose enough seats to UKIP to deprive us of an overall majority, in which case, we would end up depending on UKIP support in Parliament, the condition of which would of course (ironically) be the holding of a referendum." It was a logic based on the premise that Farage was now arbiter of Tory politics and electoral fortunes.

Farage proclaimed "a tremendous victory." And his verdict in retrospect: "It was so obvious to me at the time of Bloomberg that any argument that I should have worked from within the Conservative Party would never have worked, and actually the UKIP tactic of fighting and taking votes from the outside had worked." Now he moved in for the kill, true to the words of Kipling, beloved by Enoch Powell: "If once you have paid the Dane-geld, you never get rid of the Dane." In the June 2014 Euro elections UKIP got its best ever result: 26 per cent and 24 seats. The Conservatives came third, the first time ever in a national election that they had not come first or second. Three months later, just after the 2014 Tory party conference, two Tory MPs defected to UKIP, the first to do so. Both held their seats in by-elections, provoking panic in Downing Street that more Tory MPs might defect at any moment. The pressure was on Labour too: on the same day in October 2014 as the by-election which returned Douglas Carswell as UKIP MP for Clacton, Labour held UKIP off by only 617 votes in a by-election in Greater Manchester.

By now, Farage was playing daily variations on his anti-immigrant riff. He told *Newsweek* in November 2014 that immigrants with HIV should not be admitted to Britain. By the 2015 election campaign this was amplified to the false claim that 60 per cent of those diagnosed with HIV in

Britain were foreign and exploiting the NHS. The "Australian points system" was UKIP's magic cure to keep high-skilled migrants while weeding out the "HIV tourists."

In the run-up to the 2015 general election immigration consistently ranked in polls as one of the top or three issues facing the country, often coming top. The three mainstream parties did their best not to talk about it – "mass immigration has been all but airbrushed from this election, even by the Tories," the *Daily Mail* blazed half way through the election – but that didn't abate public sentiment.

By early 2015 UKIP was polling 17% and predicting it would win up to 20 seats in the imminent election. Its appeal went far wider than just Europe and immigration. As Lord Ashcroft said in one of his poll summaries, Farage's primary attraction was that 'he will say things that need to be said but others are scared to say.'

It was an article of faith among Tory pollsters in the run-up to the 2015 election that a UKIP vote of more than ten per cent would make it impossible for the Conservatives to secure a majority. Panicked, Cameron tacked further right. He repeated his "tens of thousands" immigration pledge for the 2015 election, despite its absurdity. Cameron had long stopped referring to UKIP as "closet racists" and was now referring to them jovially in private as "my little purple friends." He made a Brexit referendum a red line in any future coalition negotiations with the Lib Dems. When challenged directly by Farage in the one televised leaders' debate of the campaign: "Do you accept or not that in your renegotiation free movement is not up for discussion?", Cameron replied: "I don't accept that."

In the event UKIP did surge in the May 2015 election, to 12.6 per cent, by far its highest poll in any general election, pushing the Lib Dems into a distant fourth place. Through the quirks of first-past-the-post, Cameron nonetheless won a majority of seats on just 36.9 per cent of the vote. But with Clegg and the Lib Dems eviscerated, Cameron's Brexit referendum red line now applied only to himself.

One of Cameron's first acts on forming, in May 2015, the first purely Conservative government in 18 years was to legislate for the Brexit referendum. Labour and the Lib Dems voted for it, in deference to the Tory/UKIP landslide, and it passed the Commons by the overwhelming majority of 544 to 53 votes with only the SNP voting against.

Like Harold Wilson forty years earlier, Cameron set out to secure a "new deal" with the European Union that could be sold as a favourable renegotiation of terms in a referendum. His problem was twofold. Firstly, Britain already had secured almost all the opt-outs and concessions possible along with greatly strengthened measures against further integration; and secondly his party and his media had created impossible benchmarks for success that in reality could only be achieved by leaving.

Cameron won the right to red-card EU legislation, was excused from the treaty commitment to ever closer union and within the framework of freedom of movement gained some rights to control immigration even if they fell short of the much taunted emergency brake. But it appeared too little. In this it was very different from Wilson's renegotiations in 1975. Although Wilson did not secure fundamental treaty changes – he didn't want any – he got an improved deal on New Zealand lamb and butter which he paraded successfully as cheaper food in the shops and playing fair by our Commonwealth "kith and kin." Cameron had no parallel gains to parade.

Cameron should have demanded more and might have secured the "emergency brake" he sought on EU immigration had he "done a Thatcher" and brought the EU to a virtual standstill. But he didn't even try. He was also keen to move quickly on a Brexit referendum. Another Syrian and North African refugee surge appeared likely and his party was becoming more Faragist by the day. He thought time was his enemy.

So on 20th February 2016, less than ten months after the general election, a Brexit referendum was called for 23rd June. From day one, Cameron was on the back foot. The argument about a "reformed" European Union was not so much lost as never even made. Steve Baker, leader of the Brexit brigade on the Tory backbenches, called his renegotiation "like polishing poo." To the *Daily Mail* it was THE GREAT DELUSION. WHO DO EU THINK YOU ARE KIDDING MR CAMERON?, opined Murdoch's *Sun*, beside a steaming pile of manure. The *Mail* ran front page anti-immigration stories on 17 of the 23 days before the referendum.

Cameron was typical blasé about the referendum arrangements. He allowed an electoral quango, under pressure from the Faragists, to change the question from "yes/no" to "leave/remain." This decision alone probably lost the referendum given its narrow outcome: in about two-thirds of referendums the change option wins. He also sided with the Faragists in refusing to insert a threshold for a "leave" vote to take effect: only 38 per cent of the registered electorate voted Leave. He refused to allow 16 and 17 year-olds to vote, although they had been given the vote in the Scottish independence referendum two years previously and were strongly pro-EU.

No requirement was demanded of Leave to set out their stall so that voters would know what Leave implied. The "Vote Leave: Take Control" website explicitly argued that Britain would stay in the Single Market via membership of the European Economic Area, yet leaving the Single Market became a red line subsequently. And Cameron failed to legislate for any parliamentary or legal process to be followed in the event of a Leave majority, including a subsequent referendum on the Brexit deal itself, essential to allow the "sovereign people" to consider the actual divorce deal resulting from any "instruction" to Parliament to negotiate one. The long post-2016 parliamentary crisis about the handling of Brexit was largely caused by this critical omission.

It was immigration that decisively turned opinion sour. It has been rising in salience, but in 2016, on the eve of the referendum, 63% believed refugees to be one of the most important issues facing the country today, compared to just 39% saying the same for the NHS, or 33% the economy.

Even then a British Social Attitudes survey found that 43% wanted Britain to stay in a reformed EU. Much of the EU referendum would thus come down to whether or not Cameron's deal qualified, in the minds of the British people, as "reform." It did not. According to pollsters Survation, on the most important issue, immigration, just 26% felt that his renegotiation would reduce immigration, with 60% believing it would make no difference. A clear majority believed his reforms did not go far enough. Whilst in 1975, the government's renegotiation was one of the reasons why support for "In" doubled in the six months before the referendum, Cameron's renegotiation was an unqualified electoral failure. 47% said it would make no difference to their vote, and 31% said it would make them more likely to vote to leave.

A study of 268 referendums since 1990 finds that in 69% of them, the change option won. Dissatisfaction with the status quo in "left behind" parts of England made the electorate ripe for such a change vote. From a subsequent analysis weighted for turnout, it was estimated that from at least January 11th, and probably before, Leave was consistently ahead of Remain. A week before the vote on 23 June, just before the Labour MP Jo Cox's murder in her Yorkshire constituency, the Leave campaign peaked with a lead of 13.2%.

The campaign itself was a textbook disaster. The day after its launch Cameron lost the most popular Tory in the country, the outgoing Mayor of London Boris Johnson, to the leadership of the Leave campaign alongside Farage, plus a quarter of his Cabinet. Johnson spent the campaign on a bus emblazoned with "£350m a week for the NHS if we leave the EU." He was cheered by Tory activists wherever he went. Quitting the EU had long become an article of faith among the mostly retired Tory membership, dreaming of a better Thatcherite yesterday.

Nor was Labour much help, distancing itself from joining a cross-party platform in the belief that this would tar the party with a Tory brush, as the 2014 cross-party referendum campaign against Scottish independence had done. Jeremy Corbyn, the disastrous "old left" post-2015 Labour leader, was a decades old critic of the EU from the 1980s Bennite stable, who made only one speech weakly opposing Brexit throughout the entire campaign and refused to appear with Cameron.

On 16 June, Farage unveiled his BREAKING POINT poster. A few hours later, Jo Cox was assassinated by a far-right nationalist extremist in broad daylight.

Exactly a week later, 33,577,342 electors, the largest number in the history of the United Kingdom, voted.

Shortly after dawn on June 24th, David Cameron announced on the steps of 10 Downing that he would respect "the instruction of the British people" to leave the European Union. He also announced his resignation.

Nigel Farage was having breakfast at the Ritz with Freddie Barclay, owner of the Ritz and the *Daily Telegraph*. They toasted in champagne.

On 13 July Theresa May succeeded David Cameron as prime minister. But it was Nigel Farage who had become effective leader of the Conservative Party.

9

JENKINS

While I have met almost no-one more serious in their pleasures than Roy Jenkins (1920-2003), I have also met almost no-one more serious in their politics, and absolutely no-one more serious and successful at the liberal politics of creating what he called a "civilised society."

Roy used to say that history belongs to those who make the weather, not to the weathervanes. What inspired me about him, as an Oxford student when I admired from afar, through to the end of his life when we became close friends, was his combination of politician and historian; and how someone who was in many ways so Establishment could be so genuinely and constructively radical. This is my lecture on the centenary of his birth in 2020.

For those who think that in politics the art of the possible is narrow and circumscribed, unless you are a populist or a revolutionary, just look at Roy Jenkins. The legalisation of homosexuality and abortion in 1967, in the teeth of deep public and religious opposition, and well before any other large western democracy had done either, still ranks as one of the most remarkable acts of modern British statecraft. And Roy wasn't just a major force for Britain's entry into the European Union. He was also in many ways the father of today's single European currency, which in the 1970s, when he laid the path to it as president of the commission, seemed "the nearest thing to pie-in-the-sky since the invention of the pie," as one of his officials told me. Then straight after returning from Brussels he created the SDP, in its long-run effects one of the most successful insurgent parties in British history, a model – maybe *the* model – for New Labour under the leadership of his young friend and admirer Tony Blair.

As I got to know Roy well, I realised that his extraordinary blend of Establishment-itis and radicalism was a personality trait, not just a political standpoint. Indeed his political genius grew out of his personality. His life in all dimensions was an extraordinary blend of self-assurance, courage and risk, enveloped in claret, Brooks's and the Athenaeum. The Proustian *liaisons dangereuses* of his private life followed a similar pattern to his public life. Shirley Williams told me of a parliamentary trip to Greece with Roy in the 1950s. For some reason they spent a night on a ship; as she came out onto to her balcony in the early morning she was amazed to see Roy, from the high deck above, dive straight into the sea. Jim Callaghan, who had a generally frosty relationship with Jenkins, told me that he was nonetheless in awe of him standing in the Warrington by-election of 1981 immediately on his return to Britain after the presidency of the European Commission. "The sheer courage to do that at his age was impressive, after his career and with so much humiliation if it went wrong," he told me.

It was the same with his books. Who starts writing a thousand-page biography of Churchill at the age of 78?

A clue as to how Roy thought and worked is how he described the writing of *Churchill.* "It's like climbing Everest. I rarely look at the summit; just as the track ahead, and what advance can be made each day with a bit of determination and optimism." His writing and reading usually started at 6am; just before lunch he would count the precise number of words he had written and note it on a card. Usually between 500 and 1,000 words. There wasn't much writing after lunch. He told me he had only once in his life had sandwiches for lunch, and vowed never to repeat the experience.

Of course, if you are going to try and get up a mountain, it is vital to choose the right one and to know quite a lot about it before setting off. Herein, in my view, lies Roy's genius. His boldness was matched by shrewdness. He had a generally good, often brilliant sense of pace, timing and subject. He used to tell me that a good sense of proportion is the supreme attribute in politics and in life.

Where did these qualities come from? I think they had a lot to do with him being literally born and brought up in politics, and in the values and principles he held for the rest of his life. His father Arthur Jenkins was a Labour MP and parliamentary private secretary to Attlee when Roy was growing up in Abersychan in the South Wales mining valleys in the 1930s. Arthur was a unique blend of trade union leader, politician, autodidact and Francophile; mild-mannered yet administratively decisive and effective: secretary of the miners' federation of south Wales, the most important union in the country besides Ernie Bevin's Transport and General Workers' Union, alongside being a county and district councillor and then MP for Pontypool from 1935 until his early death as a junior minister in Attlee's government in 1946, two years before Roy himself became an MP.

Arthur had been jailed for incitement to violence on the picket line in the 1926 General Strike, yet insisted he had never incited anyone, was ashamed to have gone to jail, and refused to become a folk hero in much the way that the fastidious Roy, his only son, always refused to play to the gallery. Leading Labour politicians of the 1930s, including Attlee and Herbert Morrison, were constantly staying with the Jenkins family in south Wales, and from his early teenage years Roy gravitated to politics almost as naturally as a Cecil to the Tories. He first stood for parliament at the age of 24 in the 1945 election, got elected at a by-election three years later and fought 15 parliamentary elections in all, more than any political titan of the 20th century apart from Churchill, who fought 20.

Jenkins was a member or leader of major political institutions for 55 years. But more than that, his entire life was in politics, including his youth and the writing of his biographies, all of them about political leaders. Even his affairs to Lady Caroline Gilmour and Lady Bonham-Carter were with women married to MPs. Jennifer, his wife, to whom he was nonetheless devoted, was passionate about reformist politics since being a Fabian at Cambridge – the two of them met at a wartime Fabian Society summer school – and she did as much campaigning as Roy in his parliamentary elections.

Roy was born into Europe too. Arthur held that Paris was the capital of the world, read and spoke French passionately, and took Roy there when he was 17. They stayed in a modest *pension*. I simply *have* to reproduce this passage in Roy's memoirs about this youthful month in Paris in the summer of 1938, not just for the wonderfully orotund Jenkins-isms (read it aloud) but to conjure his whole world view:

I lived in an encapsulation of Third Republican Paris. Boulevard de Port-Royal, where we stayed, was redolent of seventeenth century Jansenism but its appearance was firmly nineteenth century, except for a scattering of black Citroens, red Renaults and market trucks which rolled along the wide pavé, either up the gentle slope to the Carrefour de l'Observatoire and the Montparnasse of the Coupole and Dome cafes a short way beyond, or down to join the Avenue des Gobelins which debouched into the Place d'Italie, the hub of the south-eastern and mainly working-class treizièmearronidissement.

The Boulevard de Port-Royal itself was flanked by oppressive public buildings, which seemed to me to have faintly sinister names, like Val-de-Grace ...or the Hôpital Cochin, or the Baudelocque lying-in hospital or the Hospice des Enfants Assistés. La Santé prison was just behind. I hoped I would not end up in any of them. Inside the great wooden door of No 85 ... a porte-cochere led into a not very attractive gravelled garden, around which were several separate and 1930-ish three-storeyed buildings, one of which was my pension. It was presided over by Madame Vincent, who ... who looked severe and concentrated on accurate French and a Gallic but not luxurious diet at the communal table ...

My room was basic but had an adequate cloth-covered writing table which commanded a good view of the eastern sky, in the direction of Germany I frequently thought, for both that summer, and the next one when I returned to the pension, were dominated by the threat of Hitler and the thought of the Nuremberg rallies taking place a few hundred miles away. I acquired some French but more knowledge of the topography of Paris, to match that of London ... I do not remember feeling apprehensive about the approach of

Oxford. What I did feel apprehensive about was the approach of war.

The point of all this is that by the time Roy Jenkins went up to Oxford at the age of 18, he had more political and international grounding than most politicians ever acquire. And he never shifted this ground for the rest of his life.

However, grounding is one thing, character and flair another. Fast forward 25 years, to Harold Wilson's first Labour government in 1964, and a single incident reveals Jenkins' political character like—as he might have said—a streak of lightening lights up the night sky. Starting out under Wilson as minister for aviation outside the cabinet, in January 1965, three months into the government, Wilson offered him promotion to the cabinet as education secretary. After a few hours of anguished cogitation, Roy turned the post down. Wilson was astonished. So am I, even in retrospect knowing what came afterwards. It makes Roy literally the only politician of any party I have ever known to have turned down a first cabinet post.

Why did he do it? For three reasons, he told me. First, he didn't have a reformist programme for education. Worse, Labour's policy of abolishing the grammar schools was one he disagreed with, having gone to one himself; and Jenkins rarely did what he disagreed with, and never on major issues. But thirdly, the post he wanted was home secretary, where for the previous decade he had been working out in his mind a whole liberal reformist agenda – roughly what he went on to do as home secretary. He sensed that Wilson's first home secretary, Sir Frank Soskice, nice but weak and beleaguered, wouldn't survive long, and he told Wilson straight out that the Home Office was the job he wanted if it became vacant, which is precisely what happened eleven months later. Having seen the top of politics myself, I am all the more awe-struck by this combination of poise, focus and bold but well-judged risk taking, which he was to show it again and again throughout his remaining 38 years of life – political, literary and social.

On big political questions, Roy wasn't just bold and confident; to an extraordinary degree, he was right. At least, I think so. His last speech in the House of Commons was against the restoration of the death penalty. His last speech in the House of Lords was against the looming Iraq War. The fact that he was Tony Blair's friend didn't lead him to pull his punches. This is the beginning and end of that last Lords speech, three months before his death:

> I have a high regard for the Prime Minister. I have been repelled by attempts to portray him as a vacuous man with an artificial smile and no convictions. I am reminded of similar attempts by a frustrated Right to suggest that Gladstone was mad, Asquith was corrupt and Attlee was negligible. My view is that the Prime Minister, far from lacking conviction, has almost too much, particularly when dealing with the world beyond Britain. He is a little too Manichaean for my perhaps now jaded taste, seeing matters in stark terms of good and evil, black and white, contending with each other, and with a consequent belief that if evil is cast down good will inevitably follow. I am more inclined to see the world and the regimes within it in varying shades of grey. The experience of the past year, not least in Afghanistan, has given more support to that view than to the more Utopian one that a quick "change of regime" can make us all live happily ever after ...

I am in favour of courage — who is ever not in the abstract? — but not of treating it as a substitute for wisdom, as I fear we are currently in danger of doing.

Those final words – almost the last words he uttered in public – "I am in favour of courage, but not as a substitute for wisdom" – sum up Roy Jenkins. Courage with wisdom.

On the wisdom, I was a regular go-between between Roy and Tony Blair until his death in January 2003. Month after month, letter after letter, conversation after conversation, the old leader urged the young leader to take the plunge and join the Euro; and not, as he argued, to repeat the same mistake as Attlee in 1950 and Eden in 1955 and stay out of the construction of the institutions of Europe only for Britain to have to join from a position of weakness and isolation later. Blair nearly took his advice. Nearly but not quite. Just imagine Britain and Europe today if he had taken it gone into the Euro instead of Iraq.

"Ah, but he never became Labour leader and prime minister so never had never had to make the fundamental choices needed to win and stay in power," some might say. Wilson said roughly that, complaining of Roy's refusal to budge on joining Europe after it became unpopular on the Labour left when Heath, as prime minister, applied to join in 1971. Roy himself said in his memoirs: "I may have avoided doing too much stooping, but I also missed conquering," in reference to not becoming prime minister.

However, it is not a fair criticism of Roy Jenkins that he preached but did not practice, or that he ducked difficult choices, or that he was deficient in accumulating political power. On the contrary, his capacity for turning liberal ideas into successful liberal action on the great questions of the day was to my mind his defining achievement and legacy.

In his liberal convictions, Roy wasn't a great innovator although he was a great lighthouse: rather, his genius lay in turning conviction into action and into institutions of lasting effect. The legalisation of homosexuality and abortion; the creation of the Euro; the creation of the SDP which presaged New Labour are, together, more than most prime ministers have ever achieved. So let me now seek to illuminate the Jenkins method.

It is an astonishing fact that Roy was home secretary for only one year and eleven months, from December 1965 to November 1967, and those 23 months included the 1966 general election. But in those 23 months he radically changed the face of English society for the better. Before Roy thousands of gays were prosecuted each year for their identity, and many sent to jail. Illegal abortions were running at anything up to 200,000 a year; hundreds of women died each year from criminal abortions in the most horrendous circumstances.

Before Jenkins, bill after bill had failed in the previous twenty years to legalise abortion, while on homosexuality there had been no progress whatever since the Wolfenden Report of nine years earlier. Only months before he became home secretary, a private member's bill to legalise homosexuality was defeated outright on a free vote in the Commons, after Labour had come to office. Labour whips organised against it because, as Wilson's confidant Richard Crossman put it in his diary, they "objected fiercely that it was turning our working-class support against us." It was a

1960s version of populist fears about the loss of the Red Wall.

Roy's predecessor Sir Frank Soskice wouldn't even countenance a law against racial discrimination, arguing that this might stir up racial prejudice. Instead he proposed a royal commission—knowing, as Wilson said of royal commissions, that they "take minutes and last years."

And lest there be any sense of inevitability about what happened, when Roy enacted his liberal reforms in England, Willie Ross, Wilson's secretary of state for Scotland, stopped homosexuality being legalised in Scotland for another 13 years. For a decade after 1967, French women came to England in their thousands for abortions each year because they still weren't legal in France. Ireland didn't legalise homosexuality until 1993, 36 years after the Jenkins reforms; and abortion not until 2018, half a century after England.

The first key to success is that Roy knew exactly what he wanted to do the moment he became home secretary. More, he was passionate about it, and his passion was infectious. He was especially popular among the large and young intake of new Labour MPs in Wilson's 1966 Labour landslide, who were looking for a leader and a cause. As David Marquand, one of these self-styled Jenkinsites, said: "It is hard to recapture in retrospect the excitement Roy generated as Home Secretary." Whether left and right in Labour terms, they saw Jenkins as a dynamic force and the face of the future. To extend Jonathan Freedland's insight: even career politicians mostly don't mostly believe in abstract ideas, but rather in leaders and *their* ideas.

To get an immediate grip on the notoriously hidebound Home Office, one of Roy's first acts was to replace his permanent secretary, after bitter exchanges about his desire to take advice from officials who were better informed and more receptive to his reforms. He was also one of the first ministers to use special advisers effectively. His special advisers acted as *his* agents, not vice versa like Dominic Cummings, and they worked pretty effectively *with* the civil service machine, not against it. His longest-serving special adviser, John Harris, was a smart former journalist and press aide to both Gaitskell and Wilson who represented his boss so faithfully that he came to speak like Roy, gesticulate like Roy, think like Roy, smoke and drink like Roy, even to look like Roy. He later became a successful minister as Lord Harris of Greenwich. When I first met him, in the Reform Club of course, I momentarily thought he was his ex-boss.

Roy was himself an adept media operator. David Astor, editor-proprietor of *The Observer*, wasn't just an admirer, he was a friend and hired the young politician as a feature writer, giving him far greater prominence than he would have got as a mid-ranking opposition spokesman. Roy became an accomplished journalist (he also wrote for an Indian weekly). Indeed it was *Observer* features he wrote on aviation which led Wilson to make him minister of aviation in 1964; and he only stuck with politics after the death in January 1963 of Hugh Gaitskell, his close political friend, when he told Wilson had been offered the editorship of *The Economist* and the new Labour leader, hailing from a nominally more left-wing Labour faction than Gaitskell, promised to give him a senior post if Labour won the imminent election.

On the political right-of-centre, Roy was also admired by William Rees-Mogg's *Times*. He was seen as a 1960s moderniser even by those who weren't particularly liberal, and therein lies a fourth key facet of the Jenkins method. He ran his liberal reforms alongside a radical modernisation of the criminal justice system which few doubted was long overdue. Two modernisations in particular he carried through: a rationalisation of police authorities, reducing the number from 117 to 49, the position we still have today; and the introduction of majority verdicts in trials, a controversial reform—Margaret Thatcher voted against it as an offence against the jury system—but one long overdue and which, as he took pleasure in noting, "contributed more to the conviction of professional and dangerous criminals than any of the measures introduced by Mrs Thatcher's four home secretaries." William Rees-Mogg, ex-Balliol like Jenkins, and father of you know who, wasn't remotely liberal, yet he was one of his fellow alumnus's strongest supporters out of admiration for his sheer competence, dynamism and panache.

Equally vital was Roy's parliamentary skill. He invested an inordinate amount of time in preparing set-piece speeches. His greatest parliamentary test as home secretary was after the escape of the spy George Blake from Wormwood Scrubs. Heath tabled a censure motion. In a debate of high drama, Jenkins trounced Heath and Quintin Hailsham, the shadow home secretary, by demonstrating that everything he had done and not done in dealing with prison security his Tory predecessors had done and not done worse. Crossman described it as "a tremendous annihilating attack which completely destroyed the Opposition."

All this – his command of the Home Office, of Labour MPs, of the media and of Parliament – gave Roy the political capital to move on his liberal reforms. Without them he couldn't conceivably have succeeded since he had to carry radical reform in face of deeply hostile public opinion in the case of legalising homosexuality, and in the face of strong opposition from the leaders of all the churches in the case of abortion; and—just as big an obstacle—in the face of neutrality verging on opposition from the prime minister and the cabinet. Wilson had reformist tendencies and admired Roy's sheer competence and panache, which is why he made him chancellor when Callaghan collapsed over devaluation, but his constituency as an MP was Huyton in the Catholic part of Liverpool and his social liberalism didn't extend much beyond the Beatles.

For this reason Jenkins had to reform by means of an unusual and precarious device for such sweeping reforms, backbench private members' bills, which had to be carried through parliament on free votes with no government whips applying. A critical factor in enabling Roy to succeed here was his own extensive parliamentary experience as an MP already for twenty years before he became home secretary. Moreover, he knew the private members' bill world back to front because in the late 1950s he had used it himself to abolish print censorship.

In 1959, after years of literary and parliamentary agitation, Roy had successfully piloted a private member's bill to allow a defence of literary merit in publishing books containing explicit sex. In legal terms it was a half measure, for it still allowed censorship on grounds of obscenity, but it was the best he could get in a deal with then Tory home secretary R A Butler, and without Rab's support there was no chance of getting any reform through. In the event its effect was practically to end censorship, largely because Roy himself persuaded the jury, in the famous *Lady Chatterley's Lover* trial which followed the passage of his bill, that Penguin should be allowed to publish D H Lawrence's then scandalous novel. This was the occasion the prosecution counsel asked the jury rhetorically: "Would you approve of your young sons and young daughters—because girls can read as well as boys—reading this book? Is it a book that you would have lying around in your own house? Is it a book that you would even wish your wife or your servants to read?"

Roy applied his *Lady Chatterley* experience to the legalisation of homosexuality and abortion, carefully selecting backbench MPs—David Steel in the case of abortion, Leo Abse in the case of homosexuality—to promote the bills then giving them Home Office support, including in the drafting of the bills, although the government itself was neutral. Roy then persuaded Wilson and the cabinet first to agree that despite official government neutrality, he should be allowed to speak and vote for the bills and other ministers be allowed to vote for them too; and then, when as was inevitably going to happen, the opponents attempted to filibuster the bills on the floor of the Commons because there was no government guillotine motion to limit debate, that additional government time should be made available for them. This led to a row in the cabinet, but Jenkins made it a matter of confidence in himself and Wilson supported him in giving the extra time. Wilson needed his home secretary to be a success; part of Roy's skill vis-à-vis Wilson is that he was generally a team player while also a highly successful sole trader.

On top of all this, Roy's timing and tactics were impeccable. He moved immediately after the 1966 election not just on one but on *both* legalisations, abortion and homosexuality. This obviously increased the controversy and hazard. Some of the leading parliamentary supporters of legalising homosexuality were opposed on abortion, including Shirley Williams, an observant Catholic, and vice versa. This involved, as he put it, treating the same MPs as "heroes" and "hobgoblins" on different days while retaining their goodwill. However, his judgement was that he had a narrow window of opportunity to mobilise, on the run, the 1966 influx of new and mostly liberal Labour MPs. The fact that they saw these reforms as part of a comprehensive liberal programme, including Roy's other measures to abolish flogging in prisons, end theatre censorship and introduce no fault divorce and the first race discrimination legislation, made them more not less supportive. This judgement was vindicated: both bills passed in the 1966/67 session, thanks to strong backbench Labour support for both. If Roy had phased the reforms, only one would have passed and maybe not even one. By the second parliamentary session after the 1966 election Roy was no longer home secretary; that latter-day John Bull, Jim Callaghan, was in his place, who declared "we've had too much sex" on arriving in the Home Office. By then glad confident morning was also receding fast on the Labour backbenches.

Roy didn't just get the cabinet to agree he could speak and vote for the two private members' bills on abortion and homosexuality. He spoke strongly in support of them at every stage in the Commons. On the second reading of the Abortion Bill he described the status quo as "harsh and archaic" and "in urgent need of reform." On the Sexual Offences Bill he didn't hide behind arguments about enforcement and police corruption; he stated baldly that homosexuality was a fact of life not "a matter of choice." "It is not concentrated in any particular social classes or occupational groups. The majority of homosexuals are ordinary citizens who do normal jobs" and deserved legal protection not legal oppression. No home secretary had ever spoken like this from the despatch box.

It took three all-night sittings to get the two bills through their final stages on the floor of the Commons, after months in committee. Jenkins was on the front bench throughout, voting in all 45 divisions on the two bills. The third all-night sitting, on the Abortion Bill, started at 10.15pm on a Thursday and finished at noon on the Friday. A mammoth filibuster was ended only when it was clear to the opponents that Jenkins and his team had managed to keep enough MPs in the House by lunchtime on the Friday to enable the House to sit through a second night and into Saturday if necessary to get the Bill through, breaking the filibuster vote by vote.

So it was that the Sexual Offences Bill became law at the end of July 1967, and the Abortion Bill at the end of October, just a month before he ceased to be home secretary. And a telling footnote: I said that Roy voted in all 45 divisions on the two bills. Harold Wilson voted in precisely zero. Callaghan also in zero. Margaret Thatcher in one, and that was in favour of a key illiberal amendment.

Between Roy's first home secretaryship (1965-67) and his presidency of the European Commission (1977-81) was a decade of huge political activity and strife, as chancellor of the exchequer, deputy leader of the Labour party and home secretary for a second time for another two years after 1974. But let us proceed straight to Brussels in 1977 because this was the second of his three transformational political projects.

Immediately on arriving in Brussels in January 1977, Roy spent his first months setting out, as at the Home Office, a bold fulfillable purpose to advance his central liberal conviction. His objective was, as he put it, to give "a stronger bone structure" to the European Community he had campaigned so fervently for Britain to join for the previous twenty years. And his big bold but achievable step to do this was economic and monetary union.

The idea of economic and monetary union was as old as the European ideal itself. Shelves in Brussels groaned with EMU proposals, most recently the Werner Plan of 1970, whose status was akin to the Wolfenden Report when he became Home Secretary: very worthy but nearly a decade old and unimplemented. The Jenkins coup, on the back of the ongoing economic turbulence caused by oil price shock of 1973, was to focus Europe's leaders and institutions on the creation of a viable scheme for fixed but flexible exchange rates, within carefully pre-determined bands to limit volatility, intended to lead on to a single currency thereafter. Which is essentially what happened over the next twenty years.

As ever with Jenkins, this was the coming together of vision, leadership and what Gladstone said of his career, a lifetime spent "working the institutions." Although not a technical economist, any more than any other Balliol PPE-ist, he had a sufficient grasp of the concepts; more relevantly, he was steeped in public finance experience as an ex-chancellor. From this he had a good working knowledge of international monetary institutions and cooperation; more particularly he had forged it partnership with both Giscard of France and Schmidt of Germany, his main interlocutors in the creation of the European Monetary System, both of whom had been fellow finance ministers when he was chancellor from 1967 to 1970. Indeed it was largely thanks to them that he had become president of the commission. He also played with great skill the new institution of the European Council – the twice-yearly meeting of EU heads of government, then only nine-strong – and the increasingly influential European Parliament, just as he had managed the cabinet and the House of Commons so successfully as home secretary and chancellor.

Roy's Florence speech of October 1977, a magisterial presentation of the case for his proposed European Monetary System, was full of Jenkins-isms. "Let us think of a long-jumper. He starts with a rapid succession of steps, lengthens his stride, increases his momentum, and then makes his leap. We have to look before we leap, and know where were to land. But leap we eventually must." He set out a clear road map. In his original conception this included new fiscal powers for the European Commission; these were ditched to keep the plan politically acceptable, instead strengthening the Commission's regional funds.

Another Jenkins trait we observed at the Home Office came immediately into play: his double-or-quits strategy to run one big reform alongside another, making both urgent and indispensable to each other as a programme.

A big debate in Brussels when Roy arrived in 1977, after the 1974/5 democratic revolutions in Portugal and Spain, was whether the Iberian countries should be admitted soon into the Community, or whether monetary union was the more important priority. He did both together, arguing that they were mutually reinforcing: the stronger and more vital the Community, the more essential membership would be to Europe's new democracies, soon to include Greece and, only eight years after the Jenkins presidency, also the whole of central and Eastern Europe. Thus the European strategy of "widening" and "deepening" at the same time was launched, and Roy lived with huge satisfaction to see both the Euro and the decision in principle to expand the European Union to embrace the whole continent of Europe.

The trouble is, the one country that refused to deepen, and ultimately Europe proved insufficiently wide to embrace, was his native Britain. From the outset at his commission presidency, Roy had a far closer and more productive relationship with Giscard and Schmidt than with Callaghan, Wilson's successor as prime minister in 1976. Indeed the reason why Roy was in Brussels, rather than in London as foreign secretary, was because Callaghan refused to give him the Foreign Office because he was too pro-European. Callaghan determined to keep sterling out of Roy's exchange rate mechanism or ERM, not from much grasp let alone judgement of the economics but essentially to strike a nationalist pose.

This Callaghan-Jenkins rift on monetary union, which extended to most political issues they confronted in their generation except resistance to the Labour party's far-left, was of huge significance because it established the opt-out mentality which every British government from Callaghan onwards applied to almost every new European initiative. There was nothing whatever pre-ordained about this. On the contrary, back in February 1970, when Roy and Giscard were the British and French finance ministers, he had told Giscard that if Britain joined the Community, a key reason for doing so would be to overcome the chronic monetary instability so harming the British economy. "I do not want to reserve the monetary field from the Community and we are prepared to move far in this field," he told Giscard, and this was central to his thinking at the Commission.

Furthermore, for all Callaghan's John Bull – aped by his new foreign secretary David Owen, setting himself up as Plymouth's dashing Eurosceptic Francis Drake – there was no public demand to stay out of the ERM. On the contrary, the whole purpose of Harold Wilson's successful European referendum, held only 18 months before Roy went to Brussels, was to be at the heart of the full European Community rather than continuing in the outer ring of the European Free Trade Area where Britain had previously languished. The big issues in British politics in the late 1970s were inflation and undemocratic trade union power: there was little controversy about the ERM outside the leader columns; nor was the then Tory opposition opposed in principle. The ERM could easily have been sold to the British public for what it was: part of the solution to the very problems of instability and weakness overwhelming the British economy.

But it was not to be. Callaghan opted out of the ERM as one of the last substantive acts of the Labour government before the 1979 election. We now know how this play ended. A Eurosceptic Labour prime minister was followed by a Eurosceptic Tory prime minister (Thatcher). From the launch of the ERM onwards Britain's membership of the EU was half-in, half-out, and ended up wholly out. The key point is, this happened primarily because of the leadership of its leaders not the nationalism of its people. Roy urged full participation at each and every stage, and he was right. Being half-in, half-out of Europe was fool's gold.

It was largely because Labour became so anti-European after the 1976 referendum that Roy moved to set up a new social democratic party on his return to Britain. Roy didn't vote in the 1979 election – Jennifer voted Liberal – and he gave his Dimbleby Lecture, which indicated the tentative road map to the SDP, as early as November 1979. It was a reaction more to the defeatist, do-nothing leadership of Callaghan than to Thatcher, who had only just entered No 10 and had yet to radicalise to the right. Callaghan's ERM opt-out led under his successor Michael Foot to support for complete withdrawal from the European Community, only five years after the 1976 referendum.

Jenkins had as little time for the temporising of Callaghan and Healey as the extremism of Foot and Benn. Wilson, significantly, he generally regarded more favourably. "The thing about Harold's smoke and mirrors," he told me, "is that they were genuinely clever, and after the show was over, you realised he had largely got to the right place without the other side quite realising. The problem is, while it was happening, I didn't always realise either." Indeed, on the greatest missed opportunity of the

Wilson premiership, the abandonment of Barbara Castle's *In Place of Strife* trade union reforms in 1969, Wilson supported them more strongly than did Roy, which he always acknowledged afterwards as a point against himself.

Which brings me to the SDP. The striking point about the setting up of this entirely new political party in 1981 is that the speed and decisiveness with which Roy moved was almost incredible, although it fits a pattern now that we have seen in his mode of action at the Home Office and the European Commission.

Roy's last day as president of European Commission was January 19th 1981. Just six days later, with Shirley Williams, David Owen and Bill Rodgers—the "Gang of Four"—he signed the Limehouse Declaration and set up the Council for Social Democracy. Just two months later, on March 26, the SDP was launched as a party. Just another two months later, on May 29th, the Labour MP for Warrington resigned, creating a by-election in that northern town. After Shirley Williams havered and then decided against contesting it, Roy, with no hesitation, took the plunge, and after the most intensive election campaign he had ever fought, on July 16th, less than six months after leaving Brussels in all his pomp, came within 1,750 votes of winning. It was, he said at the declaration of the vote, "my first defeat in thirty years in politics but by far the greatest victory in which I have ever participated."

Summer 1981 saw the SDP soar to 50% in the polls. Shirley Williams won the Crosby by-election on November 26th. Just a month later Roy took the by-election plunge for the second time in a year—in Glasgow Hillhead, territory at least as hazardous as Warrington. He won it by 2,000 votes on 25 March 1982, a spectacular turnaround in a seat where the Liberals had previously been nowhere. It was almost a year to the day since the formation of the SDP.

Back in Parliament, Roy was elected first leader of the SDP on 7 July 1982 and led the SDP-Liberal Alliance into the 1983 election. We know the upshot: a decisive advance for the new third force, but only 23 seats and a split opposition which saw Margaret Thatcher, by then the Boadicea of the Falklands War, win a landslide in seats. Sensing that all he could do as leader was done, he immediately resigned the leadership of the SDP to David Owen.

Roy's foundation and leadership of the SDP occupied just 29 months, about the duration of his formative leadership as home secretary, chancellor and president of the European Commission. He was only actually leader of the SDP for 341 days. One other leader of a British political party has achieved so much in just 341 days – Nigel Farage with his last Brexit party (2018/9), dedicated to reversing all that Roy had achieved in Europe in the previous generation. Imitation as flattery? Certainly an echo.

Roy never looked back in anger. After the SDP he went on to write his two greatest books, *Gladstone* and *Churchill*; to act as friend and mentor of the dominant social democratic leader since Harold Wilson in Tony Blair; and to emulate the best of Proust.

At the end of his life of Asquith, Roy cites the inscription on the Westminster Abbey tablet to the fateful Liberal prime minister who took Britain into the first world war. It from Milton's *Paradise Lost*:

Unshaken, unseduced, unterrified
His loyalty he kept, his love, his zeal.
Nor number, nor example with him wrought
To swerve from truth, or change his constant mind.

They are a fitting epitaph to Roy Jenkins himself.

10

LLOYD GEORGE, ASQUITH, GREY

Lloyd George, Asquith and Grey were the Liberal leaders who dominated politics in the first quarter of the 20th century. Two of them are members of the "club of 30" and the third nearly so, first elected to Parliament aged 27, 33 and 23 respectively. They deserve a lot of credit for launching the welfare state but a lot of blame for the first world war. Then Lloyd George's fateful decision to forge a post-war coalition with the Conservatives destroyed the Liberals as Britain's main non-Tory party, and they never recovered. In all this they yet again demonstrate that, for good and ill, political leaders shape nations fundamentally.

David Lloyd George was self-created and self-destroyed. His nemesis, after a decade in which he almost single-handedly launched the welfare state and mustered the drive to defeat Germany in 1918, can be dated to one fateful act at the end of the war: the forging of a peacetime coalition with the Conservatives, which undermined liberalism and eviscerated the Liberal party. Within five years, the Liberals were replaced by Labour as the principal non-Tory party, and there has never been another Liberal prime minister.

It started so differently. Without Lloyd George's progressive "new liberalism" before the first world war there would have been no "people's budget" of 1909, no "peers v people" elections in 1910, no abolition of the veto for the House of Lords in 1911, and no health and unemployment insurance. Nor would there have been the spell-binding popular oratory, admired by Hitler and Lenin alike and unmatched by any British politician of the 20th century apart from his fellow Welshman Aneurin Bevan. Lambasting the Boer war, fighting the Germans, excoriating the Lords and the established Church, exposing injustice: his every cause was a demotic crusade, fought ad hominem, arousing not just excitement but hysteria.

Lloyd George's achievements were vast. It wasn't just his liberalism but his oratory and his huge capacity to forge partnerships and energise government. With Asquith, he launched the welfare state and emasculated the Tory peerage. With Bonar Law, Balfour and Douglas Haig, he won the war. With Woodrow Wilson, he arbitrated the peace.

This necessarily qualifies the subtitle of Roy Hattersley's biography: *The Great Outsider.* Lloyd George became a versatile *insider*, a government man adept at compromise, constantly hankering for coalitions and combinations to co-opt the very Tories and monopolists he lambasted on the platform. He used them, but they used him just as much. Ultimately in 1922 they destroyed him, and he never returned to office.

Lloyd George's taste for coalition-building long pre-dated 1918. Throughout the fluid politics of 1910, with its two kings, two elections and constitutional crisis, he was flattering the Tory leader Balfour in private and peddling coalition schemes. It was essential, he argued, to unite "the resources of the two parties into joint stock" in order to avoid "imminent impoverishment if not insolvency." He toyed with a government "composed of businessmen which would carry enormous weight in the country."

This is the paradox of Lloyd George, outsider and insider, siren and sycophant; the paradox, perhaps, of British liberalism, as exemplified also by Gladstone and Earl Grey, the greatest 19th-century Liberal leaders, who were establishment to their core (Gladstone started out a Tory and in some ways never ceased to be one). Keynes evoked the Welsh Wizard best: "How can I convey any just impression of this extraordinary figure of our time, this siren, this goat-footed bard, this half-human visitor to our age from the hag-ridden, enchanted woods of antiquity?"

Lloyd George's pre-1914 partnership with Herbert Henry Asquith, who took over as prime minister after Sir Henry Campbell-Bannerman's death in 1908 and held the office continuously until the middle of the first world war, was one of the three enduringly successful No 10/No 11 duos of the 20th century. The other two, between Margaret Thatcher and Nigel Lawson in the 1980s and between Tony Blair and Gordon Brown after 1997, were the making of equally radical and effective governments. By 1910, the year of two narrow election victories for the Liberals, Asquith's imperturbable solidity and measured but sonorous parliamentary oratory, in the face of a raucous Tory opposition, established a hold on the political middle ground which continued until his government collapsed in December 1916 and Lloyd George took over.

"Asquith drunk can make a better speech than any of us sober," said Andrew Bonar Law, Tory leader after A.J. Balfour, in dour teetotaller admiration. This was just as well, for abstinence was not an Asquithian virtue. "It would be impossible to imagine anyone who was more obviously enjoying life," wrote Lytton Strachey after one house-party encounter. "There was a look of a Roman emperor about him." Where Lloyd George's influence ended before 1914, so did the progressive energy of the government. A partial modernisation of the armed forces took place under Haldane, and some labour and penal reform under Churchill, in his Liberal phase. But Asquith himself was rarely an independent force for bold reform, and the artful passivity which served him well vis-à-vis his chancellor was a serious weakness elsewhere.

Where Lloyd George was not engaged, nor for the most part was Asquith. In particular, Asquith resisted the suffragettes, campaigning for women to get the vote, and he let public education languish. The Balfour Education Act of 1902, passed by the previous Tory government, promoted mass state secondary education for the first time, but there was no reform impetus under Asquith, whose Balliol classical superiority gave him little interest in the progress that Germany was making in technical education. The neglect of state education was the Achilles's heel of 20th-century progressive politics: like Attlee and Harold Wilson after him, Asquith had little idea of its capacity to lessen England's debilitating class barriers and enhance its prosperity.

Equally retrograde was Asquith's failure to reform the House of Lords. The Parliament Act of 1911 simply reduced its powers, making no changes to the composition of a chamber which remained a bastion of hereditary Tory aristocrats. The position of the Lords was in flux throughout the constitutional crisis of 1909-11, with wide support at the 1910 inter-party constitutional conference for a reformed, even elected, second chamber. The moment was not seized: the entire hereditary peerage remained in the Lords for another 90 years until 1999, and a weak nominated second chamber remains in place today.

Asquith's famed imperturbability ("let us wait and see" became his catchphrase) was suffused with indolence and indifference. These were his undoing, and nowhere more so than in his chronic mismanagement of Ireland and of the European crisis of July 1914 which resulted in the first world war.

There was no better opportunity to settle the Irish question than in the year after the 1911 Parliament Act, which removed the Anglo-Irish aristocratic veto over a "home rule" settlement within a potentially federalised United Kingdom, on Gladstone's model. Yet Asquith invested neither the emotional sympathy nor the effort to frame a viable Irish settlement. It is hard to judge which he handled worse: the Curragh mutiny and the events of early 1914 that led to an effective Ulster Orange veto over home rule; or the 1916 Easter rising, where he left Dublin to a military command whose court martials and summary executions created a gallery of martyrs, catapulting Sinn Féin into the hearts and minds of Irish idealists and nationalists alike. By the time Asquith left office in December 1916, home rule was dead and Ireland seething and ungovernable by Britain, as Lloyd George found when he sent in the "black and tans" four years later. The die was cast for Sinn Féin to sweep the 1918 election outside Ulster, and for a unilateral declaration of independence and the visceral divisions and bloody conflicts which endured for the next eight decades and are not wholly over even now. Such was the Irish legacy of Asquith and Lloyd George.

Yet of even greater consequence was the chain of events that led to the outbreak of European war in August 1914—which in addition to its vast death and destruction over the following four years, eviscerated European liberalism for a generation, and far longer in central and eastern Europe. Maybe also in consequence, liberalism never took root in Russia at all.

Until recently it was taboo to question the inevitability of British engagement in the "great" war, so heart-rending for the living was the sacrifice of the dead. Even among those who believed that war might have been avoided, the conduct of British ministers was rarely impugned. Responsibility was cast on the Kaiser and/or his ministers, supposedly in the grip of a German military-expansionist complex which made full-scale European war unavoidable; or if guilt was shared, it was the system of diplomatic alliances which supposedly drove Britain into war once the dominoes started falling. Roy Jenkins, Asquith's biographer and admirer, and himself the most pacific of politicians, sidesteps the issue entirely in his 1964 biography. A mere seven uncritical pages are devoted to the events leading to war, compared to 50 pages on Ireland and 40 on the 1909-11 constitutional crisis. In those cursory pages, Jenkins treats the "plunge to war" with an air of inevitability, yet this is contradicted by his correct opening comment: "From 1911 onwards the European scene was menacing. But there was no especial menace in the first half of 1914. There was no slow, inevitable edging towards war as in 1939. Even after the murders at Sarajevo, the mood did not change." In which case, why the conflagration only five weeks later?

By contrast, Asquith himself was revealingly prolific in chronicling the run-up to war, writing long and frank letters to his 27-year-old lover Venetia Stanley, some penned in the midst of cabinet meetings and Commons debates. Now published, the letters are among the most riveting ever written by a prime minister. They show Asquith barely engaged in the escalating European crisis until its final days; Ulster was his main policy concern until the very end of July. Diplomacy was left to a vacillating and weak Edward Grey at the Foreign Office.

As late as 24 July, at the end of a letter mostly about Ulster, Asquith simply noted: "Happily there seems to be no reason why we should be anything more than spectators" in any forthcoming European conflict. Four days later he was still writing in this distant vein, even drawing comfort from the prospect that the European crisis may have the effect "of throwing into the background the lurid pictures of civil war in Ulster." Later still, on 29 July, he concluded a divided cabinet with the decision, as reported to the King, that even in the event of a German violation of Belgian neutrality—which was to become the *casus belli* less than a week later—"Sir E Grey should be authorised to inform the German and French ambassadors that at this stage we were unable to pledge ourselves in advance, either under all conditions to stand aside or in any conditions to join in." "It sounded a little pusillanimous," writes Jenkins laconically of this crucial decision in his biography, "but it was bound to be unless the cabinet was to be split." That one sentence is a comprehensive indictment of Asquith's leadership.

From his letters to Venetia Stanley it is evident that Asquith did not appreciate the magnitude of the European crisis until Saturday August 1st—three days before the German invasion of Belgium. The day before, he had been planning to attend a weekend house party with Venetia in far-off Anglesey. The miscalculation of British intentions that played a decisive part in the outbreak of war was unsurprising because those intentions were chronically unclear. As matters stood on August 4th, Britain would almost certainly have done best to stay out of the war, as Gladstone had wisely stayed out of the Franco-Prussian war in 1870. And if a firm, consistent declaration of British intentions to that effect had come earlier, the war might not have started at all.

Ernest Bevin, an acute commentator on the July 1914 catastrophe from his own later experience of containing Stalin, took this view. Inveighing against appeasement in 1936, he argued that war came in 1914 through diplomatic fumbling and weakness. "I look back to 1914. The Liberals of that day never made themselves clear. They let this country drift on until we were in it and then they used propaganda to prove it was a righteous cause."

Which brings us to Edward Grey, scion of a great aristocratic Whig family, who has the distinction of being both Britain's longest serving and most ill-fated foreign secretary. He served throughout the Liberal governments from 1905 until 1916, but experience brought neither wisdom nor strength.

Because Grey was so inoffensive, historians have mostly followed his contemporaries in excusing the reality that he was a disastrous minister. We will never know, of course, what might have happened in 1914 had British policy been more effective. But it was probably within the power of Asquith and Grey to have kept Britain out of the war. Possibly they could have prevented it entirely, either by dissuading Germany from supporting Austria in the chain reaction that led from Archduke Franz Ferdinand's assassination in Sarajevo on 28 June to the German invasion of Belgium on 4 August, and/or by making robustly clear to France and Russia that Britain would not support them in a war against Germany and Austria. Even had a war then ensued, it would been far more limited than actually happened. Had France and Russia lost such a war, the continental balance of power would have tilted to Austria and Germany. But it was a mistake to regard those two powers as a unified bloc, and almost any alternative outcome would have been better than what followed from the calamity of 1914 – namely, the start of a European Thirty Years' War featuring not just the Kaiser but in due course Hitler, Lenin, Stalin, communism, fascism, genocide, the Holocaust, slavery and the partition and subjugation of eastern Europe for a further half century beyond 1945.

Our grandparents and great-grandparents suffered so much, they wanted to believe that the mass slaughter of the western front was not in vain and that German militarism made war unavoidable. And this is what they were told by almost the entire corps of politicians and diplomats who were responsible for the war. But that does not make it true, and in my view it is probably false.

Typical of Grey's biographers is Michael Waterhouse, whose *Edwardian Requiem* (2013) has far more to say about the foreign secretary's love of fishing and the Northumbrian countryside, and his amorous affairs, than his conduct of foreign policy. Waterhouse's only judgement on Grey's policy leading up to 1914 is this:

During the decade before the outbreak of war he prepared his country for what many saw as the inevitable conflict and, although exhausted and half blind, he was the only European statesman who fought hard for peace during the July crisis.

But if Grey was exhausted and half blind, why was he in the job? And why does Waterhouse not discuss his profound ignorance of "abroad"? It took Grey more than eight years as foreign secretary to make his first overseas visit and he didn't even want to make that one (King George V's state visit to Paris in April 1914). He never visited Germany, which is incredible in nine continuous years as foreign secretary before 1914.

In the July 1914 crisis, Grey desired peace yet his policy produced world war. How far was he to blame? Waterhouse does not address this question, beyond noting Grey's irresolution on the basic issue of whether or not Britain would support France in resisting a German invasion. He says this was because of "a split cabinet". However, the point is that Grey did not seek to lead the cabinet because he himself was weak and irresolute. Only on the eve of the German invasion, on 4 August, did Grey come off the fence and seek a cabinet pledge to uphold the security of Belgium and France. By then, both France and Russia were mobilised for war, in expectation of British support.

As the armies marched in August 1914, Grey famously remarked that the lamps were going out all over Europe, while Asquith wrote to Venetia Stanley deploring the cheering crowds outside Buckingham Palace. "How one loathes such levity," he added. There was indeed nothing to cheer, but it followed a month of political and diplomatic levity by Grey and Asquith which was to destroy so much of the twentieth century's optimism and liberalism.

11

FOOT v. HESELTINE

Michael Foot and Michael Heseltine were the greatest British political orators of the last generation. Both had been president of the Oxford Union and were tipped for the top, not least by themselves. But the ultimate prize eluded them both. Foot (1913-2010) became an epically unsuccessful leader of the Labour party, losing the 1983 election to Thatcher by a landslide; seven years later "Hezza" (b. 1933) unseated Thatcher but failed to succeed her by a tantalising margin.

They leave starkly different but equally fascinating legacies. Foot's lies in great speeches and books, Heseltine's in great executive acts and institutions.

Most politicians vanish from memory as rapidly as the controversies they spin. It is heads of government and rare inspirational leaders, philosophers and institution builders that linger, and even the last of these often survive with little reference to their political careers. Who thinks of Alexis de Tocqueville as Louis-Napoleon's foreign minister, or even James Madison as a two-term president? Michael Foot and Michael Heseltine – and Roy Jenkins, the subject of an earlier chapter – are among the few post-war British politicians who will be remembered for achievements other than those of a prime minister.

Foot was a master of polemics to rival the classical 18th century Whig orators Fox and Burke, whom he admired and emulated. Reading Kenneth Morgan's 2007 biography, the only dull part is the chapter on Foot's ministerial career as employment secretary in Harold Wilson's 1974 government, where the detail of successive trade union and labour relations acts are as tedious to read as they were calamitous at the time. Had he held office for more than five years in a journalistic and parliamentary career spanning half a century, the ruin to his reputation might have been lethal. His greatest contribution to the 1964 Wilson government was his brilliant philippics against Richard Crossman's plan for a nominated House of Lords. "Think of it," began one tirade alongside Enoch Powell. "A second chamber selected by the whips! A seraglio of eunuchs!" Come a political crisis, "we would hear a falsetto chorus from the political castrati. They would be the final arbiters of our destiny."

This is Foot's celebrated defenestration of David Steel, the cherubic (but in fact 40 year-old) leader of the Liberal party, in the House of Commons no-confidence debate of 28 March 1979 which toppled Callaghan's minority Labour government and brought Thatcher to power:

> What the right honourable lady has done today is to lead her troops into battle [pause] snugly concealed behind a Scottish nationalist shield [pause] with the boy David holding her hand.

[Then, as the laughter subsided, the stiletto:]

> I must say to the right honourable lady – and I should like to see her smile – that I am even more concerned about the fate of the right honourable gentleman than I am about her. She can look after herself. But the leader of the Liberal party – and I say this with the utmost affection – has passed from

rising hope to elder statesman without any intervening period whatsoever.

And few of those who heard it (I did so around an old wireless at a friend's house) will forget Foot's call to arms in the emergency Saturday House of Commons debate the day after the invasion of the Falkland Islands on 3 April 1982. Rising immediately after a hesitant Margaret Thatcher, he captured the House and the nation:

> The Falkland Islanders have been betrayed... The government must now prove by deeds—they will never be able to do it by words—that they are not responsible for the betrayal and cannot be faced with that charge. Even though the position and circumstances of the people who live in the Falkland Islands are uppermost in our minds... there is the longer-term interest to ensure that foul and brutal aggression does not succeed in our world. If it does, there will be a danger not merely to the Falkland Islands but to people all over this dangerous planet.

Foot's rhetoric was a fusion, in Morgan's description, "of the Cornish chapels, the Oxford Union and the soapboxes of the Socialist League." He possessed an "instinctive minority-mindedness, locked into a kind of permanent self-made exile," although this was not absolute. There is the splendid example of his dogged loyalty to the beleaguered Jim Callaghan as the "winter of discontent" dismembered his minority government in 1978/9, deploying his parliamentary gifts to keep it alive week by week until the bitter end of the no confidence motion described above, which was lost by one vote in one of the most dramatic parliamentary moments of my lifetime.

Foot's loyalty to his friends—and what an odd gallery, including Max Beaverbrook, Indira Gandhi and Enoch

Powell—is equally magnificent in its way. Yet it was as the scourge of authority that Foot ranks as a supreme political artist. And his achievement was, I now realise, anything but purely negative. Such masterly parliamentary minority-mindedness helped sustain the institution of Parliament with greater credibility and legitimacy than most representative assemblies have ever achieved in other nations. There was no inevitability in the survival of parliamentary authority in the turbulent post-war decades, particularly the 1970s when, in the height of irony, Foot became a bastion both of the supremacy of Parliament and of the unaccountable excesses of the trade unions which threatened to engulf it. Fortunately for him, it is the parliamentary rhetoric which is now remembered, as he orated tirelessly to maintain the credibility of that highly conservative and unapproachable grand forum of the nation, which didn't even permit radio broadcasts until 1978 (TV cameras weren't admitted until 1989).

Foot the propagandist was equally formidable. From *Guilty Men*, his 1940 denunciation of the appeasers "responsible" for war, to his campaign against the evisceration of his beloved Dubrovnik more than five decades later, barely a week passed without a passionate broadside or opinionated review. Even as a minister he was a regular *Observer* book reviewer. Near the end of Morgan's book comes a pathos-laden image of a Lear-like Foot and his wife Jill Craigie, fronting and producing a shoestring film on Slobodan Milosevic's ethnic cleansing in Kosovo. The 80-year-old Foot, handicapped, barely mobile, blind in one eye after an attack of shingles, rails in the bitter December cold against the great dictator and his unforgivable crime against a defenceless people. It is up there with Gladstone's final denunciation of the Armenian atrocities and Chatham's dying pleas on America.

Foot's inspirations were Swift, Hazlitt, the Romantics and the humanist and revolutionary propagandists from the Levellers to the Chartists. And Nye Bevan, his contemporary hero-saint. And his father Isaac Foot of Pencrebar in Cornwall, a "west country Hatfield," inculcating five remarkable sons in the radical classics under the watchful eyes of more than 20 busts of Cromwell. Isaac fought 12 parliamentary elections over 35 years, as a Liberal, losing eight of them and holding government office for precisely one year. Like father, like son, except that Michael's 15 elections for Labour, over 52 years, yielded 12 victories. Between them, father and son fought every general election from 1910 until 1987, and both of them fought in 1935 and 1945.

Foot's last book was a biography of his father entitled *A West Country Boy – Apostle of England.* When the young Michael defected from Liberal to Labour in 1934, after a post-Oxford gap year in the Liverpool slums, Isaac's response was that "he ought to absorb the thoughts of a real radical" and "an even more intense perusal was needed of the thoughts of William Hazlitt." The perusal of Britain's great radicals of the past never ceased thereafter, and the fruits were as erudite as they were audaciously partisan. 20th century labourism may owe more to Methodism than to Marxism, but the substance of Foot's 20 books and thousands of articles testify to a wider heritage. Who but Foot could evoke the 1945 election as a British 1789 with Bevan as Danton, or write essays entitled "Byron and the Bomb" and "Swift and Europe"?

Reflecting on Michael Foot a decade after his death, I find myself surprisingly unconcerned about the merits of his specific causes. As Morgan puts it, he "commands attention, even fascination, not so much for what he did as for what he was." Or rather *is*, for, like Mr Gladstone, his righteous anger lives still.

By contrast, Michael Heseltine, although as great an orator as Foot, commands attention now both for what he did and what he was. In the brilliance of his constructive creativity, Heseltine is matched, in my view, only by Bevan, Bevin and Roy Jenkins among postwar ministers who never made it to No. 10. More shaming for the left, he was Britain's best social democratic institution builder of the 1980s.

In the Blair/Brown government, as I set about creating academies to replace failing comprehensive schools, and planning High Speed 2 – the high-speed line from London to the Midlands, the north of England and Scotland – Heseltine was an inspiration. If an entirely new city can be created on the Thames, if three million tenants can be turned sustainably into homeowners, and if a new high-speed line from London to Paris can bedriven through Kent, what can't we do to build a better future?

My dad was one of the first Camden tenants to buy his council flat under Hezza's "right to buy" legislation in 1980. No act of the state did more to transform his family's life, apart from building the flat in the first place. It was a practical and psychological liberation.

To my surprise and pleasure, I found myself campaigning alongside Michael Heseltine in favour of elected mayors for England's cities in the early 2010s, the best modern development in the governance of England. We campaigned together again after 2016 in the struggle against Brexit, which he fought with such intensity that he was expelled from the party he had so nearly led. At the age of 88, in 2021, he is still an active president of the European Movement.

Long before most others, Hezza saw that without strong, visible, democratic leadership, England's cities will never flourish as they should. As environment secretary under Thatcher in the 1980s, and again under Major in the early 1990s, he was essentially Mayor of England. "I've searched all the parks in all the cities and found no statues of committees," said G.K. Chesterton, the epigraph of this book. It is a fair bet that, a century hence, there will be a statue or two of Michael Heseltine in England's cities.

Even where Hezza failed, he was usually right. He was right to oppose Brexit, right to oppose Thatcher's poll tax, right to highlight the social crisis after the Toxteth riots in Liverpool in 1981, and right to support European industrial capability in the Westland crisis which precipitated his resignation from Thatcher's cabinet in 1986, rather than shipping helicopter and hi-tech production abroad.

Then there is Hezza as Tarzan. Foot was the better parliamentary orator, but only Tony Blair and Boris Johnson rank alongside Heseltine as modern political showmen, brilliantly creative in the exercise of democratic arts. His especial forte was the party conference speech, which became an annual performance literally upstaging both Thatcher and Major as party leader.

Hezza's first big Tory conference speech in 1976, which secured his place in Thatcher's shadow cabinet, was a theatrical attack on the beleaguered Callaghan. If the Labour government had any pride it would call an election, he said. Instead, he declaimed in tones to rival Olivier, Callaghan's was "a one-legged army limping away from the storm they have created. Left, left – left, left, left!" – as he marched left-legged across the stage. The standing ovation cemented his place as a household name and the speech itself was so popular he did a sequel nearly twenty years later as John Major's deputy, lampooning Tony Blair's New Labour. "Left, left – Left, left, left! That didn't work. About turn! Right, right – Right, right, right!"

His conference speech a year earlier, in 1994, featured a lame pun which only Heseltine could transform into a headline joke, when criticising New Labour's economic jargon:

> Neoclassical endogenous growth theory and the symbiotic relationships between growth and investment, and people and infrastructure. Clear, unambiguous and to the point. Well last week The Guardian disclosed the speech had not been written by Gordon Brown at all but by a 27 year old choral-singing researcher named Ed Ball [sic]. So there you have it the final proof, Labour's brand new economic dream, but 'It wasn't Brown's. It was Ball's!

Heseltine's rhetoric was sedulously honed. In his twenties he would listen to tapes of the mellifluous radio broadcaster Charles Hill, a Tory MP and Macmillan's minister-spokesman, and practice delivering speeches to large crowds with his solitary reflection in the mirror being the only audience. When read, his conference speeches are not outstanding. It is the sheer panache with which they were delivered that makes them – or rather him – so memorable.

Yet for all his comic oratory, Heseltine was never a comic act. His most searing Tory conference speech was his 1981 response to the racial disparities which underscored the recent Brixton and Toxteth riots in south London and Liverpool:

> We talk of equality of opportunity. What do those words actually mean in the inner cities today? What do they mean to the black communities? We now have large immigrant communities in British cities. Let this party's position be absolutely clear. They are British. They live here. They vote here. However tight the immigration legislation – and in everyone's interests they should be tight – there will be a large black community in this country tomorrow, just as there is today. There are no schemes of significant repatriation that have any moral, social or political credibility.

It was his bravest speech, facing off against his own party, many of whom were still enraptured by Enoch Powell, including ghost-at-the-feast Margaret Thatcher sitting behind him. It was, according to his memoirs, the speech about which, above all others, he "anguished so long and so hard." David Dimbleby reported that Heseltine had "picked up the Conservative Party, shaken it and put it down where he wanted it to be" on race and repatriation. In view of its record since, that accords a finality which did not come to pass, but he certainly helped slam the door on the Powellite extremes of public racism still rampant in 1980s Britain.

It was another brand of courage to lecture a Thatcherite audience in 1992 on the limits of the free market. "If I have to intervene to help British companies," he roared, "I'll intervene before breakfast, before lunch, before tea and before dinner. And I'll get up the next morning and I'll start all over again." It was Tarzan refusing to be cowed by fashionable and dangerous absolutes. His last act was to attempt the same in resisting Brexit after 2016. But by then the roar was diminished and the cause was lost.

12

CLEGG

Nick Clegg (b. 1967) was Britain's first Liberal leader to hold senior cabinet office since Lloyd George ninety years before. For all his banter with David Cameron in the Downing Street rose garden as the Tory-Lib Dem coalition was unveiled after the inconclusive 2010 election, it was not a happy experience. His party collapsed from 57 seats to just 8 in the following election in 2015, after which Cameron raced headlong into Brexit, the cause above all others which the former MEP and European official Clegg reviled. My review of a 2011 biography of Clegg, a few months into the coalition, discusses why he was already so obviously ill-fated – or misguided.

T he striking thing about this defensive biography of Nick Clegg is how much of it is spent debating whether he is really a Conservative.

The author, Liberal Democrat activist Chris Bowers, likes his leader a great deal. "Idealism in politics is at stake through the person of Nick Clegg," we are told. "He believes in the intrinsic goodness of people" and "he may yet be headed for great things, as many have believed for some time." Like the prophet, Clegg may go unrecognised in his own country; but apparently this is a problem for the country, not for him:

Clegg remains as much a challenge for the British people as they are for him. If there is any genuineness in the cries for a better form of politics, he should become popular again, as he represents something different.

But different in what respect? Much of Bowers' book consists of interviews with fellow Lib Dems and friends of Clegg, including, tellingly, Leon Brittan, for whom Clegg worked in Brussels in the 1990s when the former Tory minister was a European commissioner, and Ed Vaizey, an ex-Tory minister with whom he travelled to the Arctic Circle for a week in 2007.

The consensus is that the "something different" about Clegg is that while previous Liberal leaders had been essentially anti-Tory, he was anti-Labour and what motivated him to enter politics as a Lib Dem rather than a Conservative was not "a better form of politics" but rather one issue, Europe.

Clegg's Europeanism stems as much from a wealthy cosmopolitan lifestyle as from liberal conviction: his Spanish wife, Dutch mother and Russian grandparents, all rich, aristocratic or well-connected; his career in Brussels; his fluency in four European languages; his studentship at the College of Europe in Bruges. On losing his seat in the 2017 election – his parliamentary career lasted just 12 years – he emigrated to California to work as Mark Zuckerberg's assistant at Facebook. This accounts for the character of his liberalism, too. His free-market economics are common in right-wing liberal parties on the Continent, but have little rapport with the 20th-century social-democratic tradition that animated Britain's Liberal Party and its successors from Lloyd George, Keynes and Beveridge through to Roy Jenkins, Paddy Ashdown and Charles Kennedy. Indeed, Bowers notes that until he became an MP in 2005, after five years as an MEP in

Brussels, Clegg "had very little knowledge of Britain politically."

Thus Chris Davies, a former Liberal Democrat MEP friend of Clegg's, says: "I think of him more as a Continental liberal than perhaps a mainstream British liberal." Andrew Duff, another former Lib Dem MEP, observes: "If the Conservative Party had been how it used to be under Edward Heath, Nick would be a Tory, albeit a liberal, pro-European Tory like Chris Patten and Ken Clarke." His Tory friends agree. According to Lord Brittan, Clegg "didn't like Labour at all and didn't like the Conservatives enough. He was very unhappy with the Conservatives' European policy." Ed Vaizey says he is "essentially Tory but divided by one issue, in his case Europe." The journalist John Palmer, who knew Clegg well in Brussels, links Europe to his neoliberalism. "His work with Leon Brittan in and around the single market and competition policy probably had quite a strong influence on him. He was quite markedly to the right of some of his colleagues."

Europe apart, Clegg fits the Cameroon glove in background, outlook, style, the lot. The English side of his family could hardly be more establishment. The son of a wealthy Buckinghamshire banker, educated at prep school and Westminster School like his grandfather (his father was at another pubic school, Bryanston), he emerges from this biography as a home counties ultra-establishmentarian in largely the same mould as David Cameron and George Osborne. Which appears to be why, given the choice in 2010, he opted to form a coalition with them rather than stand aside from a minority Tory government, or negotiate a "confidence and supply" agreement with the

Conservatives, or form a coalition with Gordon Brown and Labour: all credible options.

Clegg told his party there was "no alternative." Margaret Thatcher and Neville Chamberlain said that, too, yet this is never true in politics. To govern is to choose, and the choices reveal the leader. In Clegg's case, the choice was not only to coalesce with the Tories, but also to support their austerity policy without compromise, and even to front the trebling of university tuition fees. Significantly, Bowers reports that Clegg supported tuition fees before the election, but was too weak within his own party, and too much of an opportunist, to take on the membership or tell the voters. He deserved the student protests which dogged him throughout his time in government.

Clegg's Tory inclinations are all the clearer in his statements during the 2010 election that, in the event of a hung parliament, he would negotiate first with the largest party as a matter of principle. As he knew, this was contrary to constitutional precedent and international practice. It also contradicted the position of previous Lib Dem and Liberal leaders, who had said simply that they would seek to get the best deal for the party in the wider national interest. Given that, in 2010, the Tories were very likely to be the largest party in any hung parliament, Clegg knew this would give momentum to a Tory-Lib Dem coalition above all other options. And so it proved.

Here lies a crucial point of distinction with continental politics. The major centre-right parties on the Continent – the successors to the Gaullists in France, the Christian Democrats in Germany, Italy and the Benelux countries – have tended to be corporatist and statist. Liberal parties in these countries inject a dose of market individualism into coalitions of the right as much as the left. In Britain, by contrast, the post-Thatcher Tory party is largely neo-liberal, though it is wearing a "big society" badge this time around. This means that a Lib Dem leader from the same neo-liberal stable is mutually reinforcing, not a force for compromise or innovation. Which was precisely the record of the Cameron/Clegg coalition in practice.

Why did the Lib Dem social-democratic majority put up with Clegg? It didn't quite realise that a coup took place in 2010 (I have lost count of how many Lib Dems told me: "Nick had no alternative but to go in with the Tories"). The party at large liked the idea of being in government and latched on to small mercies: a referendum on electoral reform here, a bit of Murdoch-bashing there (both equally tokenistic and unsuccessful). And they were still out of sorts with New Labour for the Iraq war and for, well, for being in government for 13 years.

Anyway, Lib Dem MPs had no choice but to fall in behind Clegg unless they got a new leader. They were not in the room when Clegg and Cameron did the deal. They are not in cabinet meetings when Tory policy after Tory policy is agreed. Also, despite policy disagreements, the Lib Dems in Parliament are as establishment as the Tories by background – indeed in 2010 they were even less diverse than the Tories in gender and ethnicity. They are largely a Home Counties and Oxbridge party, making Clegg as fitting a leader of the Lib Dems as was Cameron of the Tories. His opponent for the Lib Dem leadership in 2007 was Chris Huhne, who also went to Westminster School and Oxbridge.

Bowers invites the nation to admire Clegg's accompl-ishments. Whatever you think of his politics, he is a man apart. Not only the talented linguist and the easygoing nice guy, there is also Clegg the sage. "He has a deep-rooted love of English literature and is comfortable with demanding works." His favourite is Giuseppe di Lampedusa's *The Leopard*, "a fairly challenging Italian novel imbued with hidden meaning, and not the kind of book many would be found reading on the 7.20 into Waterloo."

That's true. On the 7.20, they are more concerned with grubby, everyday things like jobs, taxes, riots, and the state of England's schools, trains and hospitals. They may not be imbued with Lampedusa's insights into the Sicilian aristocracy and his enigmatic observation that everything must change for everything to remain the same. But they know a Tory when they see one, and they know a leopard doesn't change its spots.

13

MITTERRAND

Francois Mitterrand (1916-1996) is the most successful left-wing leader ever to have been elected to rule France, or indeed any of the largest European states, measured by longevity in power. But what was the real identity of this most sphynx-like of modern political leaders?

A front-rank politician by the age of 30 in 1946 and a senior minister in successive governments of the Fourth Republic while in his thirties, Francois Mitterrand went on to lead the French Socialist party from 1971, then to win two presidential elections and two parliamentary elections after 1981. Having condemned Charles de Gaulle's presidential Fifth Republic as "a permanent *coup d'état*" when the general assumed power in the late 1950s, he occupied the post in full plenitude for 14 years (1981-95), longer than de Gaulle himself – longer indeed than any leader of France since Napoleon III – in a political career spanning half a century. He said the most essential attribute in politics is "indifference." But the explanation for his success is that he was anything but indifferent to his career and the fabrications on which it was built.

The best biography of Mitterrand, by Philip Short, is subtitled *A Study in Ambiguity,* but it could equally be described as "a study in deception," because there was nothing ambiguous about the massive falsehoods and carefully constructed but entirely bogus images that constituted every part of Mitterrand's career. Short begins the biography with an electric account of the "observatory affair" of 1959, when Mitterrand faked an assassination attempt on himself as a ploy to regain the political initiative the year after de Gaulle – constantly escaping assassination as if by the will of God – buried the Fourth Republic and most of its political inmates. The fake was exposed and it is extraordinary that he ever recovered.

Yet the greatest deceptions were still to come. Throughout his presidency, Mitterrand lied, and ordered his doctors to lie, about his health. Diagnosed with advanced prostate cancer within months of taking power in 1981 and expected to live for only three years, he told his urologist: "It's a state secret; you are bound by this secret." With the cancer in remission, he not only stood for re-election in 1988 but struggled through the full seven-year term, although the cancer returned and, by the end, became undeniable.

His personal life was a similar fabrication. While his wife, Danielle, and their two sons were his public family, they coexisted with a secret second family of his mistress 27 years younger than him and their daughter. Mitterrand shuttled between the two families in Paris and the country, again unknown to the public, until the end of his presidency (and there were other affairs, one with a 21 year-old). His daughter, Mazarine, was named after Cardinal Mazarin, Louis XIV's wily and secretive first minister, whose precepts for the politician were taken deeply to heart by her father: "Be sparing with your gestures, walk with measured steps. Simulate, dissimulate, trust nobody."

Unsurprisingly, it is hard to pin down what Mitterrand actually believed. His ideas constantly shifted to suit the times and his part in them. Starting out as an official of the Vichy regime and an admirer of Pétain, who fronted the wartime collaborationist Vichy regime at Hitler's behest, he successfully covered this up until it was exposed at the end of his life. After the war, he was elected for a shifting array of centre-right parties of the Fourth Republic. As a minister in the mid-1950s, he was a voice not only of conservatism but of outright reaction and repression in respect of Algeria and the French colonies.

Throughout the 1960s, his big idea was anti-Gaullism, championing liberalism in the face of overweening presidential power. Socialism entered his vocabulary only as he sought a viable anti- and post-Gaullist political grouping, which, thanks to his artful machinations, came together in his Socialist Party in 1971.

Mitterrand then rose to power on the back of an alliance with the still-strong Communists. He fashioned this as tribune of a leftism that included wholesale nationalisation, a war on the rich and a huge expansion of welfare spending without any regard for conventional economics, which he professed to despise. This led to the "common programme" for the 1981 presidential election.

Elected on the rhetoric of a "complete rupture" with capitalism and the slogan "Change life", Mitterrand appointed Communist ministers to a pan-left coalition that embarked on the most radical and frenetic programme of nationalisation, state spending and cultural reform attempted by any western European government since the early postwar years. Barely a year later, Mitterrand put most of this into rapid reverse. With the franc collapsing and financial markets in revolt, economic orthodoxy returned, state spending was slashed and the Communists were ejected. Nationalisation was rolled back after the right won the parliamentary elections of 1986. Scotching the notion that he should resign in the face of this debacle, the Sphynx of the Élysée instead fashioned a new concept of "cohabitation" between a president of the left and a government of the right. He proceeded to outwit his Gaullist prime minister, Jacques Chirac, fighting him on the slogan of "Opening to the centre" in the 1988 presidential and parliamentary elections. Chirac was forced to scrap with Jean-Marie Le Pen and the far-right National Front, whose potency was largely a creation of Mitterrand's cynical manoeuvre to change the electoral system to proportional representation before the 1986 elections.

Thus reincarnated as a centrist, Mitterrand appointed a government under the social democrat Michel Rocard, including a large number of non-aligned ministers and even a handful of centre-right former ministers, before succumbing to another "cohabitation", this time under Edouard Balladur (finance minister in the first "cohabitation"), which saw out his final two years of office.

"It was not in my interests to oppose the trend of public opinion," said Mitterrand, abdicating any role in leading opinion as he drifted, with increasing physical and political infirmity. Shortly before his replacement as prime minister in 1991, Rocard described his rival and nemesis as "cynicism in its purest sense". During his 14 years in the Élysée, Mitterrand got through seven prime ministers, each the product of labyrinthine political calculations worthy of

Mazarin, the subtlety of which was mostly lost on the participants and victims. Simulate, dissimulate.

Mitterrand's ideas are an endlessly turning kaleidoscope. I cannot think of a modern democratic leader who has made so successful a career from trading rival policies to suit immediate political convenience. In the British context, over the course of his career, he was Tony Benn, Clement Attlee, Harold Macmillan, Harold Wilson, Tony Blair and Enoch Powell, all rolled into one, yet done with immense intellectual engagement and apparent conviction. In Mitterrand, the academic scribbler was the servant of the practical politician, not vice versa. A big part of "brand Mitterrand" was an ostentatious intellectualism giving depth and sincerity to whichever creed he was peddling at any given time, however great the difference with the last one.

Mitterrand said he needed to read for two hours or more a day "to oxygenate the brain." Many of his major shifts in ideas were accompanied by a book or pamphlet by the maestro – including his remarkable 47-page "Letter to all the French," written as a manifesto for his "opening to the centre" for his 1988 re-election, advertised with little modesty as covering "all the big subjects which are worth discussing and mulling over between French men and women." "The night before it was to be published he stayed up till 3am at the printing press correcting the proofs, like a neophyte brooding over a first novel," writes Short, a brilliant detail. During tedious cabinet presentations, Mitterrand annotated antiquarian book catalogues and on presidential flights would sometimes ask the pilot to circle before landing so he could finish a chapter.

Is Mitterrand's legacy an object lesson in intellectual manoeuvring, with no inner core, as the method of a politician supreme? It is more than that in four respects. First, however labyrinthine his methods, there is a substantial progressive legacy from which the French left takes inspiration, including the abolition of the death penalty, significantly raising the minimum wage, equal rights for women and minorities, decentralisation and numerous beneficial *grands projets*, including the TGV.

Second, the 1982-83 reversal had the effect of demonstrating to the European left that "socialism in one country" didn't work. Pragmatic social democracy is the successful face of "Mitterrandism", although there wasn't the clear break with the doctrinaire past of the German SPD in the late 1950s and the British Labour Party in the mid-1990s. But then the contemporary SPD and Labour Party aren't much to boast about.

Third, there *was* a Mitterrand core: peace with Germany and projects to entrench European peace and security, from the European Communities in the 1950s to the single currency in the 1990s. A survivor of European war and its horrors – including time as a prisoner of war – Mitterrand never allowed the central pillars of a pro-German and pro-US foreign policy to become part of the game of "simulate, dissimulate." Ironically, it was de Gaulle who played dangerously in that arena. With Communists in his government and the left triumphant, Mitterrand's first move in 1981 was to assure Ronald Reagan in unequivocal words and actions that France was a reliable ally. He did the same with Margaret Thatcher during the Falklands war a year later, and also with Helmut Kohl, after an initial wobble, on German reunification in 1990. It was ambiguity at home but clarity abroad – and clarity in the cause of European peace and stability. Hence the most enduring image of Mitterrand: hand in hand with Helmut Kohl before two huge wreaths at Verdun in 1984 at a ceremony to seal Franco-German reconciliation.

Fourth, throughout his life and career, Mitterrand had a patrician sympathy with the underdog. The son of a stationmaster who inherited a family vinegar business, he served in the ranks in the war, having failed the competition for a commission, and developed a contempt for hierarchy and authority (besides his own) and a social sympathy for the less fortunate that was genuine and lasting. His political initiation – and his early political power base – was in organisations for returning prisoners of war. This need not have led him to the socialist left but it helped him accomplish the transition with an authenticity born to some degree from experience. No feats of intellectual and political gymnastics can substitute for, or detract from, personal experience. In Mitterrand's case, it was his intimate experience of a France prostrate, impoverished and divided, that dominated his twenties and shaped him fundamentally.

Philip Short suggests another attribute of Mitterrand the leader: natural authority rooted in an "inner solitude" – "a part of his being that was locked, inaccessible to others, which is one of the characteristics of uncommon leaders everywhere" (he is also the biographer of Pol Pot and Mao Zedong) – and which came in part from a long period in the political wilderness (the 23 years from 1958 to 1981). He draws the parallel with de Gaulle in the wilderness in the 1950s; Churchill in the 1930s also comes to mind.

Perhaps. Yet Mitterrand showed himself to be a notable leader as a prisoner of war and an organiser of fellow returnees long before his wilderness years. Maybe it owed more to Cardinal Mazarin, whose further advice for politicians was to "maintain a posture at all times which is full of dignity. Each day spend a moment studying how you should respond to the events which might befall you."

In the last months of his life, Mitterrand's doctor told him he was a mixture of Machiavelli, Don Corleone, Casanova and the Little Prince. When the patient enquired, "In what proportions?" the physician replied, "That depends on which day."

14

GEORGE III

Most of this book is about modern politicians coming to power through fairly free and representative elections and parliaments. But the roots of the modern western politics go deep into monarchies, oligarchies and dictatorships. Two seminal shapers of the transition to modern politics were Britain's King George III, who reigned for 60 years between 1760 and 1820, and Napoleon Bonaparte, the French military leader who seized power in 1799 and created a dictatorship, albeit one accepting many of the social changes of the revolution. For most of his 16-year rule Napoleon was at war, including with George III. This chapter and the next tell the story of these two rulers, reviewing biographies of them by Andrew Roberts.

On 14 July 1789, the Bastille prison in Paris was stormed and the ancient French Bourbon monarchy descended into an orgy of revolution and bloodshed, culminating in the guillotining of King Louis XVI and Queen Marie-Antoinette amid virtually lawless terror. It took a decade before stability was ruthlessly imposed by Napoleon's military dictatorship, but that too collapsed in a megalomaniacal European war and for the next century and a half France lacked fundamental strength and legitimacy of government.

On 14 July 1789 King George III was on holiday in Weymouth. Tens of thousands turned out to cheer the King's carriage on its way to and from Windsor. "The King bathes, and with great success," wrote a companion of Queen Charlotte, to whom he was uxoriously devoted.

A machine follows the royal one into the sea, filled with fiddlers, who play 'God Save Great George Our King' as His Majesty takes the plunge! They have dressed out every street with labels of 'God Save the King': all the shops have it over their doors; all the children wear it in their caps, all the labourers in their hats, and all the sailors in their voices for they never approach the house without shouting it out loud.

Well into a third century later, Britain remains a popular monarchy, reigned over in the national mind from Buckingham Palace, which George bought and invested as his headquarters in his capital, by his great-great-great-great-granddaughter Elizabeth II, whose benignity, moderate splendour, longevity and moral rectitude make her reign – like that of her equally adamantine great-grandmother Victoria in the intervening century – in some ways a continuation of his, except that he ruled as well as reigned and was significantly better educated than either Elizabeth or Victoria, with far greater interest in science, architecture, agriculture and the arts. He was Victoria and Albert, Elizabeth and Charles, rolled into one.

Andrew Roberts makes a strong revisionist case for George III, and I am largely persuaded by it. "George III more than filled the role of King of Great Britain worthily; he filled it nobly," he concludes. It was nobility with Lear-like pathos, which Roberts attributes to bipolar disorder not the blood disease porphyria of Alan Bennett's *The Madness of George III*, although both give due recognition to the early mental health specialist Dr Francis Willis, who saved the king's life from the ravages of his quack physicians. However, until his final confinement at the age of 73, after half a century on the throne, George's episodes were incapacitating for a total duration of less than a year, so to describe him as the mad king is as historically misconceived as to regard his major legacy as losing America.

George III was an improbable success. Half a century before his accession, his great grandfather was an obscure German protestant princeling recruited in a dynastic crisis to fill a chronically unstable British throne. Two recent occupants had been beheaded or expelled, the first (Charles I) after a full-scale civil war won by the military dictator Oliver Cromwell, a descendant of Thomas Cromwell of *Wolf Hall*, who had more besides in common with Napoleon. Both Oliver Cromwell and Napoleon founded "new model" martial dynasties and were hero-worshipped by adherents who saw them as cleansing royal Augean stables.

George I of Hanover spoke little or no English and was in two minds on whether even to reside in his new kingdom in 1714. He immediately faced an armed uprising, led by the son of the ousted James II claiming legitimacy and popularity, particularly in Catholic Ireland and disaffected Scotland. His son George II faced another rebellion in 1745, led by James's grandson with French support, while his own son died prematurely leaving the succession in 1760, in the middle of yet another war with France, to a priggish 22 year-old grandson who appeared clueless about government and quickly fell out with the aristocratic magnates indispensable to managing the oligarchic but highly disputative parliament required by law to meet annually after the 1688 "Glorious Revolution" which removed James II.

The linchpin of mid-18th century government was a monarch who, while head of government as well as state, church and armed forces, had to engage an effective aristocratic parliamentary manager to secure majorities by hook or crook in the two houses of Commons and Lords in support of the crown's financial and other demands, adjusting them as necessary. Hence the new office of "prime minister." For most of the reigns of George I and II there were just three dominant premiers – Sir Robert Walpole, a brilliant, thuggish aristocratic manager who wisely steered clear of wars to stabilise the new dynasty, succeeded by two of England's principal oligarchs, the Duke of Newcastle and his brother Henry Pelham, who recruited talented lesser aristos of parliamentary standing when needed to deal with emergencies, notably William Pitt during an initially disastrous war with France in the late 1750s. "I am sure I can save this country and no-one else can," the inspirational Great Commoner boasted, and he was probably right.

Obtusely, within two years of his youthful accession, as soon as that war was won, George III dismissed both Newcastle and Pitt, replacing them with his ex-tutor Lord Bute, a dilettante Scots peer devoid of parliamentary skill who urged his pupil to "be a King" but himself became a national hate figure and was soon pleading to be released. Within a decade, a struggling George was on to his seventh prime minister, Lord North, another childhood friend, who was as clueless as his royal master as to how to handle a growing dispute over self-government with Britain's increasingly self-confident American colonies.

Drifting aimlessly into a long trans-oceanic struggle to avoid separation but with no clear view of what continued union actually meant, George and North proceeded by 1782 to lose the American war to George Washington. "Upon military matters, I speak ignorantly and therefore without effect," North told the King, of which Roberts observes: "That sentence alone ought to have disqualified him as leader in a time of war." Forced to stop the war at the hands of bitter parliamentary opponents led by Charles James Fox, George contemplated abdication. Indeed he was a constant, frenetic monarchical melodrama to his ministers even when not bipolar, dating all his letters to the minute ('0759' typically heading the day's first screed), with declarations like: "I shall never lose an opportunity in declaring that no consideration shall ever make me in the smallest degree an instrument in a measure that I am confident would annihilate the rank in which the British Empire stands among the European States, and would render my situation in this country below continuing an object to me."

It is debatable whether the dynasty would have long survived George's abdication at the end of the American war in 1792, or his reign ending when he nearly died later in the decade, and was equally nearly replaced by his son during his most serious four-month bipolar episode of 1788/9. The vast licentiousness of the then 26 year-old Prince of Wales would have known few bounds as Regent, not least because he would have appointed his equally licentious friend Fox as prime minister. Fox was also a supporter of the unfolding French revolution.

Instead, and amazingly, the next 22 years were the apotheosis of George III. By the time his by now 48 year-old son finally took over in 1811, after the death of both Fox and Pitt, there were no tremors of state or changes of policy or ministers and the Hanoverian dynasty was so strong that it withstood even George IV's extravagances. Roberts attributes this to three essential causes, all of which are convincing.

First, for all the melodrama and poor judgement of his early years, George III's rootedness in the 1688 version of limited monarchy – instilled in him by his tutor Bute, ironically – constituted a sheet anchor in the alarums and excursions of national strife and international revolutions. Although an opponent of further reform, and prepared to fund the corruption of the age, George never sought autocracy or to abolish or seriously undermine parliament, which met freely in every year of his reign.

"George was not a reactionary so much as a natural conservative," says Roberts. "He did not believe in the Divine Right of Kings, but he did believe in the near-divinity of the British constitution." His anti-revolution-itis faced all ways: against the American separatists and the French Jacobins, but equally against populist anti-Catholic demagogues at home like Lord George Gordon, and against fellow monarchs going despotic. "I will never acknowledge that the king of a limited monarchy can on any principle endeavour to change the constitution and increase his own power," he declared after Gustav III overthrew Sweden's constitution in 1772.

Roberts demonstrates, article by article, that virtually all the charges against "the tyrant" George III in the American Declaration of Independence were fictitious. The issue was a simply one of whether the King-in-Parliament had continuing legislative power of any kind over colonies with their own elected assemblies. He gives a moving account of

John Adams's reception by George as the first American ambassador to the Court of St James. The King received him with a "gracious and heartfelt" speech, declaring:

> The separation having been made ... I have always said, and I say now, that I would be the first to meet the friendship of the United States as an independent power. The moment I see such sentiments and language as yours prevail, the moment I shall say, let the circumstances of language, religion and blood have their natural and full effect.

British-American equality and friendship are rooted in that moment.

Adams called George "the most accomplished courtier in his dominions," and therein lies his second essential strength. However beleaguered, he not only avoided despotism, but he was thoroughly professional and generally popular, outside parts of the "liberal metropolitan elite." In particular, he was quintessentially English and proud of it. He never travelled outside southern England, and while that was a weakness, it was less so than the opposite of not being a royal John Bull. "I glory in the name of Briton," his accession declaration, became ever more poignant as Britannia struggled for survival against Napoleon and threatened invasions. He was personally brave, generous and affable, with a reputation as the farmer's friend. After one of many assassination attempts – at the Theatre Royal Drury Lane in 1800 – the playwright Sheridan, formerly a bitter critic, penned a new verse to "God Save the King" which captured the popular mood:

> From every latent foe
> From the assassin's blow,

God save the King!
O'er him Thine arm extend,
For Britain's sake defend,
Our father, Prince and friend,
God save the King!

The fundamental stability and constitutional consensus of George's reign within England, Scotland and Wales was a vital platform for economic progress, investment, trade and industrialisation. Ireland, forced by George III and William Pitt into a colonial-type union with Great Britain in 1799, remained semi-revolutionary and economically undeveloped, of huge import to the evolution of British politics and the British state ever since. But across the rest of the United Kingdom an industrial revolution flourished during and after long after George III's rule, with its roots in his reign and policy. And for all the loss of America, the colonisation of India advanced dramatically, and that was to endure for another century and a half.

The third factor in George III's ultimate success is that at last, in 1783, after 23 years of almost continuously weak, divided or disastrous governments, he found his ministerial match in William Pitt the Younger. And having appointed Pitt – prodigy son of his first prime minister, whose vast egocentricity he had admired and reviled in equal measure back in 1760 – he backed him to the hilt for the next 17 years. Barely older than George had been himself in 1760 but already an accomplished parliamentarian of conservative but not reactionary disposition, with shrewd political judgement, Pitt was prime minister for most of the rest of George's effective reign. The two men were never friends but the mutual respect was formidable. Pitt became "the pilot who weathered the storm" of the Napoleonic wars. In the process he established the modern form of

Cabinet government, progressively removing the monarch from the business of government and leading the way to kings and queens who reigned but not ruled.

If George III came back today, he would recognise so much. Buckingham Palace. Windsor. Eton. The state opening of Parliament, the changing of the guard, trooping of the colour, public rituals still adorned by the music of Handel, his favourite composer and another German immigrant, who wrote what Roberts calls the "dynastic soundtrack" for the Hanoverians. Oh, and a vituperative popular media and the "heirs and spares" trashing the good name of a popular, dutiful, aged monarch. As the *Guardian* concluded in its obituary in 1820: "In the perplexity of nations, the throne of the King of England was the only one unshaken, and its stability was the work of his virtue."

15

NAPOLEON

The French historian Élie Halévy asked the rhetorical question: comparing France and Britain in 1750 and 1850, which country seriously modernised? It was obviously the nation of shopkeepers, not the descendants of Napoleon "the Great" (1769-1821), as Andrew Roberts ordains him. As a leader, Napoleon was mostly a failure, and the title of "founder of modern France" belongs far more to Charles de Gaulle, who rebuilt both the idea and the reality of France in the three decades after Hitler's invasion and occupation in 1940. But the sheer chutzpah and grandiloquence of Napoleon's leadership dazzle far beyond his accomplishments, and his political legacy endures in much of the map and political mentality of modern Europe.

In 1750 Louis XV's France was the magnet of Europe. By 1850, Victoria and Albert's Britain was the workshop of the world, leading an industrial and agrarian revolution that France had barely begun. Britain was also, outside Ireland, a stable constitutional monarchy, whose political class took the decisive steps towards fully representative government with virtually no bloodshed, no reactionary backlash and no military coups. France, by contrast, lurched from revolution to revolution, and coup to coup, in the 70 years after the 1789 meeting of the Estates-General which began the undoing of Louis XVI and the absolutist Bourbons.

For all Napoleon's brief colonisation of much of Europe, by the time something resembling stability was achieved under the Third Republic in the 1870s France was the economic inferior of Britain, the military inferior of a united Germany, and beset by internal crises that constantly threatened further revolutions. It took another general-turned-president, Charles de Gaulle, finally to end this cycle, and that was another 70 years, and two European wars, later.

In this longer view, what was the legacy of Napoleon's 1799 coup and 16-year reign? Some improvements to French law and infrastructure, an emphasis on meritocracy; but the broader political, economic and military effects were retrograde. Napoleon's regime was not even the longest lasting of the revolutionary era. More enduring were both the July Monarchy of Louis-Philippe (1830-48) and the reign of his adventurer nephew Louis-Napoleon (1848-70), whose empire crumbled equally fast on the battlefield against Prussia.

Andrew Roberts brings Bonaparte to life a military commander and public administrator of immense skill, energy and resourcefulness who took control of France in a military coup only six years after entering the country as a virtually penniless political refugee. But Napoleon "the Great"? The challenge Roberts has in establishing this claim is summed up by this sentence in his conclusion: "Although his conquests ended in defeat and ignominious imprisonment, Napoleon fought 60 battles and sieges and lost only seven."

In other words, Napoleon's legacy was one of comprehensive failure, but with success and glory *en route*. What's more, these seven military losses include neither his naval failures nor the overwhelming disaster of Russia.

Roberts does not even attempt to justify Napoleon's strategic and tactical errors of 1812-13, from the initial decision to invade Russia right through to the mistake of retreating from Moscow by a northern rather than a southern route. Instead, he cites the emperor's motives and state of mind. He had not intended a deep invasion, but rather expected Tsar Alexander I to sue for peace. Similarly, he did not expect Alexander to order the burning of Moscow – "an event," Bonaparte said, "on which I could not calculate as there is not, I believe, a precedent for it in the history of the world." Poor excuses for monumental military and diplomatic misjudgements.

The truth is that Napoleon was a megalomaniac who had constantly to be at war and to enlarge any war in which he was engaged – and this overwhelmed his debatable talent for administration and institution building. In his military trajectory, he bears striking similarities to Hitler 130 years later, complete with a Russian invasion.

The Dutch historian Pieter Geyl, writing during the German occupation of Holland in the early 1940s, portrayed Napoleon as a totalitarian dictator, the harbinger of the concept and method in modern times. Roberts attempts to defend Napoleon against this Hitler parallel. It is true that there were relatively few political executions, in France at least, and although representative government was one of the first casualties of the Napoleonic coup, he was not totalitarian in all aspects of civil life. There was a right to private property, some religious tolerance and some aspects to the rule of law in the civil sphere. But this is a paltry defence, and it was all mostly true of Hitler too. Both leaders ruled their occupied territories brutally as colonies and extended slavery within them.

Roberts says more than he perhaps realises in arguing that Napoleon saw his ideal of France as an extension of the army: "It was very much as a French army officer imbued with the military ethos that he rose, seized power and then maintained his rule." (Hitler similarly saw his Reich as an extension of his army). Fortunately for France, General de Gaulle, in his Napoleonic moment in 1958, took a broader view and sought to contain not extend French military and colonial megalomania. He also made genuine peace with Germany – and with democracy. He became a statesman, not a warrior.

16

THATCHER

Early in her premiership, Margaret Thatcher (1925-2013) demonstrated, for the first time in most people's observation, that strength and dominance can be female as well as male traits in political leadership at the highest level. By the Falklands War of 1982, three years into her eleven years of continuous rule, she had established a reputation as the Iron Lady at home and abroad, and Britain's most resolute leader since Churchill. There was soon a debate on whether "cabinet government" had been replaced by "prime ministerial government," to which I contributed in this excerpt from my book on the rise and fall of the poll tax, the controversial reform which proved to be her nemesis in 1990.

For more than a century, commentators have debated whether British government should be described as "cabinet government," "prime-ministerial government," or even "presidential government."

The view that the prime minister is only first among equals, propagated in the late nineteenth century by Walter Bagehot and A.V. Dicey and still largely supported in the 1930s by Sir Ivor Jennings, has long since been abandoned. It was little more than an Aunt Sally by the time Crossman made his celebrated attack on the idea in the 1963 reissue of Bagehot's *English Constitution*. Indeed, Dicey himself did not fully adhere to it. "The sovereignty of parliament is still a fundamental doctrine of English constitutionalists," he declared in 1885, but developed the point thus:

this sovereignty can be effectively exercised only by the Cabinet, which holds in its hands the guidance of the party machine. And of the cabinet which the parliamentary majority supports the Premier has become at once the legal head and, if he is a man of ability, the real leader.

Dicey's contemporary, John Morley, moved from his earlier description of the premier as "the keystone of the cabinet arch," to writing in his biography of Sir Robert Walpole that the power of the prime minister was "not inferior to that of a dictator, provided the House of Commons will stand by him." Indeed, Gladstone, the subject of Morley's more famous biography, was periodically described as a "dictator" by his colleagues and contemporaries, as was the other great late-Victorian prime minister, Lord Salisbury, who combined the office with that of foreign secretary for most of his tenure, so that he could direct the entire British empire unimpeded. Gladstone was the last prime minister to combine the premiership with the chancellorship of the exchequer, so that he could determine his government's entire fiscal and economic strategy personally.

The effective power to appoint and dismiss fellow ministers also dates back to Walpole himself in the 1720s: this is partly what made him "prime" minister. And all the leading premiers since Walpole have dominated the media of their day and often taken key decisions after consultations with only a few colleagues, sometimes with one or none. Once the cabinet secretariat and prime minister's policy unit (then dubbed the "kitchen cabinet") were established by Lloyd George after 1916, all the essentials of the modern premiership were in place.

So the rise of the British presidency is not a recent development. But in reality, now, as in times past, there are some strong prime ministers, some weak ones. The strong are able to dominate their cabinets and parliaments to a dictatorial degree; the weak are highly dependent on the consent of party elders, and/or of fickle parliamentary majorities and outside forces, whatever the media illusion of centralised and personalised power.

Of the 15 prime ministers since Churchill in 1940, only two (Thatcher and Blair) have been unambiguously "strong" for the entirety of their tenure. Another two (Douglas-Home and Callaghan) were unambiguously weak throughout, with the majority oscillating between strong and weak at different stages of their premierships. This includes the present incumbent Boris Johnson, and indeed Churchill himself, the supreme leader of 1940 who, through illness, age and lethargy, was a virtually a ghost in the middle of his last premiership in 1953.

Under Thatcher, fewer and fewer matters had much discussion in full cabinet. According to Nicholas Ridley, a long-standing minister and acolyte:

> She did not see the cabinet as a body to take decisions, except decisions of the gravest importance. She saw it as a forum in which all important activities were brought together and reported upon. She saw it as the body to approve individual ministers' policies. She used it as a tactical group to discuss the immediate problems of the day.

Despite the pressure of business, the full cabinet met for fewer hours in the 1980s than in any decade of the 20th century. Typically Thatcher held between forty and forty-five meetings a year, barely half the number under

Churchill and Attlee. (Blair governed on the Thatcher model). The number of cabinet papers circulated in the 1980s represented only a sixth of the annual tally in the late 1940s and early 1950s. It was not just to cabinet committees that decisions were devolved: Thatcher increasingly utilized ad hoc committees and 'bilateral' meetings with individual ministers to decide policy. As Nigel Lawson observes: "What had started off as a justified attempt to make effective decisions in small and informal groups degenerated into increasingly complex attempts to divide and rule." He later remarked that in the "long-drawn-out final phase, she had become reckless over Europe, reckless over the poll tax, reckless over what she said in public, and reckless over colleagues."

'Twas not ever thus. Despite her famous remark in an *Observer* interview shortly before the 1979 election that she could not "waste time having any internal arguments," first-term Thatcher was careful to keep the Tory party's power-brokers, notably her initial deputy leader Willie Whitelaw, with her on key decisions. But as she grew senior to all her colleagues and more certain of what Douglas Hurd, her last Foreign Secretary, called her "individual powers" following her defeat of the cabinet "wets" in 1981, General Galtieri in 1982, and of Arthur Scargill in 1985, she relied less and less on the advice and confidence of ministerial colleagues and made her impatience increasingly plain. The near disaster of the Westland affair in 1986, when Michael Heseltine resigned and festered, was followed by a brief period of caution, but after her third election triumph, in 1987, she came to believe, as one colleague put it, that she could "walk on water". Her dramatic falling out with previous stalwarts Lawson and Geoffrey Howe between 1988 and 1990 sealed her fate.

Thatcher was not the first Prime Minister to have highly – and publicly – strained relations with senior colleagues. "What I have done is to surround myself with friends and to isolate Callaghan," Harold Wilson brazenly told the cabinet of his 1966 reshuffle, moments before the Chancellor entered the room. But under no other premiership since the second world war had relations at the top broken down so spectacularly.

The poll tax, Thatcher's last great reform battle, exemplified and to a large extent caused her demise. The insignificance of the full cabinet to decision-taking is well attested by the poll tax. The cabinet did not so much as discuss the proposal for the tax until January 1986, fifteen months after a coterie of advisers had been tasked with devising the monstrosity and more than seven months after the key decision of principle had been taken by a cabinet committee. The full cabinet merely rubber-stamped the draft of Kenneth Baker's Green Paper *Paying for Local Government*. Nigel Lawson, a strong opponent of the proposals at every earlier stage, did not even bother to register dissent at the full cabinet. It was not just that by now it was too late: as Lawson put it, "the cabinet is far too public a forum for the Chancellor to announce his disagreement with the Prime Minister on a key policy – unless he wants it to be across the world's press the next day, making his or the prime minister's position untenable."

But if the cabinet was irrelevant as a decision-taking forum, the cabinet structure, as an umbrella embracing the dozen or more key ministers and meetings between them, was fully engaged at every stage in the rise and fall of the poll tax. Nearly half of the cabinet was present at the

Chequers meeting of 31 March 1985, which gave the initial impetus to the policy. More than half of the cabinet was involved in the cabinet committees which successively endorsed the principle of the scheme (May 1985), agreed the worked-up plan of the Green Paper (December 1985), and supervised the drawing up of legislation first for Scotland (summer 1986) and then for England and Wales (summer and autumn 1987). John Major's decision to scrap the poll tax and replace it with a revamped property tax, taken in the spring of 1991, was also agreed by a cabinet committee comprising half the cabinet.

Only at the implementation stage, between autumn 1988 and the downfall of Thatcher in November 1990, was a smaller number of ministers involved. Key decisions about transitional funding arrangements, and the several internal reviews of the operation of the tax, were taken in small groups, some in bilaterals chaired by the Prime Minister (or, in the case of the bitter dispute over funding between Chris Patten and Lawson in September 1989, by Howe as deputy prime minister). But the overall policy had been endorsed by a wider group. There was no pressure among other ministers for a wider re-assessment, and the speed with which many of the financial decisions had to be taken made such a reassessment impractical. Indeed, the most important financial change – the switch of £4.5bn. of local authority spending from the poll tax to VAT in March 1991 – was made by John Major and his first Chancellor Norman Lamont in the annual budget, which by long convention is never discussed in cabinet.

The poll tax would almost certainly not have happened without Thatcher in third term hubris, but "it is quite untrue to say that her Cabinet colleagues were 'bounced' into accepting it," notes Lawson. "Despite her profound personal commitment, she observed the proprieties of cabinet government." Apart from Lawson, all Thatcher's key ministers, from across the cabinet's departmental and ideological spectrum, endorsed the tax once it had strong prime ministerial backing, including pragmatists like Whitelaw and Scottish secretary George Younger. There was a Scottish dimension to their support. For historic and demographic reasons, the domestic property rating system bore more heavily on the Scottish than the English middle classes, and Younger was described by a colleague as "hell-bent" to have the poll tax introduced into Scotland as early a possible, without any of the transitional arrangements or safeguards envisaged in the original scheme devised by Kenneth Baker. "Anything but the rates" became the mantra: a dangerous case of policymaking taking the form of "anything but the status quo," when the cure turned out to be worse than the supposed disease.

In a 1993 lecture on cabinet government, John Wakeham, a loyalist "fixer" who spanned the Thatcher and Major cabinets, noted that "many commentators who bemoan what they see as the decline of the cabinet as a decision-taker fail to appreciate its significance as the cement which binds the government together." The poll tax sage supports Wakeham's observation. In particular, it highlights the interplay of formal and informal procedures which lie at the heart of cabinet government in Britain.

As I have described, the cabinet, through its committees, was fully and formally engaged in all the decisions which led to the poll tax. It would, however, be simplistic to believe that the move towards the poll tax was conducted wholly within the formal decision-making structure of the cabinet and its committees. In reality, a parallel set of informal forums played a critical role in the evolution of the policy. Some of the forums involved ministers alone and some a combination of ministers and advisers; but all were outside the regular cabinet structure, often dovetailing awkwardly with the formal structure.

The most obvious such forum was the Chequers gathering of Sunday 31 March 1985. Although not a formal meeting of a cabinet committee, it played a critical role in the evolution of the policy, and is regarded by Thatcher as the occasion on which the poll tax was truly born. There is nothing new in day-long meetings at Chequers to thrash out major policy departures. Wilson and Callaghan both took to holding meetings there on a fairly frequent basis, as did Blair thereafter. Yet in the case of the poll tax – and other policies with a similar genesis – the effect of such informality was to give momentum to the prime ministerial policy.

The March 1985 Chequers meeting on local government finance reform was so informal that its significance was underrated even by those invited. Lawson was absent, "having been assured that this was simply a preliminary discussion at which no decisions would be taken." No papers were circulated before or at the meeting, and few of those there had any idea what a full-fledged poll tax might actually look like. The only information available to ministers on the day was that supplied by Kenneth Baker and William Waldegrave in their slide show setting out the original poll tax plan. By the time the policy began to go through the established cabinet machinery, with papers supplying details, it had already achieved critical momentum.

But there is rarely such a thing as a "preliminary" prime ministerial meeting, particularly if it lasts for a whole morning like this one. In key decision-making terms, it was to be the first and last meeting that mattered in the launch of the poll tax. It is often remarked that the power of the Prime Minister lies in his or her ability to control the agenda of meetings. Just as important is their control of the forum in which decisions are taken. The Chequers meeting is but one instance of that in the poll tax saga. No less important was the initial decision, in autumn 1984, to opt for a "quickie" review of the alternatives to rates. Thatcher and environment secretary Patrick Jenkin wanted to have the investigation over in a matter of months, and feared that any quasi-independent inquiry would reaffirm the existing system of property rates. The Layfield royal commission report on local government finance was only ten years old, and it had taken eighteen months to report. Jenkin's "studies" team managed to undo its work in less than five months.

The use of informal forums and procedures had another significant bearing on the outcome of the 1984 rates review: it enabled the environment department to keep at arm's length all other departments, particularly the Treasury, normally all-powerful on tax reform. at arm's length. Other departments were excluded from all the formative work of the 1984 review until it became agreed policy – on the basis that it had yet to go through a formal inter-departmental and cabinet process which, when it came, was too late to stop the policy.

In the case of the poll tax, therefore, John Wakeham's "cement" served to bind the cabinet as a whole to maybe the most controversial tax of the 20th century, generated in a matter of weeks by a tiny group of Thatcherite enthusiasts whose scheming was initially in advance even of the prime minister herself.

"Procedure is the best constitution we have," remarked the Bagehot scholar Norman St John-Stevas, ironically an early Thatcher minister sacked for insufficient zeal long before her third term. The poll tax was not an exercise in prime-ministerial autocracy, but a classic product of prime-ministerial power and procedure.

17

SCHOLZ

Olaf Scholz (b. 1958) is set to become Germany's ninth post-war chancellor, unexpectedly seizing the crown laid down by Angela Merkel after 16 years. However, to describe Scholz as "continuity Merkel" – his brand in the 2021 election – confuses his consensual, understated style with his actual record as a social democratic reformer over a decade as finance minister and mayor of Hamburg. He has the makings of a shrewd successor to the run of outstanding leaders since the federal republic's foundation in the unpromising conditions of the Bevin v. Stalin cold war of the late 1940s, described in Chapter 3.

Before Olaf Scholz became its candidate for chancellor in the federal election of September 2021, Germany's social democratic party (SPD) was attracting not votes but obituaries. A year before it had sunk to fourth place in the polls on just 11 per cent, behind the far-right AfD party and with no respite in view. Its junior status in Angela Merkel's fourth coalition looked like the final death embrace. I was told of the advice that Merkel gave to David Cameron, when he was faced with the necessity for a coalition in 2010: "You hug your smaller party close, then squeeze them dry." She did this to the SPD not once but three times during her 16-year reign.

So riven and demoralised was the SPD as it embarked on its last "grand coalition" with Merkel in 2017 (strong far-right and far-left contingents in the Bundestag making this the only way to secure a majority government), it wouldn't even elect its senior minister in that coalition—and Germany's vice-chancellor and finance minister—to be one of the party's co-leaders. Instead, it opted for two hard-left rivals.

Scholz was the leader rebuffed. He is now on the brink of becoming Germany's chancellor, having led the SPD to a remarkable victory after a long and highly personalised election campaign in which the party started in third place, running not only behind the Christian Democrats (CDU) but also the Greens. The winning margin was narrow, but Scholz was able to mobilise prestige and momentum from an astonishing electoral turnaround. Even putting aside the SPD's dire last decade, it was an exceptional result to overtake the CDU. In the seven-decade history of the federal republic, the SPD topped the ballot on only three previous occasions; the CDU, in their alliance with the more conservative Christian Social Union (CSU) in Bavaria, did 16 times. In today's fractured political scene, neither main party is as big as it used to be, but the swing between them since Merkel's last win in 2017 was a substantial 7 percentage points, the biggest two-party shift ever witnessed in a single election in a federal republic renowned for continuity and stability.

How did this sober and taciturn 63-year-old pull off such an extraordinary coup? Simple: Scholz was the best candidate in the 2021 election. As voters increasingly appreciated during the campaign, he had the best credentials and capacity for the chancellorship. He'd been highly competent as finance minister for three years and, for the seven years before that, as mayor of Hamburg,

Germany's second city and a federal state in its own right. He looked tailor-made for the job.

Go further back and you find a lifetime's political experience. A virtually full-time student politician at university in Hamburg, the city he grew up in, he rose to be vice-president of the international union of socialist youth when barely out of his teens, putting him alongside Biden, Blair, Obama and Modi in the "club of 30" of leaders described in earlier chapters, all of them first elected to public office or seriously engaged in politics by the age of 30. In his late twenties he went on to build a successful labour law practice which, much like the young Boris Johnson's *Spectator* journalism, was politics by other means. Returned to the Bundestag in the election which brought Schröder to power as Kohl's successor in 1998, he was thereafter in public or political office continuously until his own bid for the chancellorship 23 years later.

After two decades at the top of German politics, Scholz remains strikingly well-liked, with few enemies. His personal life is discreet and modest. He doesn't own a house but rents flats in Potsdam and Hamburg with his wife Britta Ernst, another lifelong SPD politician, now education minister of Brandenburg. He doesn't have a doctorate, unlike many German leaders, but he is well able to hold his own in intellectual discourse and would be at ease discussing John Rawls and Michael Sandel with Gordon Brown or Barack Obama. "He is equally at home talking to dockers in Hamburg harbour, then an hour later meeting Navid Kermani [Germany's foremost thinker on the interaction between Islam and the west]," says Michele Augur of the Friedrich-Ebert-Stiftung centre-left think tank.

So once again, "It's the Leader, Stupid".

It was said that Scholz was lucky in his 2021 election opponents. The floundering, gaffe-prone Armin Laschet vainly attempted to occupy Merkel's CDU shoes while AnnalenaBaerbock, the initially popular Green leader, proved to be green as well as Green, wilting in the limelight from inexperience and an inability to reconcile her party's centrist and radical wings.

But life's spoils are claimed by those who are present and able to dominate. In an election without Merkel, Scholz was the most senior incumbent from a generally respected government, and he was shrewd to portray himself as the continuity candidate. "He's the closest thing to a political automaton," an ex-colleague said to me, "and I'm only slightly exaggerating." True, like Britain's Clement Attlee, who sprung from the effective if unglamorous discharge of the deputy prime ministership during the second world war to lead Labour out of a long electoral wilderness in 1945, Scholz is more naturally suited for governing than campaigning. But also like Attlee, his cut-through as a candidate and campaigner came by demonstration of governing competence. It worked in 2021 because he reflected the spirit of the moment, in a broadly stable and economically successful Germany nonetheless timid and worried as it emerged from Covid and the prospect of government without Merkel.

Leadership, then, explains 2021 the election result: all else is embellishment and detail. But read on, because it is vital to understand that Scholz is not continuity Merkel, as most commentators said at the time, to his electoral satisfaction. Like her, he subscribes to Germany's post-war "social market" model of state in equilibrium with free enterprise. But he is also a radical who thinks deeply about reform to tackle deep-seated challenges, and he has demonstrated a capacity to effect successful change. His agenda is not Merkel's and, in the endgame of her chancellorship, it was he who squeezed her dry and not vice versa, while uniting his own party's centre and left behind an inclusive slogan of "respect."

This had much in common with how he unexpectedly won the mayoralty of Hamburg from the CDU in 2011, with a modernising, socially activist but business-friendly programme oozing reassurance and reform in equal measure. He was easily re-elected to a second term in the city and left only when destiny and Berlin called in 2018. By then he had a strong personal reformist brand, which has grown since to include his part as a consensual but innovative finance minister during the pandemic.

It would, however, be wrong to discount the SPD from brand Scholz. Keenly aware of the political traditions he grows out of, they condition his whole outlook. The SPD is Germany's oldest democratic party, boasting—despite the rarity of its outright wins—three considerable chancellors since the war: Willy Brandt and Helmut Schmidt (1969-82) after Adenauer, and Gerhard Schröder between Kohl and Merkel (1998-2005). For all its vicissitudes, including its recent spell of left-wing Corbyn-style leftism before Scholz became "chancellor candidate," the party never lost its governing aura, not least because it is long-established at running many of Germany's 16 federal states as well as government in Berlin.

Parties have a kind of charisma as well as their leaders, a charisma conferred by past leaders whose shadow persists. Scholz owes a drink to Schröder, whom he served as SPD general secretary in the early 2000s, and should lay red roses on the graves of Brandt and Schmidt, the latter his youthful mentor who, before becoming chancellor, was also a fellow Hamburg city father. A longer shadow extends back to Otto Wels, the only party leader to speak out in the Reichstag against Hitler's Enabling Act of 1933, earning the nearest thing to immortality for any political party in modern Europe. "You can take our lives and our freedom," Wels told the dictator to his face, "but you cannot take our honour." The SPD has a trans-partisan place in the story of democratic Germany, hence the striking image of Merkel attending the SPD's 150th anniversary celebration in Leipzig in 2013. There is Hamburg microcosm here: the much-admired SPD mayor of Hamburg in the 1980s, Klaus von Dohnanyi, was grandson of Hungarian composer Ernst von Dohnanyi, whose father and uncle were executed in 1945 as members of the anti-Nazi resistance. Like Scholz he was a centrist reformer of powerful appeal to left and right in a decade of social and economic turmoil.

What makes the "continuity Merkel" label fundamentally misleading is the record of Scholz's three stints in government, totalling 13 years in Berlin and Hamburg.

Here goes, in staccato summary, so you get the cumulative effect.

As mayor of Hamburg, a city suffering the full range of industrial and millennial challenges typical of large western cities, Scholz launched a housebuilding programme of 6,000 new homes. It expanded to 10,000 to accommodate the refugee influx post-2015 which he welcomed, writing personally to all non-Germans who had been resident for more than eight years urging them to seek citizenship and organizing citizenship ceremonies in the town hall to welcome them, giving Hamburg the highest naturalisation rate of any region in Germany. He abolished student university fees, lengthened the school day and greatly expanded free childcare. He appointed Hamburg's most senior business leader—Frank Horch, president of the chamber of commerce and former manager at the shipyard Blohm+Voss—as a non-party economy secretary charged particularly with carrying through the controversial and previously stalled expansion of the river Elbe to maintain Hamburg's status as Germany's premier port.

The Elbe project—a massive 116km deepening and widening of the whole fairway of the Elbe from its North Sea river mouth into the port of Hamburg, just completed—is vital to the city's capacity to handle the largest modern international container ships. It was a business imperative opposed by the Greens and by much of the SPD. He and Horch got it through by patient explanation and negotiation, in the city and with its neighbouring federal states of Lower Saxony and Schleswig-Holstein—which were opposed—as well as the Berlin government and the European Commission to gain the necessary exemption from the EU's habitats and other environmental directives. Scholz even got the Greens to join his second term coalition as mayor, despite their former opposition.

Then a string of new railway stations were opened across Hamburg as part of a public transport infrastructure strategy, and thanks to Scholz construction is beginning of a new 24km metro line going east-west across the city, like London's Crossrail. He also sorted out the notorious inherited crisis in the financing and construction of Hamburg's new concert hall, the Elbphilharmonie (popularly called the "Elphi"), part of the regeneration of the declining and seedy HafenCity port district and now a jewel in the city's crown. A friend who attended the opening jamboree, on a boat touring the port, encountered the mayor on the top deck surveying his city, cigar in hand, "beaming and proud." He was sitting alone.

As Schröder's SPD general secretary, and later labour minister in Merkel's first grand coalition, Scholz played a formative part in the controversial "Hartz IV" reforms that squeezed unemployment benefits, but ultimately made the German economy more competitive. Merkel's domestic project has basically been to embed and embellish the Hartz reforms. Scholz is equally clear that it is time for workers to share in the fruits of their earlier sacrifices: the introduction of a statutory national minimum wage in 2015 was rooted in his plans as labour minister, and one of his key election pledges is to increase it to €12 an hour.

As finance minister, Scholz oversaw the EU's €750bn post-Covid recovery fund—the biggest step so far towards an EU-wide fiscal capacity, the absence of which had previously been the greatest structural weakness in the single currency, and a weakness that Berlin had previously been the mightiest obstacle to fixing. He oversaw, too, Germany's plans, broadly adopted by the EU, for a banking union and for global digital taxes. He also breached the German elite's attachment to *schwarze null* ("black zero")—an allergic aversion to public debt that has particularly hampered infrastructure investment. As pandemic finance minister, he suspended Germany's constitutionally enshrined debt-brake rule for two years in a row. This was a "historically exceptional situation," he explained. Permanent innovations often start with those words.

Of course, much of the credit for all this is collective, and there have been Scholz failures too. Financial regulation, notably the accounting scandals that led to the insolvency of the German payments company Wirecard, dogged him as finance minister, and his plan for Hamburg to bid for the 2024 Summer Olympics were overturned in a referendum. But he may have been right on the Olympics—how many Londoners regret hosting the 2012 games, despite all the prior controversy over the costs? Moreover, the episode again makes the real point. Whereas he has stylistic similarities to Merkel—subscribing to her mantras "in calmness lies power," and always taking care to present his ultimate course as so obvious and commonsensical that it is *alternativlos* ("without alternative")—in his activist "do-something" instincts and his determined, hands-on reformism of spirit, he is her antithesis. Formidable as she may be, she rarely makes a decision until she has to (another Merkelian motto is "give time to time") and almost never makes a move of any significance without consulting the polls. Her management, or mismanagement, of the Euro crisis largely consisted in kicking the can down the road, and putting up with a miserable drift that it is hard to imagine Scholz could have borne.

"I have worked for him for 20 years and stayed because he has an extraordinary capacity to make change happen," says Wolfgang Schmidt, Scholz's chief strategist and deputy as finance minister, and a former state secretary in Hamburg. He identifies Scholz's essential qualities as *Vernunft* (passionate reason) and *ordentliches-Regieren* (leading a sound and reliable government), which reminds me of Roy Jenkins and his social democratic concept of radical, competent centrism.

Schmidt highlights Scholz's "transformational approach" during the Hamburg mayoralty. By contrast with his time as Merkel's deputy chancellor, back in Hamburg

> he was unambiguously in charge and responsible, which is akin to the post he is now likely to assume. From the outset he conceived his role as changemaker not just administrator, while patiently yet systematically building the broadest possible consensus for change. I think he will do that too as chancellor.

For all the criticism of his finance ministry's handling of the Wirecard and other serious financial regulation problems of recent years, "no one believes he is personally on the make," says Schmidt, "and his whole lifestyle cries against it."

The Scholz years in Hamburg were marked by its social and industrial advance. Amid the post-Covid turmoil of Europe and Germany the hope must now be that he can do for his country, and for his continent, what he did for his city.

18

VON DER LEYEN

If you had to design a president of the European Commission from scratch, you might come up with Ursula von der Leyen (b. 1958). Trilingual in English, German and French, she studied in Hanover and London, lived in California and was a right-hand ministerial colleague of Angela Merkel in Berlin. She was even born in Brussels, the daughter of a founding Eurocrat.

But therein lies her Achilles's heel. Von der Leyen went into politics in the footsteps of her father, a power broker in Germany's dominant centre-right Christian Democratic Union; but, for all her connections, experience and ambition, high-level political talent has never been evident. She is Europe's Hillary Clinton. Within months of taking office her bungling of vaccine supply and the Irish border tarnished the Commission, but her very Europeanness may still enable her to make a mark.

Down the ages, nepotism has more often benefitted mediocre men than mediocre women: in elective politics alone, George W Bush and Rajiv Gandhi spring to mind as lesser copies of their father and mother respectively. But Ursula von der Leyen's mode of entry into a male-dominated political world creates a parallel with Hillary Clinton who, as the failed presidential candidate put it revealingly in her memoirs, had a "20-year career in government as first lady, senator and secretary of state." As first lady, she was simply the spouse of the first man. At the crunch Clinton couldn't get herself elected to the top job, failing repeatedly in 2008 and 2016.

Von der Leyen is the first female European Commission president, after 12 men since the office was created. But the crucial difference with Clinton is that she didn't have to be elected by the people—she was simply appointed, then confirmed by a wafer-thin majority in a European Parliament presented with no alternative. "She was pulled like a rabbit out of a hat," in the words of Christian Lindner, leader of Germany's liberal Free Democrat party.

Von der Leyen's shortcomings immediately encouraged the "other" EU president—European Council president Charles Michel, a former prime minister of Belgium—to assert himself at her expense. Since the inception of a separate Council president in 2009, that job had been more chair than chief executive—specifically, presiding over sessions of EU heads of government. Michel, however, had bigger ideas. This is the significance of "sofagate," the now iconic meeting of the two EU presidents with Erdoğan on 7 April 2021. In front of the world's cameras, Michel made a beeline for the gilded chair next to the Turkish leader, relegating von der Leyen to a distant sofa. "I felt hurt, and I felt alone, as a woman," she said. But as one EU ambassador said to me: "I don't think Angela Merkel would have gone to the sofa."

To understand Ursula von der Leyen and her impact on contemporary European leadership, you need to start with her late father, Ernst Albrecht. The Albrechts were princelings of Europe: a great north German Hanseatic dynasty with ancestors from royal diplomats. Born in 1930, Ernst just avoided fighting in Hitler's war but he experienced its full devastation. He studied law and economics first in Tübingen in southern Germany and then, more significant in raising his sights, at Cornell University in New York (one of his grandmothers came from a prominent plantation-owning family in South Carolina). Ernst was determined to become an architect not only of a new Germany but a new Europe. Hence his master's thesis at the University of Bonn, the capital of Konrad Adenauer's new federal republic of Germany on the subject: "Is monetary union a prerequisite for economic union?"

Soon a protégé of Adenauer's circle, Ernst was appointed one of Germany's founding officials in the European Commission while he was in his mid-20s. In an iconic photograph of the signing of the Treaty of Rome in 1957, he is standing directly behind Adenauer. Ursula, the eldest daughter among his seven children, was born in Brussels the following year and went to its international school. (A few years later, in the mid-1970s, Boris Johnson did a pre-Eton spell there.)

Ernst's last job in Brussels, head of competition policy, was a principal construction site of today's EU. He left it in 1970 to forge a political career in his native Lower Saxony, the northwest German state that borders the Netherlands and Hamburg. Double-hatting for a few years as a CDU member of Lower Saxony's state parliament while chairing a food company—a talent for publicity earned him the nickname "cookie monster"—he soon held the highest position in the state: minister president. He put himself forward as a candidate for federal chancellor in 1980 but lost and, in any case, the CDU did not prevail that year. When it was back in government in 1982, Helmut Kohl was in charge, but Ernst remained in the party's higher echelons even after losing the 1990 Lower Saxony state election to Gerhard Schröder, the charismatic SPD leader who went on to succeed Kohl as chancellor.

So, while he did a succession of big jobs, Ernst never made it to the very top. His chances were not helped by successive political scandals during his 14 years running Lower Saxony. But he didn't fail in his youthful ambitions. Under Adenauer, Brandt and Kohl, he was a proud and successful pioneer of today's democratic Germany within a democratic European Union, powerfully allied to the United States.

Ursula, Ernst's favourite child, imbibed it all, and was to replay it all, including the scandals. When the CDU won back Lower Saxony in 2003, the new minister president, Christian Wulff, was a protégé of Ernst's. Ernst even appeared at Wulff's first cabinet meeting, in a kind of laying on of hands, with his daughter present.

But that is getting ahead of the Albrecht story. Teenage Ursula started down a similar academic route to her father—law and economics at Göttingen university. At that time, the far-left militant group Red Army Faction was targeting the families of German politicians, and for her safety Ursula switched to the London School of Economics, under an assumed name. Returning to Hanover to study medicine, she pursued a doctorate on "births in warm water baths" (later the subject of a controversy over plagiarism, which she narrowly survived). She met Heiko von der Leyen, a German physician from an aristocratic family of silk merchants, and they married in 1986. An almost exact replica of family Albrecht, they now have seven children.

The von der Leyens went to America—as Ernst had done—when Heiko got an academic post at Stanford University, and they lived there for four years.

When they returned to Hanover in 1996, Ursula, now in her late thirties, launched into politics in Ernst's Lower Saxony fiefdom. By the early 2000s the political pendulum in the state was swinging away from Schröder's Social Democrats and Christian Wulff needed a prominent woman in his team for the upcoming state election. Who better than the immaculate daughter of Ernst, summed up by her debut at a national CDU conference in which the totality of her speech was: "My name is Ursula von der Leyen, I am social minister in Lower Saxony. My husband and I have seven children."

Ursula took up the brand that Ernst had launched. Back then, "the new *Landesvater* with his happy family" had been the theme of one much-replayed televised profile of the "father of the state," with Ursula and one of her brothers singing songs to him like the von Trapps. Twenty years on, her first campaign slogan was: "The future starts at home." There was national media coverage of Ursula and her family, including an iconic photo of mother with twin daughters feeding baby lambs with a bottle. It was image magic for the staid and male CDU and it caught the eye of Angela Merkel, who had become leader of the CDU in 2000, after the political demise of Helmut Kohl.

"Her publicisation of her family is too much for some," write von der Leyen's biographers Ulrike Demmer and Daniel Goffart. But it wasn't too much for Merkel, who badly needed other female faces in her CDU line-up, especially one who, unlike her, was a mother with west

German roots. So in 2005, after Merkel narrowly defeated Schröder, the "social minister from Lower Saxony with seven children" took up the same job at federal level in Berlin; and there she stayed, later as labour and then defence minister, becoming Merkel's longest-serving cabinet minister until her elevation to Brussels in 2019.

Von der Leyen was a star of the early Merkel era. With an inherited touch for pragmatic CDU centrism, she was presented as a new force—a *female* one—of smooth, reassuring competence. This worked best on her home territory of social policy, exemplifying the *Heimat* and happy nuclear families beloved of Germany's Christian right.

"I turned into the family policy I did," she told Charlie Rose, the US talk show host. Classic von der Leyen was her campaign to curb child sexual abuse imagery on the internet: a modest policy change making waves in the media and sparking a typically German controversy about censorship, and giving her the nickname "Zensursula" (*Zensur* is the German word for censor). More generally, her policies amounted to incremental, overdue improvements in support for Germany's new generation of working women, marred by botched larger schemes for hot school lunches and extra nurseries—and welfare cuts affecting poorer women. Hard-up families didn't feature in those photoshoots with lambs.

In positioning, it was of a piece with Hillary Clinton's use of the African proverb "it takes a village to raise a child," which she adapted for the title of the 1996 book she used to signal her independent political launch. Both women sought to use social policy to break through the "glass ceiling." And indeed, both did break through. Hillary became Obama's secretary of state; von der Leyen, defence minister in Merkel's third term. However, as they rose higher, insufficient political skill became their real glass ceiling. Perhaps because, in both cases, their rise wasn't purely meritocratic—in contrast to Margaret Thatcher and Merkel, who, before them, went through not just the glass ceiling but also the roof.

At the German defence ministry, a faltering von der Leyen soon lost any prospect of succeeding Merkel. Her career seemed all but over, until she was plucked by EU heads of government for Commission president in the last-minute horse-trading of top EU jobs in the middle of Merkel's fourth and final term in 2019.

Von der Leyen got the job largely because of who she wasn't: namely, one of the three candidates (*Spitzenkandidaten*) promoted by the main party groups in the European Parliament, none of whom had enough support in either the European Council or the parliament itself. In different ways all three were, in Vatican terms, *non-papabile*—too forthright for the top job, at least for the taste of President Macron in France and the eastern European premiers, Hungary's authoritarian Viktor Orbán in particular. And once France's Christine Lagarde had been nominated to succeed Mario Draghi as president of the European Central Bank, a German also fitted the power-balancing "grid."

A constant problem with von der Leyen is style over substance. In nearly 20 continuous years in government, there have been neat media launches and soundbites at every turn. As defence minister she even coined a slogan for reforming the German army, "*Activ, Attraktiv, Anders*" ("active, attractive, different"), with a trademark plan for better living conditions and family support for soldiers. Most of this modernisation was necessary, but the execution was botched, and military leaders mocked that triple-A strapline as a "slogan for IBM."

When attacked, she exhibits what Robert Birnbaum, a longstanding observer at Berlin's *Tagesspiegel*, calls a "glassy brittleness." "She is self-disciplined and over-perfect in all aspects of presentation and doesn't like to admit mistakes in public or even reflect on them." Equally brittle is her tight-knit personal team. Jens Flosdorff, her media manager, has been with her since her social minister days in Hanover.

In Brussels, von der Leyen was soon a byword for misjudgments under pressure—threatening Northern Ireland with a hard border to stop vaccine exports from the EU, despite Michel Barnier's three long years of negotiations to guarantee that such a border was avoided, then blaming the vaccine companies and even the EU's trade commissioner for procurement mistakes that were equally her fault. But those who know von der Leyen's backstory, familiar as they are with her habit of passing the buck, were less shocked. As defence minister, when faced with a scandal of right-wing extremism in parts of the German army or *Bundeswehr*, she blamed the generals. "The *Bundeswehr* has an attitude problem, and it appears to have weak leadership at various levels," she announced, to a predictably enraged top brass. Exorbitant fees paid to consultants to reshape the German military, as a means of sidestepping existing officialdom, provoked a huge storm.

When auditors revealed shady procurement, she declared that mistakes had been made "far below my level."

Von der Leyen's statement to *Le Monde* on 1 February 2021, as the EU's vaccine failure swept the media, is another classic:

> Some countries [ie the US and Britain] resorted to emergency, 24-hour marketing authorisation procedures. The Commission and the member states agreed not to compromise with the safety and efficacy requirements for the authorisation of the vaccine. Time had to be taken to analyse the data, which, even minimised, takes three to four weeks. So, yes, Europe left it later, but it was the right decision. I remind you that a vaccine is the injection of an active biological substance into a healthy body. We are talking about a mass vaccination here; it is a gigantic responsibility.

Every one of those assertions was wrong, complacent, contested, or all three. Taken together, it was a breathtakingly misplaced argument that, in a public health emergency, speed is cavalier and dangerous while delay is safe and wise. Had she made such statements before taking the job, she would have been unappointable. "Only the Pope is infallible," Commission spokesman Eric Mamer said in a press conference defending a boss who evidently did not agree.

Rarely had an EU president looked more precarious on the 13th floor of the Commission's Berlaymont headquarters than von der Leyen in the summer of 2020. As the virus wreaked havoc, she proclaimed Covid-19 to be "Europe's moment." She reached repeatedly for that clanging phrase, with an almost compulsive weakness for slogans and a general lack of political touch.

And yet to survive in politics for 20 years, especially with seven children, you need something—particularly stamina and friends, and von der Leyen has plenty of both. For all the controversy, she lasted six years in the German defence ministry and was reappointed by Merkel to a second term, whereas her three predecessors had been forced out early: one over a failed drone programme, another for plagiarism in his doctorate, and the third over civilian deaths from a German airstrike in Afghanistan. Von der Leyen weathered her equivalent of all three scandals. Below the radar, over her six years, she secured a one-third increase in the military budget, thanks partly to a strong rapport with Wolfgang Schäuble, the veteran CDU finance minister.

She has none of the lethargy or isolation of the one and only Commission president to be forced out early—Jacques Santer, sacked for administrative cock-ups in 1999. Rumours of her political demise are almost certainly exaggerated.

Writing in late 2021, the significant question about von der Leyen is not whether she will survive, but what she signifies about leadership in today's EU. In particular, why did Macron promote her, while the leader who knew her best—Merkel—temporised before only reluctantly acquiescing in the final stages of the 2019 horse-trading?

Von der Leyen had real attraction for Macron not only for what she *wasn't* but also for what she *was*: a consensual and supremely Euro-networked German straight out of Merkel's governing Berlin; a woman in an era committed to equality; and a pragmatic but determined pro-European, who—like her father—is also strongly pro-American.

This mix is well suited to Biden's Washington and Macron's Paris. She supports Nato while, like Macron, pushing for a greater defence capability for the EU. The one occasion I have met her was at a US-European forum, where this was her theme. It was from defence discussions with von der Leyen, in French, that Macron lighted on her as a possible Commission president. "He liked the style, even if there wasn't much substance," says a French diplomat. "He intended to provide the substance." Macron also saw von der Leyen as an instrument for tying Germany into new European projects acceptable to France.

Conversely, this is partly why Merkel was cool about her appointment. As a German diplomat put it to me:

> Merkel wasn't wild about *any* German as president of the Commission, not just von der Leyen. Most of Europe's problems and Europe's bills end up in Berlin anyway; she didn't particularly want a second postbox for sending them to Berlin via a German president who would add some of their own too, plus some special pleading.

There was also the characteristic German worry about seeming too dominant, which is why until von der Leyen there had only been one previous German Commission president: Walter Hallstein, its founding head, for whom Ernst Albrecht worked six decades ago.

In other words, much of the explanation for—and doubts about—her rise are as much geopolitical as personal. But for von der Leyen, the geopolitical is the personal, and now that she is in post, her personal geopolitical instincts that are all-important. And on European integration these instincts are—as with the transformational Commission presidents Roy Jenkins in the 1970s and Jacques Delors in the 1980s—just in advance, but not too far, of most of the EU's national leaders of her generation. Above all, she is profoundly German yet profoundly European at the same time. A spiritual daughter of her father's ideals, she often cites her father's words to describe the EU's success: "We are trading with one another again and when countries trade they build up friendships, and friends do not shoot one another." She adds her own pietistic gloss: "We can count on one another in good times and bad, because we know that we may argue but can make up again, and because we never forget why we entered into the union in the first place."

Von der Leyen talks of the EU's "holy trinity" of peace, prosperity and democracy, and has certainly not given up on the Treaty of Rome's cause of "ever closer union." On the contrary, for all the vaccine controversy, the long-term story of the COVID19 crisis may be that, thanks in part to her, the EU became, in key respects, a health union, and just at the point when it was becoming an environmental union, too, in response to the climate emergency. The Commission's €1.8 trillion post-Covid recovery plan may be just the start.

So, "Europe's moment" may be a jarring way to describe a human tragedy, but the COVID19 challenge, like the collapse of the Berlin wall, may prove to be another EU staging post, and von der Leyen's presidency could—almost despite her—yet come to be seen as an evolutionary phase of European integration as great as the Jenkins-Delors legacies of the single currency, single market and social chapter.

Oliver Wendell Holmes said of FDR that he had "a second-class mind but first-class temperament, and it's the temperament that counts." In the case of Ursula von der Leyen, unusually for a leader, both the mind and the temperament are second rate, and but for her father she probably wouldn't have got anywhere near the top. But— partly also inherited from him—her European ideals are first rate, and in a European Union which distributes its leadership across so many people and institutions, that may be enough to squeak through.

19

JOHNSON

Never underestimate the capacity of Boris Johnson (b. 1964) to win from a tight corner, and all his corners are tight. In his 13 years at the top of politics, since he became mayor of London in 2008, he has despatched all his rivals in dramas whose common theme is the extraordinary self-belief, exhibitionism and sheer entitlement of the Prime Etonian.

Tory leaders and prime ministers Cameron and May, opposition leaders Corbyn, Swinson and Farage, mayor Ken Livingstone, a litany of chancellors, foreign secretaries, ministers, MPs and permanent secretaries – all lie side by side in the Westminster graveyard, joined recently by Dominic Cummings and co-conspirators. Keir Starmer, an initially promising Labour leader, is now on the danger list. Not even the closest proximity or the highest duty instil obligation, not excepting the Queen, brazenly manipulated en route to the 2019 election, let alone the wife swapped for a younger one, like Catherine of Aragon for Anne Boleyn, while actually occupying the supreme office.

In accumulated political power, post-vaccine Boris Johnson in 2021 rivals post-Falklands Thatcher and pre-Iraq Blair. So it is time to take the Johnson phenomenon seriously and seek to explain it. Here goes, from one who knows him fairly well.

Boris isn't a conventional political project, but a personal project for supremacy and celebrity. Most leaders at least claim to be servants of ideas and causes, whereas he grabs contrasting ideas and causes as if choosing vegetables for a ratatouille. "I haven't got any political opinions", he told a friend when seeking to become an MP. All that matters is that the colours are bright, and that the chef is glorified.

Even Brexit, perhaps his one enduring legacy, turned on naked self-advancement. My last one-to-one meeting with him, on 3rd February 2016, notionally to discuss the Crossrail project with London's still-mayor, soon turned into an agonised discussion of political options. It was moments after he had left the House of Commons chamber, where he had offered a fence-sitting response to Cameron's statement of his EU renegotiation terms and the setting of the referendum date for 23rd June. Pacing around his office, hand ruffling hair, he told me that he was "buggered" if he knew which side to take.

"Isn't the right thing to say that it's high time we started to lead in Europe, as your hero Churchill would have led?" I said. "Yes, well no," he stammered. "That means Cameron leading, and that won't work." Wouldn't work for him, I think he meant, rather than for the country. He also trialled on me a populist riff about "shaking these grand corporate and diplomatic panjandrums out of their complacency" – a dress rehearsal for the "fuck business" of 2018 when its leaders pressed to stay in Margaret Thatcher's EU single market.

Trump is often cited as a populist parallel, but Boris pulled it off in a parliamentary system where it is virtually unprecedented to win from the outside. He triumphed because he is modern England's supreme insider and outsider *at the same time*. Electorally, he was the first politician to carry a UK-wide referendum against a prime minister, reaching downtrodden parts no other modern

Conservative politician has reached. Bolsover, Bassetlaw and Blyth Valley are all Boris blue, as now is Hartlepool, a rare and remarkable government by-election gain in May 2021, won by running as an insurgent in power. But socially and psychologically, he imbibed and exudes Etonian elitism to an extreme degree, emerging from the school in Thatcher's decade of widening inequality, part of the vanguard of a new generation of Etonians asserting a right to rule and dominate. An extrovert by nature, he built himself a disarmingly popular, seemingly apolitical one-man band on these Etonian foundations, a sort of Bertie Wooster meets Henry VIII, bumbling and disarming yet cunning, ruthless and lethal.

Back in the late 1970s, when Boris started at the school, many thought there would never be another Etonian in No 10. Thatcher's meritocratic Tories were thought to be too canny for that, learning from Sir Alec Douglas-Home's defeat in 1964 by Harold Wilson, a Yorkshire middle class grammar school boy.

Douglas-Home made a good joke in reply to Wilson's jibe about being a 14th Earl — "I suppose when you think about it Mr Wilson is the 14th Mr Wilson" — but he still lost, and was rapidly replaced by a Tory grammar school boy, Ted Heath, who in turn was succeeded by the most famous bourgeois grammar school girl in history. And the coup de grâce, so it seemed, was the Tory leadership election after Thatcher's defenestration in 1990. John Major, a Brixton grammar school boy who hadn't even gone to university, aced it over both Michael Heseltine (Shrewsbury and Oxford) and Douglas Hurd (Eton and Cambridge). His three successors as Conservative leader –

William Hague, Iain Duncan Smith and Michael Howard – all attended state schools of different types.

When the Tories elected David Cameron as leader in 2005 – overtaking the favourite, another grammar school boy, David Davis – I thought Eton might be his undoing. He half-suspected so too, hence the scramble to buy the copyright of the famous Bullingdon club photos of him with privileged friends in Etonian-style evening dress, and the intimations that the little Camerons would be sent to state schools (His son was quietly put down for an Eton feeder prep school shortly before his father left Downing Street.) Gordon Brown's government, two years later, is the only government in British history not to have contained a single Etonian.

But then history slammed into reverse. In 2010 Cameron squeezed into No 10, courtesy of the Lib Dem leader Nick Clegg (Westminster School and Cambridge, portrayed in Peter Brookes's cartoons in the *Times* as Cameron's Eton fag). Then, after the Theresa May interim in which he loomed large, Boris. *Floreat Etona* ("May Eton Flourish") turned out to be more a command than a motto. And if there were to be a vacancy at No 10 any time soon, Rishi Sunak (Winchester and Oxford) only looks downmarket to, well, an Etonian.

So what happened? The story of Johnson and Cameron is also the story of the resurgence of Eton, not only as a school but as a caste of unrivalled wealth and prestige. Eton endowed Johnson both men not only with the will to power but the means to conquer it, even to compete for it between themselves as if No 10 were an Eton prize.

Poring over the data, I now realise that even in the supposedly meritocratic 1980s, Etonians never left the Tory high command. They just didn't, for a while, become leader. Even as their demise was supposed, fully 61 Etonians served as ministers over the Thatcher and Major years, about the same number as under the string of Etonian prime ministers (Eden, Macmillan, Douglas-Home) in the 1950s and early 1960s. And under the cover of Major, who said his mission was to create a "classless society," fully 10 per cent of Conservative MPs in the 1992 parliament were Old Etonians.

"Thatcher didn't mind toffs as long as they did not attempt to patronise her," says William Waldegrave, Etonian younger son of the 12th Earl Waldegrave and a minister for almost the entirety of the Thatcher/Major era. Waldegrave is now provost of Eton — a post unique to that school, a kind of full-time "chancellor" with a palatial residence in its medieval quad, where he gives dinners to students, tutors and distinguished guests, like the head of an Oxford college. His recent memoir frankly parades the fact that, like Boris, "ever since I could remember one consciously constructed goal [to become prime minister] had been the magnetic pole around which everything I did was centred."

In the Labour-dominated 1960s and '70s, Eton's leadership saw the meritocratic threat clearly. So having been for centuries essentially a comprehensive school for the aristocracy, they turned Eton into an oligarchical grammar school. With the incomes of the super-rich racing ahead, especially after Thatcher's tax cuts for the wealthy and "big bang" deregulation of the City, the sky was the limit for both fees and resources. By the 1980s, most boys were getting top A-level grades, a quarter of the teachers had PhDs and the facilities were world class.

Just as Eton and the other top public schools were mutating into warped meritocracies, the grammar schools were abolished, so the competition largely left the field. It was strangely unrealised by Labour politicians of that era that the *esprit de corps* and academic prowess of the grammar schools had been vital to the left's ability to take on the Tory public school elite on equal terms. The main political casualty of Labour's comprehensivisation of education turned out to be the Labour party itself, which thereafter lacked leaders with the confidence to match the gilded grammar school generation of Wilson, Healey and Jenkins, while the new breed of "meritocratic" Etonians and fellow public school boys – girls were still rare, and girl Etonians non-existent – remained deep blue.

Ironically, or maybe logically, Labour's only successful leader after Wilson came from Fettes, dubbed "the Eton of Scotland," although far less rich and establishment. Tony Blair's headmaster there was Eric Anderson, who went on to become the modernising headmaster of... yes, Eton. Unsuspectingly, Blair legitimised the political rehabilitation of Tory public school leaders, and Eton promptly reverted to type in providing Cameron and Johnson as successors to its 18 prime ministers since the very first, Robert Walpole, in 1721. That total of 20 Etonian PMs is more than one in every three of the total of 55, compared to one Etonian in every 30,000-odd years if prime ministers were randomly drawn from across all UK secondary schools.

"The age of earnestness began," wrote Anderson in his history of the school. Actually, it wasn't that earnest, more a case of some things changing so that most things could stay the same. Under this more exam-driven regime, a few sons of Etonians had to slum it in lesser public schools. But feeder prep schools like Boris's Ashdown House in Sussex raised their game and for those who got in to Eton, which included most of the type who would have gone to the school previously, the social ethos scarcely changed. "One retiring Bursar," Anderson recalled, "compared his job with running a resort town with 25 small hotels and a university campus." In one respect it became grander still: Princes William and Harry donned Etonian tailcoats in the 1990s, the first royal heirs to do so. Anderson, who died in 2020, summed up his mission for Eton – "on the road from Windsor to Westminster" – in a phrase that could have applied to any of the last five centuries: "the habitual vision of greatness."

Like a Zoom backdrop, this resurgent Eton is inseparable from Boris and his personal vision of greatness. While not from pure aristocracy or plutocracy, he is a classic Eton type: a bright boy from a thrusting Tory family – father Stanley a minor public school (Sherborne) Tory MEP of exotic international pedigree, whose grandfather was the last Sultan of Turkey's interior minister; mother Charlotte the artist daughter of a President of the European Commission of Human Rights – entering Eton from a top prep school by way of one of the 70 King's scholarships which date back to the school's foundation by Henry VI in 1440. It was an ascent analogous to that of Douglas Hurd, Thatcher's last foreign secretary, who like Boris became Eton captain of school (head boy), and was a notable booster for Johnson during his rise, comparing him flatteringly to Disraeli as a Tory romantic touched by genius.

Such patronage helps explain why Boris, like generations of Etonians before him, gravitated naturally to political leadership. It is wrong to consider him a journalist who went late into politics. He first tried to become a Tory MEP at the age of just 29 – and so join the "Club of 30" which is a recurring theme of this book on political leadership – in the footsteps of his father and personally encouraged by Hurd. Then, alongside Cameron, he tried to enter the Commons in 1997, at 32. They both lost in the first Blair landslide but landed rock-solid Tory seats in the following 2001 election. Boris's was Henley-on-Thames, 15 miles upriver from Eton; Cameron's was a bit further into Oxfordshire – Hurd's old seat of Witney. By now, after a decade at the *Telegraph* demonising Brussels for effect while honing an Etonian clown act on television, Johnson was continuing in this vein as editor of the high Tory *Spectator* magazine. The point is, journalism and politics were the same activity, both geared to becoming a Tory celebrity and then leader.

It is moot how far Boris was created, and how far curated, by Eton. Either way, the outsized egotist, with a "vision of greatness" anchored in the Greeks and Romans, was fully formed by the time he left for a gap year working at the private Geelong Grammar School – "Australia's Eton" which, as his most insightful biographer Sonia Purnell puts it in *Just Boris: The Irresistible Rise of a Political Celebrity*, was "another demonstration of the Johnsonian fondness for the wealthiest and best (no sign of building latrines for starving Africans)." From there it was Balliol College,

Oxford, where he was one of about 150 Etonians at Oxford in the mid-1980s.

The school report written by Boris's Eton housemaster is often cited, denigrating his

> disgracefully cavalier attitude to his classical studies. Boris sometimes seems affronted when criticised for what amounts to a gross failure of responsibility (and surprised at the same time that he was not appointed captain of the school for next half): I think he honestly believes that it is churlish of us not to regard him as an exception, one who should be free of the network of obligation which binds everyone else.

The same could be said of every phase and every job in his life, again in his father's footsteps.

However, the striking thing is that Boris *did* become captain of school, at the second attempt. He has a knack of winning top positions at the second try, including the premiership, precisely *because* he believes it churlish not to regard him as an exception. The caricatures of him as lazy are themselves lazy. Certainly, he disdains details that doesn't impinge on his interests, yet he is assiduous at both his vocation and his pleasures, but he divides his efforts between them about equally when on a roll. On the rebound from failure, his work ethic is ferocious and focused. Far more significant than a report for parental eyes is what Eton said about him publicly. When asked by Anthony Howard, a 1980s journalist and friend of Stanley's, who was the most interesting student of his time, headmaster Anderson replied: "Without a doubt, Boris Johnson. Anyone who's spent an hour with Boris never forgets it. All I have to say to you about him is positive."

Another reason Boris is so good at winning second time around, as he is doing now (in 2021) in reinventing his premiership post-Cummings, is that his obligation to people and causes is so weak to start with. This too started young. At Oxford, when he first ran to be president of the prestigious Oxford Union debating society, he was outsmarted by a Liberal grammar school boy who ran an anti-toff campaign and won a mass of Liberal-SDP votes. The centrist parties were riding high in mid-1980s Oxford, and unlike Labour students didn't boycott the Union on social grounds. Boris's response? To run a second time allied with the SDP student faction, claiming to be a supporter and speaking passionately in a debate the night before the vote on the motion: "This House has had enough of two party politics." "I never realised until then just how intensely focused and determined he was," said his opponent. "Sure he's engaging, but this guy is an absolute fucking killer." Dominic Cummings should have checked his form.

Boris's sheer chutzpah is as potent as it is because of Eton. The institution is not just a school for boys, it is a freemasonry for life. Cameron's break into politics started with a mysterious call from Buckingham Palace to Conservative central office suggesting this was a "remarkable" young man to watch. In Johnson's case, Hurd and Anderson's leg-up was only the first instalment, and throughout his career the help was extended – and continues to extend – from the wider establishment, itself still mostly public school and Oxbridge. The importance of this top public school freemasonry struck me while watching Cummings's six-hour, search-and-destroy mission against his former boss before a parliamentary committee in May 2021. His dire imprecations reminded me of the similarly Baroque denunciation by Max Hastings in July 2019 in the *Guardian*, on the eve of Boris's triumphal entry into No 10.

Re-reading Hastings, I recalled with a start that the key figure identified by biographer Sonia Purnell as launching Johnson's career and fostering the whole incarnation as today's "Boris" is… the same Max Hastings who was here describing his one-time protégé as "a cavorting charlatan" exhibiting "moral bankruptcy rooted in a contempt for truth" caring "for nothing but his own fame and gratification."

"I have known Johnson since the 1980s, when I edited the *Daily Telegraph* and he was our flamboyant Brussels correspondent," wrote Hastings, launching his ineffectual thunderbolts. Only after reading this sentence twice, and referring back to Purnell's book, did I realise that Hastings (Charterhouse and Oxford) didn't just *know* Johnson in the 1980s: he *appointed* him as his paper's "flamboyant Brussels correspondent," where Boris made his name and brand by flamboyantly inventing stories about EU plans to ban bent bananas, standardise condoms and achieve federal domination.

Moreover, Hastings didn't just send Johnson to Brussels, he recruited him for the *Telegraph* days after he had been sacked by the *Times* for making up quotes. Although the graduate Johnson had lasted only a week in management consultancy, he had soon – through family connections – landed a coveted traineeship at the *Times* before spectacularly blowing this chance. Then Hastings, who had met Johnson when speaking at the Oxford Union, rode to the rescue. "Without Hastings' patronage," Purnell writes, "it is quite possible that Boris would have been lost forever to journalism."

If Johnson's ethics, which Hastings now deplores, weren't sufficiently apparent at the start, they were soon made crystal clear to him. We know this because Purnell documents that he was sent personally—and anonymously—the notorious tape of the phone conversation in which Boris and his Etonian friend Darius Guppy discuss hiring a heavy to "beat up" a journalist who had crossed Guppy's path. "Ok, Darry, I said I'll do it and I'll do it. Don't worry," says today's prime minister.

What happened next – before "Darry" went to jail for serious fraud, that is? "Hastings' response was to fly Boris back to London for a serious discussion," writes Purnell. "Anyone might have expected a dramatic showdown and even a resignation or a sacking at the end of it." But by Hastings' own account, the "interrogation" brought out "all Boris's self-parodying skills as a waffler. Words stumbled forth: loyalty... never intended... old friend... took no action... misunderstanding. We dispatched him back to Brussels with a rebuke." "And so Bumbling Boris won the day," Purnell relates.

Again, there is no making sense of this great escape without understanding Etonian presumption. James Wood, a literary critic who was in Cameron's year, writes of "the Etonian's uncanny ability to soften entitlement with charm." He recalls: "we were told to be wary of misusing our superiority, but we were not told we didn't have it." The sheer entitlement is what amazes.

A recent memoir by Musa Okwonga, Ugandan son of doctors and rare black Etonian, who is a novelist in the school's alienated counter-cultural tradition (think George Orwell), sheds some light: "I ask myself whether this was my school's ethos: to win at all costs; to be reckless, at best, and brutal, at worst. I look at its motto again — 'May Eton Flourish' — and I think, yes, many of our politicians have flourished, but to the vast detriment of others. Maybe we were raised to be the bad guys." In a telling riposte from the citadel, Etonian Tory MP Bim Afolami, reviewing Okwanga, blithely dismisses its discussion of politics as "the weakest part of the book." Eton's genius lies, rather, in giving politicians like Afolami "a huge appetite for hard work and a fierce competitive streak" plus a pure "belief in the importance of public service."

For Etonians, this belief in the importance of public service naturally and almost invariably takes the form of being Tory and a resolute if genteel defender of extreme elitism. As Tony Blair's schools minister I was once invited to discuss education at Eton's political society. "Sir, the headmaster said you're not one of those really red ones who wants to abolish us," began the first questioner, to titters. "But you do realise that if you tried, we would be very angry, because we are really good for the country."

For the recanting Hastings read also the destroyed Cameron, who gave Boris his break to run for mayor of London in 2008 then tolerated his leadership of the Leave campaign in 2016, and the ejected Cummings, mastermind of Leave and Boris's takeover of No 10. Boris is "a pundit who stumbled into politics," began a recent Cummings philippic against his own creation. If he believes that, then rarely has one public schoolboy so misjudged another. Johnson is a literal class act.

Now, in 2021, that Brexit is "done" and the pandemic muddled through, where does the Prime Etonian go next?

Unlike post-Falklands Thatcher and pre-Iraq Blair, post-vaccine Johnson apparently has little he wants to accomplish with his immense stock of power, beyond keeping the celebrity show on the road and striking Churchillian poses. "The fatal thing is boredom. So I try to have as much on my plate as possible," is the most insightful line *by* him I have found, in a 2002 *Times* "A life in the day" column.

The best line *about* him is by a critic quoted by Purnell: "like Lord Palmerston, Boris does not have friends, merely interests." Interests need sedulous cultivation, more so in many ways than friends, and he is devoting the full resources of the honours system, public appointments, the planning system and a good deal of public policy to the task.

What of his plan for the country? Union jacks with everything is the main discernible theme. In place of strategy, we have a handful of populist catchphrases – "Global Britain," "levelling-up," "war on woke." Typical of the paltry resulting policy is the much-vaunted Australia trade deal, which offsets Brexit trade losses in Europe with an increase in national income of perhaps 0.02 per cent. It's part of a "tilt towards the Indo-Pacific," which also includes the despatch of the Royal Navy's new aircraft carrier HMS *Queen Elizabeth* to cruise around the Indian Ocean for no essential purpose. As for flagship legislation, parliament is engaged with trivialities like the Higher Education (Freedom of Speech) Bill for free speech czars on university campuses, hiding the absence of substance by stoking a culture war vigorously supported by the new Fox News lookalike GB News.

To observers of his London mayoralty, the lack of interest in social policy is no surprise – witness his neglect of affordable housing, perhaps the most pressing issue in the crowded and extortionately expensive capital. However, in my experience, Boris does believe in one thing: *grands projets* with his name emblazoned. He doesn't much mind what the *projets* are, but the grander the better. As mayor of London, as well as a double-decker bus and bike hire scheme named after himself, his biggest projects, in tandem with the Blair-Brown government, were the London Olympics and Crossrail, the £16bn east-west London commuter line. At the launch of the Crossrail construction at Canary Wharf he quoted Juvenal to me in Latin. I can only remember the English: "Give them bread and circuses and they will never revolt."

One of the few politicians Boris consciously imitates is Michael Heseltine, maybe the best modern prime minister we never had. "Canary Wharf – Hezzagrad, as people call the great city that has arisen in docklands – is thanks to his energy and drive," he said admiringly in his maiden speech as an MP.

But there is a key difference with Hezza. "Bozza" isn't unduly fussed if his projects are any good or don't end up happening – "Boris Island" airport, a mooted bridge to France, and the garden bridge across the Thames never happened – so long as they get people talking. About to join the list is his huge bridge or tunnel across the Irish Sea, a wacky idea to maintain the Union with Northern Ireland, which the Treasury and transport officials are quietly killing off. But if there is a big infrastructure scheme that's ready to go, he would generally rather make it happen than not. Tellingly, the one major issue on which he overruled Cummings in 2019/20 was HS2, the £100bn high-speed line from London to Birmingham, Manchester and Leeds. There are now 250 construction sites on the route through the Chilterns.

It is often said that Boris is a big spender and that battles with Rishi Sunak will loom large post Brexit. I'm not so sure. Boris likes certain *grands projets*, and bungs for whatever he judges electorally vital like the NHS, yet beyond that he is an inegalitarian Tory by Etonian pedigree. He has always been surrounded by the rich and enjoys it. In response to George Osborne's "omnishambles" 2012 budget, he argued the chancellor should have cut the top rate of tax even more deeply. Social justice is one of his supreme unconcerns. His *Telegraph* column defending "sickeningly rich people" on the grounds that "if British history had not allowed outrageous financial rewards for a few top people, there would be no Chatsworth, no Longleat," comes straight from the Etonian heart. So too does the one which began: "Cancel the guilt trip. Africa is a mess, but it is not a blot on our conscience. The problem is not that we were once in charge, but that we are not in charge any more." The big cuts in overseas aid in 2020 were prompted, not opposed, by No 10.

I suspect post-pandemic Boris will be largely politics by populist gesture, some costly but most costless. No previous government has spent so much on opinion surveying, as the prime ministerial WhatsApp messages released by Cummings attest. In the grim depths of the first lockdown, Boris asks his strategist whether something unspecified was "from tonight focus group and polls?" Cummings responded: "it was from a whole run of them."

A minister tells me that the first thing Boris looks at each morning is the latest private polls. He allowed Sunak to veto the £15bn education catch-up plan after COVID19, despite having pledged support to his own education recovery commissioner Kevan Collins, because private polling showed a longer school day, a key part of the plan, to be unpopular, particularly with working-class parents in the "red wall." "Why battle with Rishi for billions for stuff which might be good for the punters but which they don't even want?" one No 10 pollster told me. Overseas aid is equally unpopular – and therefore dispensable by a prime minister who doesn't give a fig.

However, much depends on who "runs" Boris after Covid. When he was mayor of London, *consigliere* emerged after initial turbulence: Simon Milton and Edward Lister, Tory ex-leaders of Westminster and Wandsworth councils, filled this role successively at City Hall. The Cummings mayhem in No 10 had method as well as madness: only by shock and awe was it possible to get Brexit "done" after he took over in July 2019 with no parliamentary majority and a large Remain group of Tory MPs, some inching towards a second referendum. But with Brexit done, the chief strategist was also done.

So far, no post-Cummings *consigliere* has emerged. No 10 is a court of jostling factions, including rival ministers (Sunak vs Raab vs Gove), rival advisers (Treasury civil servant Dan Rosenfield vs civil service-haranguing adviser Simone Finn), and inexperienced Cabinet secretary Simon Case. The strongest emergent figure is Boris's new 33 year-old wife Carrie Symonds, a former party press officer, whose father Matthew Symonds is a biographer and friend of American tech billionaire Larry Ellison (net worth reported as $92bn) and was director of Ellison's charitable foundation before it was shut down last year. "The strongest feature of Carrie by far is her fierce intent to keep him in No 10," says a friend. Apart from a tribal conservatism and a millennial passion for animal rights, she comes with no pre-determined agenda beyond Boris's quest for fame and fortune.

Eventually, an opposition leader will get the measure of Boris, or a corner will be simply too tight. But he is still on the up, and he has the great institutions at his beck and call. He even got the Catholic church to marry him for the third time, while prime minister, thanks to a loophole by which the Vatican does not recognise his earlier non-Catholic marriages—a supremely ironic and characteristically Johnsonian manipulation of a venerable institution even older than Eton College. As he put it in his maiden speech as an MP, in perhaps the only pure statement of his political philosophy: "There is a hidden wisdom in old ways of doing things."

ACKNOWLEDGEMENTS

I am hugely grateful to Nathan Lloyd, Norman Harris and Will Dry for help and to Clive Cowdery and Tom Clark for commissioning me to write a series of profiles for *Prospect*, which comprise seven of my chapters here.

Chapter 1 draws on my article 'Forget ideas—do the maths, and it's clear political leadership always comes down to character' in *Prospect*, 9 September 2017.

Chapter 2 draws on my essay 'Gladstone, Marx and Modern Progressives' in *Liberal History*, 8 September 1995.

Chapter 3 is an edited version of 'Stalin' from my book *Ernest Bevin: Labour's Churchill* (Biteback, 2020).

Chapter 4 (Biden) first appeared in *Prospect*, March 2021.

Chapter 5 (Modi) first appeared in *Prospect*, May 2021.

Chapter 6 is an edited version of my essay 'Tony Blair' in *The Prime Ministers*, edited by Iain Dale (Hodder & Stoughton, 2020).

Chapter 8 is an edited version of the chapter 'How Mr Farage became leader of the Conservative Party' from my *Saving Britain* (Abacus, 2018) with Will Hutton.

Chapter 9 is my Roy Jenkins Centenary Lecture 'Courage with Wisdom', delivered at King's College London, 17 November 2020.

Chapter 12 is an edited version of my review of Chris Bowers' *Nick Clegg: The Biography* (Biteback, 2011) in *New Statesman*, 5 September 2011.

Chapter 13 is an edited version of my review of Philip Short's *Mitterrand: A Study in Ambiguity* (Bodley Head, 2013) in *New Statesman*, 21 November 2013.

Chapter 14 first appeared in *Prospect*, December 2021, as a review of Andrew Roberts, *George III: Britain's Most Misunderstood Monarch* (Allen Lane, 2021).

Chapter 15 is an edited version of my review of Andrew Roberts' *Napoleon the Great* (Allen Lane, 2014) in *New Statesman*, 20 November 2014.

Chapter 16 (Thatcher) is an edited version of a passage from my book *Failure in British Government: The Politics of the Poll Tax* (OUP, 1994) with David Butler and Tony Travers.

Chapter 17 (Scholz) first appeared in *Prospect*, November 2021.

Chapter 18 (von der Leyen) first appeared in *Prospect*, June 2021.

Chapter 19 (Johnson) first appeared in *Prospect*, August 2021.

And huge thanks and appreciation to Alice, Ed and Ian, for being with me on the journey, particularly in Borghino, where the manuscript was turned into a book between August and October 2021. I took to heart the wisdom of Keynes: "I only start writing with the proofs."

Borghino, 10 October 2021.

INDEX

Haldane, R.B 200
Halifax, Lord 48
Hallstein, Walter 277
Hamilton, Nigel 139-42
Hannan, Daniel 154
Hardie, Keir 24
Harriman, Averell 50
Harris, John 183
Harris, Kamala 97-8
Hastings, Max 290-3
Hattersley, Roy 124-5, 198
Hawke, Bob 4
Hazlitt, William 211
Healey, Denis 68, 193, 264
Heath, Edward 7, 10, 12, 180, 219, 283
Henderson, Sir Nicholas 87
Henry VIII, King 283
Heseltine, Michael 207-16, 248, 283, 295
Hitler, Adolf 30, 33, 36, 41-2, 48, 83, 177, 198, 205, 225, 243, 247, 260
Hobbes, Thomas 2
Holland, Francois 5
Holmes, Oliver Wendell 279
Hopkins, Harry 98
Horch, Frank 261-2
Howard, Michael 7, 128, 155, 160, 284
Howe, Sir Geoffrey 248
Hugo, Victor 119
Huhne, Chris 221
Hull, Cordell 97
Humphrey, Hubert 11
Hurd, Douglas 248, 283-4, 287-8, 290
Hussein, Saddam 135-6
Hynd, John 55-6. 68

Ignatieff, Michael 5
Irvine, Derry 123

James II, King 233
Jenkin, Patrick 253
Jenkins, Arthur 175-7
Jenkins, Jennifer 176, 193
Jenkins, Roy 124, 133-4, 173-96, 202-3, 208, 212, 218, 264, 268, 277-8, 286
Jennings, Sir Ivor 245
Jinping, Xi 114

Johnson, Boris 7, 9, 24, 124, 171, 213-4, 247, 257, 269, 281-97
Johnson, Lyndon Baines 2, 7, 9-11, 91, 93, 103-4, 140-47
Johnson, Stanley 287
Joseph, Sir Keith 156
Juvenal, Decimus 285

Kelly, Dr David 136
Kennan, George 32
Kennedy, Charles 218
Kennedy, Jacqueline 143
Kennedy, John F. 6, 7, 11, 91, 96, 103, 140, 145-7
Kennedy, Robert 94, 145
Kermani, Navid 257
Kerry, John 7, 97
Keynes, J.M. 2, 40, 48, 199, 218, 300
Kilroy Silk, Robert 158
King, Martin Luther 144
Kinnock, Neil 7, 11, 94, 124-5
Kipling, Rudyard 166
Kissinger, Henry 24
Kohl, H. 131, 152-3, 228-9, 247-9, 259
Krushchev, N. 147

Lagarde, Christine 274
Lamont, Norman 250
Lampedusa, G. 221-2
Laschet, Armin 257-58
Lawrence, D.H. 186
Lawson, Nigel 154, 199, 248-52
Lenin, V. 205
Le Pen, Jean-Marie 158
Letwin, Oliver 165
Lewis, Julian 156
Lincoln, Abraham 139, 147-9
Lindner, Christian 268
Lippmann, Walter 146
Lloyd George, David 26, 121, 126, 197-206, 217-8, 246-7
Louis XV, King 241
Louis XVI, King 231, 241
Louise-Philippe, King 242
Lutyens, Edwin 116

Machiavelli, N. 2
Macmillan, Harold 7, 285
Macmurray, John 123

Macron, Emmanuel 5, 113, 273, 277
Madison, James 207
Major, John 7, 9, 124-5, 127-8, 131-3, 154, 156, 162, 250, 283, 285
Makarios, Archbishop 112
Mandelson, Peter 125
Mansfield, Mike 147
Marie-Antoinette, Queen 231
Marquand, David 182
Marshall, George 70-82, 85-88
Marx, Karl 15-30, 212
Masaryk, Jan 78
May, Theresa 7, 9, 12, 151, 172, 281, 284
Mazarin, Cardinal 224, 226, 230
McCain, John 7, 9, 102
McCarthy, Joseph 66
McConnell, Mitch 97, 105
McKibbin, Ross 23
McNamara, Robert 147
Mendes-France, Pierre 137
Merkel, Angela 4, 11, 112, 163-4, 249-51, 255-65, 276-7
Metternich, Prince 16
Michel, Charles 268
Miller, Arthur 101
Milosevic, Slobodan 97, 105, 211
Milton, John 195-6
Mitterrand, F.152-3, 158, 223-30
Modi, Narendra 4, 107-20
Molotov, V. 33, 37, 49, 52, 58, 70-1, 76, 82
Monnet, Jean 81
Montgomery, Bernard 45, 48, 58-9
Morgan, Kenneth 208-12
Morgenthau, Henry 43, 98
Morley, John 246
Morrison, Herbert 68, 125, 176
Murdoch, Rupert 129, 133, 154, 169

Napoleon Bonaparte 5, 231, 241-4
Napoleon III, Emperor 207, 223, 242
Nehru, Jawahalal 109-110
Nenni, Pietro 78
Newcastle, Duke of 234
Nicolson, Harold 82
Nixon, Richard 6, 7, 9, 11, 66, 135, 140
North, Lord 234-5

Obama, Barack 7, 9, 10, 12, 91, 94-5, 98, 105
Okwonga, Musa 292-3
Orban, Viktor 273
Orwell, George 292
Osborne, George 165, 219, 296
Osnos, Evan 95
Owen, David132-3, 192, 194-5

Palmerston, Viscount 122, 294
Parnell, C.S. 26
Patel, Priti 114
Patten, Chris 156, 219, 250
Peel, Sir Robert 28
Pelham, Henry 234
Perkins, Frances 98, 101
Petain, Philippe 225
Peterson, Sir Maurice 69
Pitt, William (Elder) 234
Pitt, William (Younger) 236-9
Powell, Enoch 153, 155, 159, 166, 208, 210, 215
Proust, Marcel 195
Purnell, Sonia 288, 291-2

Raab, Dominic 192, 297
Reagan, Ronald 2, 5, 7, 10, 102-3, 140, 228
Rees-Mogg, William 183-4
Ridley, Nicholas 247
Roberts, Andrew231-43
Robertson, Brian 59, 68, 89
Rocard, Michel 226
Rodgers, Bill 194
Roosevelt, F.D. 2, 5, 9, 10, 31, 34, 36, 43-4, 50, 91-6, 99-106, 134, 140, 143
Roosevelt, Theodore 102-3
Ross, Willie 182
Roth, William 101
Rumsfeld, Donald 135

Salisbury, Marquess of 2, 26, 246
Sanders, Bernie 104
Santer, Jacques 249
Sargent, Orme 56
Sarkozy, Nicolas 164
Scargill, Arthur 248
Schauble, Wolfgang 264
Schmidt, Helmut 191, 259-60

Schmidt, Wolfgang 264-5
Scholz, Olaf 4, 124, 255-65, 269
Schroeder, Gerhard 134, 248, 259-60
Schumacher, Kurt 83
Schuman, Robert 46
Seward, William 148
Shah, Amit 110, 115
Sheridan, R.B. 237-38
Short, Philip 223-30
Singh, Jagmeet 8
Singh, Manmohan 117, 119
Sked, Alan 156
Smith, John 123, 125-6
Sorensen, Ted 144-5
Soskice, Sir Frank 178, 181
St John Stevas, Norman, 254
Stalin, Josef 24, 30, 31-89, 205
Stanley, Venetia 202-3, 206
Starmer, Sir Keir 281
Steel, David186, 208
Stettinius, Edward 50
Strachey, Lytton 199-200
Suetonius, Gaius 139
Sunak, Rishi 284, 296-7
Symonds, Carrie 296-7
Symonds, Matthew 297

Tebbit, Norman 161
Thatcher, Margaret 2, 5, 7, 10, 108, 121, 125, 151-9, 168, 184, 188, 193, 195, 199, 207, 209, 213-6, 220, 228, 245-54, 273, 281, 283-3, 287, 293
Thomson, Peter 114
Tocqueville, Alexis de 19, 207
Trudeau, Justin 4-5, 10
Truman, Harry 7, 10, 11, 31-7, 40, 44, 50-54, 61-2, 65-6, 70, 73-4, 86, 140
Trump, Donald 3, 4, 7-12, 91-2, 98, 105, 110

Vaizey, Ed 218-9
Vandenberg, Arthur 56
Victoria, Queen 15-6, 28-9, 232, 241
von der Leyen, Heiko 270-1
von der Leyen, Ursula 267-79

Wakeham, John 251
Waldegrave, William 251-2, 285
Walpole, Sir Robert 234, 246-7, 286

Washington, George 235
Waterhouse, Michael 205-6
Wels, Otto 260
Whitelaw, William 248, 251
Wilders, Geert 160
Wilhelm II, Kaiser 202
Williams, Francis 66, 73-4
Williams, Shirley 174, 187, 194
Willis, Dr Francis 233
Wilson, Harold 7, 9-10, 12, 168, 178, 183, 185, 188, 192, 195, 200, 208, 248-9, 252, 283, 286
Wilson, Woodrow 24, 198
Wood, James 292
Wulff, Christian 270-1

Yellen, Janet 97
Yew, Lee Kuan 112
Younger, George 251

Zuckerberg, Mark 218

Printed in Great Britain
by Amazon